MAKING
STAINED GLASS

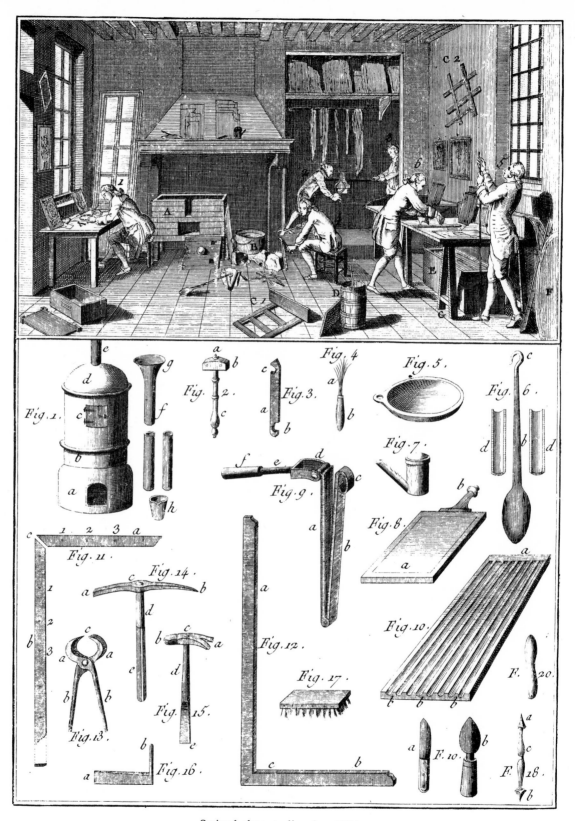

Stained-glass studio, circa 1774

Robert and Gertrude Metcalf

MAKING STAINED GLASS

A HANDBOOK FOR THE AMATEUR AND THE PROFESSIONAL

DAVID & CHARLES : NEWTON ABBOT

ISBN 0 7153 5494 9

Set in Plantin
and printed in Great Britain
by Redwood Press Limited, Trowbridge, Wiltshire,
for David & Charles (Publishers) Limited
South Devon House Newton Abbot Devon

For James, Robert, and Cynthia

CONTENTS

Preface —11

Glossary —12

Origin and History —15

Historical Beginnings
Definition of Stained Glass
Classification
Prestyle Windows—11th Century
The Middle Ages
Early Period—12th, 13th Centuries
Middle Period—14th, 15th Centuries
Late Period—16th Century
Contemporary Period

Glass and Glass Making —37

Lead —45

Iron —49

The Studio —52
Office
Drawing
Glass Work

Firing
Etching
Packing and Storage
Glazing and Cementing
The Drawing Wall and other Heavy Equipment
Fluorescent Lights
The Glass Easel
The Selecting Table

The Kiln —60

The Sketch —63

The Template —65

The Cartoon —67

The Cut Line —71

Glass Cutting —76

Selecting
Waxing up
Glass selecting
Care of the Wheel

Sharpening the Wheel
Gauge Cutting and Temporary Glass

Glass Painting —95

Binders for tracing color
Binders for Matt
Practice
Tracing
Matting
Mahlstick
Texture
Patina
First Painting
Second Painting

Additional Methods of Glass Painting —111

Scratch out Method
Painting up
Etching

Firing —113

Glazing —116

The Lathykin

The Stopping Knife
The Lead Cutting Knife
Lead Stretchers
The Process of Glazing
Cementing
Setting

The Evocative Technique —126

Project No. 1
Project No. 2
Project No. 3
Project No. 4
Project No. 5

New and Related Techniques —142

Dalle de Verre
Applique Technique
Laminated Glass
Sculpture Relief
Stained Glass Sculpture

Bibliography —151

Sources of Supply —153

Index —155

PREFACE

This book is directed to those persons who would like, for one reason or another, to practice the art of stained glass. It is based upon trustworthy professional studio practice, both traditional and contemporary. It is presented as simply as possible; a minimum of technical terminology is used and only when essential.

Specifically, this book should appeal and be useful to the layman who is searching for a new and significant form of expression; to the patron who is planning the purchase of a window and would like to know the merits of a good one; to the architect who is considering the use of stained glass in a structure; to the young apprentice working in a stained glass studio who is eager to learn more about the art; to the teacher who would like a new approach to the art of painting; and, particularly, to the gifted painter or designer who would like to try a socially significant, as well as remunerative, art.

The book is divided into four major sections: the origin and history of the craft; materials; shop practice, past and present; and what we call the "Evocative Technique." Included in the first section is a classification of the periods, styles, and the various types of windows. There is nothing to compel the reader to follow this sequence. He should feel perfectly free to read the sections in whatever order he may choose.

The authors would like to express their gratitude to those who have helped to make this book possible: Jessie Treichler and Alistair Reid, for their help in editing the manuscript; William Blenko, Jr., for permitting us to photograph the process of antique glassmaking; the Willets, for giving us the opportunity to photograph the *dalle-de-verre* technique; to the Steuben Glass Company, James Metcalf, Robert R. Metcalf, Robert Sowers, Conrad Schmidt, and Arthur Norris, for permission to reproduce their works. Special thanks are due to our many students, who worked with us both in our studio and at Antioch College, and last but not least, to Gerda Oldham and Ernestine Brecht, for typing the manuscript.

GLOSSARY

ANTIQUE GLASS   Hand-blown colored glass.

ARMATURE   Iron or aluminum framework in the form of T bars into which a window is set.

BADGER   A brush about 4″ wide of badger hair used to stipple or smooth out a wash of glass paint.

BRIGHT   A short-haired flat bristle brush.

CAME   An H-shaped lead used to bind together pieces of a finished window. Other archaic spellings are karm, calm, carm, and kam. The English use calm and the Americans came.

CARTOON   A full-sized working drawing in black and white or color which indicates the exact design and glass shapes of a finished window or panel.

CRUCIBLE   A vessel of metal or refracting material employed for heating substances to high temperatures.

CULLET   The remaining small pieces of glass after a window has been cut.

CUT LINE   The carboned outline of individual pieces of glass made from the cartoon. One outline is used for patterns, the other for glazing.

DALLE-DE-VERRE   French name for 1″-thick slabs of glass.

ETCHING   Process of removing, with hydrofluoric acid, a film of glass on flashed glass to produce two colors on one piece of glass.

FLASH GLASS   Glass which has been thinly coated with a second color. Combinations of red on blue, green on gold or white; blue on white and green on white are available.

FLUX   A substance added to assist in the reduction of metal by fusion. In the case of glass paint the flux acts as an adherent of the paint to the glass.

FURRING STRIP   Narrow strip of wood used as a guide in glazing.

GLAZING   On stained glass the process of leading together pieces of glass for a

	window opening. Broadly used to designate the process of closing a window opening no matter what the material.
GROZER	Pliers used to bite or grind away uneven edges of a cut piece of glass to make it accurately fit the pattern from which it has been cut.
KILN	The oven in which painted glass is fired.
LAMINATING	The process of adhering pieces of glass in layers with resin glues.
LIGHTS	Another term for windows.
LANCET	A long narrow window opening with a pointed rounded top.
LASTING NAILS	Glazing nails—nails used to hold together a window while it is in the process of being glazed and before it is soldered.
LATHYKIN	A small wooden tool of hard wood either heart-shaped or oblong used to open the flanges on lead cames.
MAHLSTICK	A round, wooden stick used as a guide for the hand in painting.
MATTING	The process of laying on a thin film of glass paint.
MULLION	A metal division between panels of a window and tracery.
PATINA	The accumulation of a whitish coating on the exterior of a window due to a lichen growth.

QUARRIES	Square- or diamond-shaped pieces of glass used for plain glazing.
RABBET	A channel, groove, or slot cut along the edge or face of a piece or surface of wood or stone.
SILVER STAIN	A silver-nitrate mixture which produces a yellow color varying from light yellow to deep orange when painted and fired on glass.
TINNING	Coating the tip of a soldering iron.
T BAR	(Armature in the shape of a T on which to rest glass sections in a window opening.
TEMPLATE	A paper pattern of the exact shape of a window opening.
THUMB WAX	A soft wax made of beeswax and other ingredients to secure pieces of glass to plate glass.
TRACERY	Geometric shapes used above the lancet openings.
STIPPLING	A process in glass painting achieved by stabbing a wet matt with a brush.
STOPPING KNIFE	A knife with a short blade curved and rounded on the end to push the leads tightly against the glass.
WAXING UP	The process of dropping hot wax on the corners of pieces of glass assembled on a sheet of plate glass for painting to secure them temporarily to the plate.
WHITING	Fine quality of calcium carbonate.

ORIGIN AND HISTORY

Historical Beginnings

"Stained glass is a lost art." That should have a familiar ring to most readers. The only trouble is that it is not true; it is simply an old wives' tale. Stained glass is no more a lost art than fresco painting or mosaic. But the romantic will persist: "That beautiful blue glass of Chartres Cathedral can never be duplicated!" Nonsense! There is no color ever produced in glass that cannot be duplicated. What is more, technical progress and scientific knowledge have made it possible to produce an almost infinite number of subtle variations of any basic color. However, the persistent repetition of the lost-art myth most certainly would suggest some foundation in fact. It does, but it is not technical knowledge that has been lost; rather that the simple direct-ness of expression, so often found in the early stages of a developing culture, was replaced in the sixteenth century by chiaroscuro forms unsuitable to stained glass.

In the following pages, beginning with a brief account of the history of glass and particularly of stained glass, fragments of the true story may come to be understood and reassembled into a coherent picture of what really did happen and is still happening.

It is not known for certain just where glass originated, but it is well known that almost the first examples were those made to imitate precious or semiprecious stones.

Quite early in their history the Egyptians had colored glass perfume bottles and cosmetic jars, along with the ever-present imitation jewels.

Signs of actual glass manufacturing were not discovered in Egypt until the Eighteenth Dynasty, which would place the time as somewhere between 1510 and 1349 BC. These were found at Tel el 'Amarna. They were sophisticated and represented a late stage of development. Since no primitive or evolutionary stages of development have ever been found here, one can only conclude that the knowledge of glass-making was imported. Pliny the Elder, the Roman historian, says with some degree of firmness that "the Syrians originated its manufacture"; he places its origin at the foot of Mt. Carmel, that mountain of biblical fame.

Materials needed for the making of glass were at hand—odd lumps of manufactured glass are still frequently found in that area. Pliny tells a story of the Phoenician mariners who propped up their cooking pots with blocks of natron upon a sandy beach. When their fires were burning brightly they were surprised to find that the sand had melted into a stream of liquid glass. This is not as improbable as it might seem, for natron is a form of carbonate of soda which, when combined with silica sand, can act as a flux to melt the sand into glass. It is equally likely that a wood ash deposit under their pots could have caused the same result, for

15

potash is an alkali (potassium carbonate) and is also used to lower the melting point of silica sand. However, it is extremely doubtful that glass pieces of any significant size could have been formed in this manner.

The Romans occasionally used colored glass for making windows; when they did, they generally set the individual pieces into a lattice of bronze.

It was not until the first century of the Christian Era that the Romans discovered the art of glass blowing. There is every indication that the art was known at a much earlier date by both the Egyptians and Syrians. The Romans, however, must be credited with the making of glass large enough in size to be usable for windows.

Caligula was one of the earliest Roman emperors to use glass windows in his palace, but Caligula's unsavory character did not encourage imitation by succeeding emperors. It was generally believed that glass windows were examples of the former emperor's unnecessary extravagance.

Windows have been found in Pompeii in houses buried beneath tons of volcanic ash, some of them set in wood as well as the usual bronze.

By and large, the Romans practiced the splitting of alabaster into thin sheets, using these instead of glass. There are windows made of alabaster in San Apollinare Church in Classe, the port city of Ravenna; when used for windows, the material emits a beautiful soft warm light.

When the remains of the Romano-British town of Calleva Atrebatum were uncovered at Silchester in England, glass windows were discovered among its ruins.

In 323 AD, a momentous decision was made by the Roman Emperor Constantine, a decision which changed the whole direction of history in the Western World. Constantine, observing the rapid Christianization of so much of the Eastern World and realizing that the killing of Christians had reached the law of diminishing returns, decided to follow the old adage, "If you can't beat them, join them." He proclaimed himself and all of his subjects to be Christians, resolving to move his capital to the small Greek town of Byzantium, thereafter to be known as Constantinople (now Istanbul). Six years later he carried out his intention, and Byzantium became the Eastern capital of the Roman Empire.

For the first time in history, the East and West were united in a friendly manner under a single ruler with a universal interest in the new and growing Christian faith. The cross-fertilization made possible by a union of the mystical East and the classical West was bound to produce a cultural-artistic amalgam destined to grow into unprecedented proportions—leading finally to the art of stained glass. Strangely enough, the art did not have its inception in Byzantium, that source of so much rich promise, but ultimately in France or possibly in Germany.

In less than a hundred years after the establishment of the Empire at Constantinople, warriors from the northern provinces of Western Europe began to overrun Rome itself. Constantinople rapidly became the only part of the Empire able to withstand the invaders' attack.

In the sixth century, during the reign of Justinian and Theodora, a renaissance of the arts took place in Constantinople. The Church of Santa Sophia, along with many other splendid buildings, was erected. Their walls were covered with the finest of frescoes and mosaics.

Justinian, projecting his influence westward, had the now-famous Church of San Vitale designed and built in Ravenna. Its walls were covered with the finest examples of Byzantine mosaics.

After Justinian's death, Theodora, his queen—and undoubtedly the stronger character of the two—directed both her interest and affections toward her Eastern neighbors. Throughout recorded history, some elements in Eastern cultures had maintained a consistent and persistent opposition toward representative art in any form for religious usage. They particularly objected to the use of the human figure for this purpose. With the appearance of Mohammed and the rapid growth of his new faith, the Eastern iconoclasts acquired a growing body of supporters. The Eastern emperors, frightened by the pressures of Mohammed's followers, added their support to the iconoclasts within their own ranks. In 726 AD, a law was passed by the Eastern emperor, which was known as the Iconoclast Edict. This edict specifically prohibited the representation of the human figure in religious art. The reaction to the edict was instantaneous and violent; the immediate result was the creation of a spectacular polarization of opinion. Naturally, since there was a reasonable number of Western partisans living in Constantinople, the division of opinion was expressed primarily along East-West lines.

Those clerics with Western affiliations maintained that with such a large proportion of the population unable to read or write, it was not only helpful but necessary to use pictorial means to illustrate the stories of Christian faith. They flatly insisted that without the right to use human representation to illustrate the stories of Christianity, they would be stripped of their most effective educational tool.

It must be remembered that the Gothic tribes had been introduced to the Christian religion by Arius of Alexandria (d. 336 AD); it was Arius who did not accept the divinity of Christ, believing that the Son was created by and hence inferior to the Father, and not God in the fullest sense. This attitude, inherited from the teaching of Arius, placed

16

the Gothic tribes in the forefront of a humanizing movement. On the other hand, the Eastern Church adhered to the theory of the absolute divinity of Christ. Riding halfway between these two antithetical points of view, the Roman Catholic Church accepted the idea of the Trinity, which considered that Christ was both human and divine and that He represented both the human and the divine natures in man. Justinian, forced to settle the dispute, ruled that the Pope of Rome was the head of the Christian Church, and so ruled in favor of the Trinity. For some time, the Arian Goths of the West and the Monophysites of the East were held in delicate balance by the Roman Catholic Church. Eventually, the Arians, expelled from Ravenna, retreated to their Gothic positions north of Rome.

At this point it should be noted that the mosaics which they had put in San Apollinare Nuovo, their Arian church in Ravenna, represent the type of humanistic expression which they later contributed to thirteenth-century Gothic art.

Following upon the heels of the Iconoclast Edict came an inevitable period of destruction: frescoes were painted over and mosaics were ripped from the walls. Fortunately, the vandals did not carry on their operations as far west as Ravenna and the mosaics in her magnificent churches were spared.

For a time the artists and craftsmen of Constantinople attempted to go underground. They substituted illuminated manuscripts and icons for their larger frescoes and mosaics, for these could easily be concealed when the necessity arose.

By 800 AD there occurred a complete break between the Eastern Church of Constantinople and the Western one at Rome. By personally crowning Charlemagne Holy Roman Emperor, the Pope affirmed the ultimate decision-making authority of the Church in both civil and ecclesiastical affairs.

Encouraged by the Pope's act, the artists and craftsmen of Constantinople began their trek westward to Rome, so that they might again be free to carry on their crafts without political or religious persecution.

That some glass windows had been set in Constantinople's more important buildings is evident from the various remarks attributed to members of the court; there were vague and intangible rumors that some had even been installed in the great Church of Santa Sophia. But since no vestige of such work exists, we must assume that there is a reasonable doubt that any important windows had ever been placed in this famous Byzantine church.

Colored windows are found in a number of later Eastern mosques where they are invariably of two types: one, geometric; the other, organic in design. The second type generally consists of a somewhat stylized floral spray

a   b

fig 1
a) Muslim geometric-type window b) Muslim organic-type window

arranged geometrically in a bowl-like vase. Both types are set either in alabaster or a deep fretwork of stone. The pieces of glass are small and usually of poor quality. They do, however, illustrate the important fact that when the pieces are kept small, the resulting effect is good despite the inferior quality of the base material. There is an example of this glass in Lord Leighton's house in London.

The Venerable Bede, in his history of the English abbots, mentions that his teacher, the Abbot Biscop of Monkwearmouth, had the monastery chapel fitted with windows; in addition, he had skilled glassworkers from Gaul come to teach his people the art. This would place these windows in the early part of the eighth century. Since no mention is made of symbols or subjects, we can only assume that the windows were plain and contained no painted work.

In the eleventh century the windows of the chapter house at Monte Cassino were said to have been filled with colored glass "glazed with lead and fixed with iron"; at the time referred to, Pope Victor III was the Abbot of Monte Cassino (Abbot Desiderius). A short time later, in 1087, he was elected Pope.

The above quote is significant in that in addition to glass it spoke specifically of lead and iron as structural materials for windows. Only one factor is now missing to make a true stained-glass window; there is still no mention of painted details.

The Byzantine artists and craftsmen did not terminate

17

their westward journey at Rome but continued onward into central France. They brought with them highly perfected skills in illumination, in fresco painting, and in the making of mosaics, but what is more important to us, their skill in the art of enameling.

There are three main threads of history leading directly to the origin of stained glass: (1) the discovery and making of glass, the material; (2) the early references to windows made with plain or colored glass; and (3) the story and origin of the art of enameling. The discovery of glass and its early production has just been told. The making of the particular glass used in stained-glass work will be covered under the section on materials.

The art of enameling, the third and final thread leading to the very first authentic stained glass, might well be considered the most important link, for it is to this art that we owe the possibility of giving definition and detail to what heretofore could only be classified as plain glazing.

The first known examples of the art of enameling found in the Western World were those used to define ornamental details upon the robes of metal sculpture, and were found as early as the fifth century BC in Greece. It was also customary at this time to define the whites of the eyes as well as the irises by the use of colored enamels on the same metal sculptures. Since all of the colors were separated by narrow strips of metal, the enameling technique used would qualify as cloisonné.

Slightly later, enamel was used by the Romans. After a short time, enameling seems to have disappeared or at least to have fallen out of general use in Rome. It again appears in Celtic Britain and Ireland around the third century AD. The enamel work of the Irish is considered to be far superior to that of their British cousins.

The art of enameling may be defined as the process of applying a thin coat of glass (in powder form) to a metal, which, when heated to a temperature of around 1400° Fahrenheit, melts and fuses to the metal. There are two types of enameling which are of interest to us for their relation to the art of stained glass. The first type is known as champlevé, which literally means to gouge out. The second type is called cloisonné. Champlevé is made by carving away metal areas, then filling the hollows with enamel. One way is to pour the molten enamel into the hollows; the other is to fill the same hollow areas with powdered enamel and to heat this sufficiently to bring the enamel to the melting point. Cloisonné is made by soldering narrow strips of metal (*cloisons*), placed on end, to a metal-base plate, filling the areas between the strips with powdered enamel, and bringing the enamel to the melting point. Champlevé may be distinguished from cloisonné in that champlevé enamel will always have large areas of metal showing; in cloisonné there will be no areas of metal seen except the narrow strips used to divide one color from the other. Many times a combination of both types is used on the same piece.

In making either type of enamel it usually is necessary to repeat the process several times, as the powdered enamel, when melted, shrinks considerably. After a sufficient level of enamel has been reached, which means that some or most of the metal will be partially covered, it will be necessary to grind down the entire surface evenly. The surface is then completed by polishing.

From the champlevé enamels of third century Ireland to the first stained-glass windows appearing in France in the eleventh century, quite a span of time elapses. During this interval the art of enameling traveled eastward from Ireland and ultimately to Constantinople. In similar fashion, an identical enameling art moved westward from Persia, where in due time it also found its way to the Eastern capital. Artists and craftsmen, inundated from both the East and West by the new art of enameling, embraced both champlevé and cloisonné methods. In a

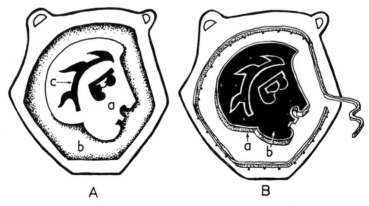

A—Champlevé enamel
a) Raised metal section
b) Shallow area either carved or etched out
c) Area filled in with colored enamel, fired and ground level with the metal

fig 2

B—Same design done as a cloisonné enamel
a) The cloison
b) Black area; colored enamel placed between the cloisons, fired and ground down

18

relatively short time they brought both techniques to an advanced state of sophistication and perfection.

The exact origin of the first stained-glass window will always remain conjecture; chauvinistic claims and counter-claims will appear from time to time. What we do know is that plain colored-glass windows were constructed as early as the middle of the first century AD in Rome, and that glass set in lead may have existed by the ninth century if not earlier. What really interested the clergy, as well as the cathedral-builders, was a means of telling the story of their religious beliefs in a vivid pictorial manner. They were also looking for a way to fill the ever-growing size of the window openings in their new cathedrals and, incidentally, to find some material which would keep out the weather without obscuring the light.

Making windows of colored glass joined together with lead cames (grooved rods of cast lead) may well have been suggested by the cloisonné and champlevé enamels. While the breaking of the glass into relatively small pieces could have been derived from the Byzantine mosaics, it is quite certain that true stained-glass windows were not made until the use of the monochrome brown enamel was borrowed from the contemporary enamelist. Stained glass is not one of those arts which has enjoyed a long period of evolutionary growth from primitive beginnings to a perfected peak. It burst forth as a *fait accompli* almost overnight. To accomplish this extraordinary feat, the budding stained-glass artist was compelled to seek for his designs patterns, ideas, and examples from among already existing arts. It is now fairly clear that four main types of art were drawn upon as models for this new technique: first, the mosaics; second, the enamels; third, the frescoes; and fourth, the illuminated manuscripts.

Definition of Stained Glass

Just what is stained glass? Whenever an attempt is made to define such a complex medium, there is always a temptation to define each separate operation. The following definition, though not perfect, at least may be accepted as a reasonably adequate one. Stained glass is a fabric composed of many small pieces of colored glass, painted with a monochrome enamel, fastened together with narrow strips of lead, and held in place with crossbars. It becomes necessary almost at once to elaborate the bare definition.

The very name "stained glass" will seem to the new-comer a fallacious nomenclature when he is told that scarcely any of the glass used for windows is stained; the color is in the glass. Only a monochrome brown enamel is applied to the colored glass. Its purpose is twofold: one, to add details, such as hands, feet, and drapery; the other, to add tones for the modulation of forms. N. H. J. Westlake calls the art "stained and painted glass," naming his famous four-volume work *History of Design in Painted Glass*. The Germans call the art "*Glasmalerei*," and the French call it "*vitraux*," which means a stained-glass window and nothing else. To better understand the term stained glass we can turn to our own history of the late 1600s which records numerous references to signs "stained" for the local inns. Staining, as one can see, is only an earlier parlance for coloring.

To change from definitions to factual participation, let us move from the sunlit courtyard in front of a cathedral through its small side door and into its lofty, dim, and twilit interior. The observer will almost certainly find himself staggered by the dramatic effect and the overwhelming power of the stained glass.

In the clerestory, saints, prophets, and lesser personages drift past in an almost endless procession, while lower down in the nave, window after window filled with medallions join the parade. They pass before the rapt observer, a veritable picturebook of colorful and forgotten saints. Here and there will be seen a remembered name, but many of them will be familiar only to the antiquarian. The observer confronted with such a vision will find it hard to believe that these same figures which seem to twinkle and float in space are composed of such uncompromising materials as glass, lead, and iron; but it is by knowledge and the proper use of these same materials that the great windows of the Middle Ages were created.

Stained glass is many things. First of all, it is essentially, at least at the outset, a Christian art; it had its inception completely in the Christian Era. Secondly, it is an architectural art, or at least it serves best as a handmaiden to architecture.

Thirdly, it is a hybrid art; like most hybrids it could acquire the best features of its parents or the worst. Just what does hybrid mean in this context? It means that stained glass is a combination of crafts: of the art of enameling and of painting; not ordinary painting, but painting made with light pouring through the color. It is not completely fair to judge art by its size, but no one can deny that a ten-inch enamel getting its effect from reflected light is no match for the identical composition made in transparent glass ten feet high. It so happens that stained glass is one of those fortunate hybrids where the whole is infinitely more effective than the sum of its parts. Stained glass can be either transparent or translucent; when transparent, it can be seen through but it is never seen through clearly—the shapes behind it are vague, blurred, and distorted; they constantly change in color from light to dark. Each passing cloud alters the effect of a window. When, on the other hand, the glass is so treated as to be translucent, it will transmit light and, under certain circumstances, it can seem to hold the light within itself—to glow like a jewel.

These properties which we have just mentioned greatly increase the potential for expanding the dimensions of the medium. They give to it a mystique which could add subtle innuendos to the "lost-art" myth. We may be helped to a better understanding of this phenomenon if we take as an illustration a simple formula used in photography. Let us say that we are setting up a comparative scale to determine both light and dark (value) and color intensity (brilliance); also, that we assume that in nature we can recognize the greatest number of gradations in both value and intensity. If we now assign to nature a figure of 1000-to-1, we will then find that a transparency in color will be 250-to-1; if printed on photographic paper, it will be 50-to-1; and if painted, it will be 25-to-1. If we correctly accept the phototransparency as being approximately the same as a miniature colored-glass window, then we are confronted at once with the fact that a transparent window can be ten times as brilliant as a painting of the same subject. It should be apparent that the stained-glass artist has at his fingertips a medium capable of producing images that are ten times as intense as those of a painter. This does not mean that painting on canvas is only one tenth as good as glass painting. It simply means that for certain kinds of work glass can solve problems that easel painting can not. It also means that a good stained-glass window is not an easel painting lit from behind.

Failure to understand this simple fact was the chief cause of the downfall of the art in the sixteenth century; but more about this later, when we discuss sixteenth-century glass painting. It should be enough to say at this point that the glass artist will have no difficulty in attaining great brilliance; his real problem will be to keep from over-coloring his work.

Classification

Setting up a classification chart for the various periods of stained glass is a somewhat difficult task because there is no clear-cut demarcation between one style and another that follows it. In a certain area a style may linger on for as much as twenty-five years after a new one has begun elsewhere. For instance, in one area of France, as at Poitiers, the artists may have continued to work in a twelfth-century style long after they had been making thirteenth-century windows in Chartres. It is this fact that accounts for the difference in opinion as to whether the great Crucifixion window in Poitiers is a hold-over from eleventh- and

twelfth-century styles executed in the thirteenth century, or an authentic eleventh-century window with twelfth- and thirteenth-century additions.

Studying the various periods and styles of stained glass serves a dual purpose. It enables us to follow the growth and evolution of window making. It also provides a storehouse of technical craft knowledge which can be adapted to new as well as old ways of making stained-glass windows.

There is still another difficulty to cope with: in Germany there is no thirteenth-century Gothic, and in Italy there is no Gothic at all. Charles Winston, in his writings on stained glass, used the English architectural classification established in about 1825 by Thomas Rickman. The table shows the English periods with those of the French opposite.

English	*French*
1) Early English, 1189–1307	Early Gothic
2) Decorated, 1307–1377	Middle Gothic
3) Perpendicular, 1377–1530	Late Gothic

Westlake further subdivided the Rickman classification to the point of utter confusion, adding a new transitional division every time a glass painter's brush slipped.

Herbert Read, in his excellent book on English stained glass, greatly simplified the period divisions as follows:

1) Age of Reason, 1150–1350 (the rise and fall of the classical epoch of Christian art)
2) Age of Sentiment, 1350–1500 (rise and establishment of Humanism)
3) Age of Fancy, 1500–1900

These three periods correspond roughly to a classification of "early," "middle," and "late," and relate to recognizable visual differences. While those of Read call for the acceptance of his personal aesthetic judgments, we feel that the following classifications are more immediately acceptable for our purposes. The classification, with its visually recognizable characteristics, would be as follows:

Period	*Type of Drawing*	*Color*	*Architectural Relationship*
Early Eleventh– twelfth– thirteenth centuries	Archaic	Pure and primary	Complete affirmation
Middle Fourteenth– fifteenth centuries	Naturalistic	Secondary color and a lot of white	Affirms but deviates
Late	Realistic— chiaroscuro form	Literal	Ignores architecture

fig 3
A head of Christ from a twelfth-century fresco in Rovio, Switzerland

fig 4
Early glass painting in the style of the Rovio Christ

Although one window can serve to illustrate the dominant characteristics of a period with regard to color, the type of drawing, or the quality of architectural affirmation, it will not suffice to explain the important variables affecting the general style of a window. Ignoring these variables can lead to recognitional confusion. In other words, it is relatively easy after studying windows for a short time to be able to say whether the window in question belongs to the early, middle, or late period. But when the next question is asked— "Is it eleventh, twelfth, thirteenth, fourteenth, fifteenth, or sixteenth century?"—the problem becomes increasingly more complex.

The particular way the flesh is drawn and painted will often provide a very useful clue, not only to the period, but even to the century and to the decade of the window's execution. Heads are generally more closely examined by the uncritical observer than other parts of a figure or composition. For this reason we are including a series of heads from the various periods reflecting different styles of painting.

fig 5
A head of Christ from Hamma Divinity Chapel, Wittenberg University. Done by the authors in the manner of the earlier glass painting

21

fig 6
A thirteenth-century head from St Nicholas Church, Wilton, Wiltshire, from Charles H. Winston

fig 7
A fourteenth-century head from Westlake

fig 8
A modern head by Arthur Norris executed in a fourteenth-century manner

fig 9
A fifteenth-century head from Canterbury

fig 10

A modern head from the Ascension Window, Church of the Ascension, Middletown, Ohio, showing a number of historic styles combined to create a new modern style of painting. By Robert M. Metcalf

fig 11

A modern head by Arthur Norris done in a fifteenth-century manner

A series of questions, in simple outline form, arranged so that they will lead to an ever-increasing body of useful knowledge will help direct your attention to these variables. It should be understood that all questions cannot possibly apply equally to all periods, but the following should be of assistance in considering this problem:

1) Style—Is the window (a) early (b) middle (c) late
2) Century—Is the window (a) eleventh century (b) twelfth century (c) thirteenth century (d) fourteenth century (e) fifteenth century (f) sixteenth century (g) later
3) Type of window—Is the window (a) medallion (b) single figure (c) subject window (d) grisaille (e) quarry (carres) (f) rose (g) combination
4) Source—(a) France (b) England (c) Italy (d) Germany (e) Switzerland (f) modern
5) Position in building—(a) clerestory (b) transept (c) apse (d) apsidal chapel (e) crypt (f) special chapel (g) other
6) Source (city)—(a) Chartres (b) Bourges (c) York (d) Canterbury (e) other
7) Church or Cathedral—(a) All Saints [York] (b) Saint Pierre [Chartres] (c) Cathedral of Notre Dame [Chartres] (d) Saint Chapelle [Paris] (e) other
8) Type of Subject—(a) The Life of Christ (b) The Life of the Virgin (c) The Passion (d) The Miracles (e) The Parables (f) Jesse Tree (g) Historical (h) Saint (i) Martyr (j) Prophet (k) Evangelist (l) Latin Doctors (m) Allegorical (n) Disciples (o) other
9) Recognition of Specific Windows—(a) What is its historical significance? (b) What is its iconographical content? (c) What is its symbolism? (d) What is its other significance?
10) Esoteric Information—(a) Who was the artist? (b) Who was the donor? (c) What was the particular technique? (d) What was other significance?

Prestyle Windows

There are very early windows in France at Le Mans, Chartres, Angers, Vendôme, Châlons-sur-Marne, and the crypt in Saint-Denis; in England at York Minster and at Brabourne in Kent; and in Germany at Augsburg and Tegernsee. Out of this group there are three windows that have been selected as possible firsts; or rather, it would be more accurate to say that there are two windows and a third group of five (which may be considered as one example since they belong together).

It would be appropriate to mention here that in the Victoria and Albert Museum, in London, one may see a colored drawing of a panel. It forms a pattern of light-colored glass interspersed with small pieces of color. What is important is that the colored pieces have rosettes painted on them in what originally may have been a brown enamel. The original may possibly have been from the eleventh century and could vie for position as one of the earliest stained-glass windows. However, since there is no exact record of its date, it has never been given too much attention. Let us, therefore, consider the first of the acceptable windows.

The small Ascension window located in the old part of the cathedral of Le Mans in central France is justifiably listed first. It is roughly five and a half feet high by slightly less than four feet wide. It depicts the Virgin Mary and the Twelve Apostles shown in the attitude of gazing upward. Each figure stands on an individual stylized hillock, and is superimposed upon alternating blue and red rectilinear areas of color. The window in its present state is obviously not complete, as there must have been an ascending Christ in the original. The elongated sinuous figures are stylized in a manner reminiscent of Byzantine mosaics, frescoes, and particularly of the sculpture at the Abbey of Vézelay. The large-scale bold pieces making up the blue and red background seem to be out of scale with the rest of the window, causing the figures to seem insignificant by comparison.

Since decisions made by scholars as to the proper dating of early windows are based upon Byzantine stylizations, they are justly open to question. The only reasonably accurate placements are those in which dated, documented, historical records are available. Bishop Hoel, who was Bishop of Le Mans Cathedral in the early part of the eleventh century, describes a series of windows which were made during his tenure. Bishop Hoel's account, which was recorded in the thirteenth century, is preserved in the cathedral library. There is every reason to believe that the little Ascension window at Le Mans is one of the windows described by him. There are certain scholars who contend that the technique of stained glass was suggested by the cloisonné process exclusively. Whether or not this is really the case may be open to serious argument

If one compares a detail of the great Poitiers Crucifixion (Plate 3) with the champlevé enamel of a Crucifixion in the Metropolitan Museum (Figure 12), one can scarcely deny the similarity of composition, but in addition he will have to admit that the Christ in this window is an almost perfect blow-up of the Metropolitan enamel. It may well be that the cloisonné system played a most important part in creating our first windows. If this is entirely so, it is strange that one of our earliest windows follows the design of a champlevé enamel. In a sense, this is needless quibbling; there really is not that great a difference between the two

types of enamel. Le Mans, the city where our first example is located, is about 120 miles southwest of Paris. Poitiers, the home of our second example, is 125 miles directly south of Le Mans. This places Poitiers slightly west of central France. The city is historically famous. It was here, in 732 AD, that Charles Martel, the grandfather of Charlemagne, met the advancing Moorish army. He defeated and turned back the invaders. For this he was acclaimed the savior of Christendom. Charles was accompanied by his grandson Charlemagne, who was destined to play such an important part in the building of the Holy Roman Empire.

The Cathedral of Saint Pierre was built in 1162 by Henry II of England atop an earlier Roman basilica. The great Crucifixion window dominates the east end of the cathedral. The present window has been altered somewhat. Originally the window included only the Crucifixion and Ascension sections, as can be seen in the illustration; at the foot of the Cross on the left side stands the Virgin Mary and one Roman centurion, while on the opposite side appears Saint John the Evangelist and the second centurion. In the upper half of the Crucifixion are shown the Twelve Apostles, six on either side of the Cross. They gaze upward with rapt attention at the ascending Christ which is placed in the section above. He is enclosed in a full-length nimbus (*mandorla*) and in turn is flanked on either side by single angels.

A typical twelfth-century border was added later; still later, in the thirteenth century, a medallion depicting Saint Peter crucified upside down was included in the new composition. The addition of Saint Peter shown in his traditional martyrdom changed the window from a simple Crucifixion with the promise of the Ascension to a strange type and anti-type form. The usual type and anti-type composition uses an example of a figure from the Old Testament and a figure with a similar or parallel experience in the New Testament. In this case, both Saint Peter and Christ properly belong to the New Testament. The figures, though still highly stylized in the Byzantine manner, are much better drawn than those of the Le Mans Ascension window. Also, the scale of the background pieces to those of the figures is better in the Crucifixion window. As in most of the better twelfth- and thirteenth-century windows where blue and red were placed in juxtaposition, the reds selected contained no vestige of blue in their composition. At the same time, the blues which were used were ever so slightly greenish in character. This set up a subtle complementary color combination which kept the windows from vibrating into an unpleasant Easter-egg purple.

The third group of windows may be considered separately or as a group. There are five remaining windows which are

24

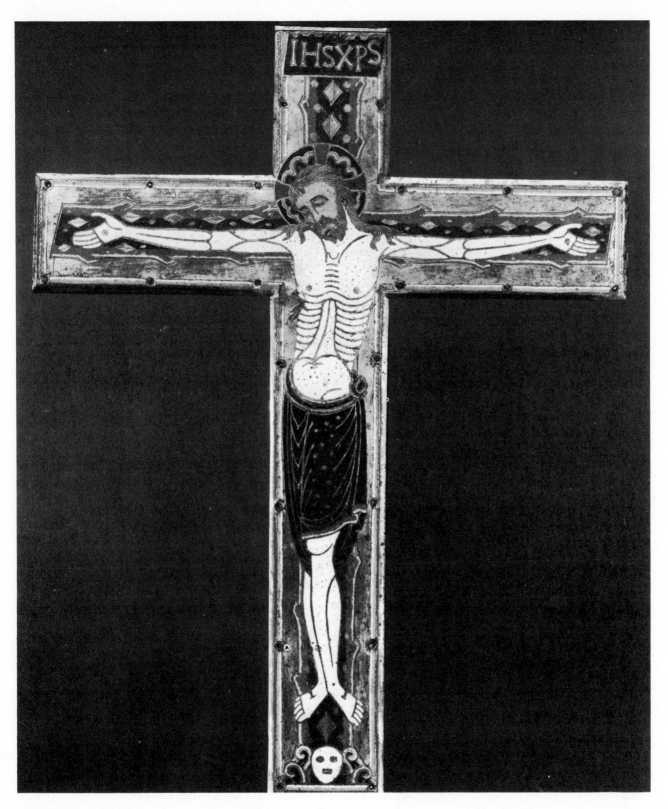

fig 12
Enamel crucifix about 1200

The Metropolitan Museum of Art, New York

25

presently located in the Dom in Augsburg. Their effect is somewhat marred by being placed too high up on the wall of the thirteenth-century cathedral. Originally they had been set in the adjacent, much older, church of which now only the foundation remains. These windows have no direct documentation, but it is well known that the first monasteries founded in Germany were established by Irish monks who brought their own Celtic manuscripts with them when they came to Germany. If one looks at any one of these remaining windows, comparing it with a typical page from the Celtic *Book of Kells*, the influence and resemblance to the illuminations will prove startling.

To some art historians these windows are Romanesque. Since about the only clear definition of the term Romanesque which can universally be accepted without serious controversy is that the round arch was used in its architecture, the term has come to be a kind of catchall for Western art between Byzantine and Gothic. It brings to mind some rather caustic remarks made by the music critic Deems Taylor during a symphony broadcast. He was speaking of the theme played by the shepherd in *Tristan and Isolde*. He noted that the theme was being played on an English horn; the instrument, he said, was called English because it was invented by a Frenchman, and a horn because it was a reed instrument related to the oboe. If we accept Saint Trophime at Arles, the abbey at Vézelay, and the cathedral at Autun all as French Romanesque, and if we also recognize the extreme difference in style between the classical character of the sculpture at Saint Trophime and the elongated expressionistic sculpture of Vézelay and Autun, then all that remains is the round arch. It is true that all three have vitalistic animal details included, but these same animal forms are characteristic of similar sculpture from the Han Dynasty in China, the Scythian area around the Black Sea, and, combined with an elaborate ornamental interweave, are dominant features of Celtic art. It would seem much more appropriate to call these Augsburg windows Celtic in origin rather than by the less definitive term of Romanesque, particularly as these windows are unique not only to Germany, but have no further counterparts elsewhere.

Originally, these five remaining figures were apparently a part of a much larger series. There does not seem to be any particular schematic order or theme in the selection of King David, Daniel, Moses, Joseph, or Jonah. If one examines the illustration of the Jonah panel at a close range, he will note a fragment of a sixth figure glazed into its base. The section has been glazed upside down. It shows a part of one red leg and the base of a hair coat invariably worn by Saint John the Baptist. All five figures face forward and are quite similar in composition. When seen together, they produce a rhythmic vertical repeat. The

change of color, along with the variable placement of the scrolls which each figure holds, add just enough variation to produce a needed foil to the potential feeling of monotonous verticality. The heads in these windows are drawn and painted in a manner much more like those in the *Book of Kells* than those in either of the two Byzantine-influenced examples which we have been studying. Compared to the dominant deep reds and blues used in both the Le Mans Ascension and the Poitiers Crucifixion, the Augsburg ones have a fresh gay color quality. Only one of the Augsburg windows contains a reasonably large area of pure red. This fairly light red has been used in an overmantle on the David figure. The other figures are colored with combinations of gold and green, with an occasional area of maroon. The fact that they are set down upon a white background adds lightness and a strong resemblance to the Celtic illuminations from which they were derived.

The series of windows which we have just discussed brings to an end the consideration of the prestyle examples. Since they have acquired their design format from other arts, they have a somewhat static formal quality. What is good about them is what is good about Byzantine and Celtic art. The twelfth- and thirteenth-century windows which follow them have in many ways design weaknesses not found in the prestyle group; but these deficiencies are compensated for by their exuberant vitality.

The Middle Ages

A true understanding of the Middle Ages is not easily acquired. There are several reasons for the apparent difficulty which many viewers encounter when studying the art of the Middle Ages. A major one is due to the fact that the Middle Ages are sandwiched in between the two so-called peaks of Western culture; that of Greece and Rome on the one side, and of the Renaissance on the other. As a result, the medieval period is unfavorably compared to these classical cultures.

Italian scholars of the time had nothing but contempt for the new architectural style coming out of the North. To them, all people from the north—Goths, Franks, or Lombards—were barbarians. They chose a name at random from among the barbarian tribes and labeled the new art "Gothic." Little did they realize that the new style for which they expressed such disdain would prove to be a new breath of life for the expiring body of late Roman art.

We of the twentieth century have inherited an almost slavish belief in classical Western culture. In fact, we consider the Renaissance and its works as very nearly sacred.

It is understandable, in the light of the Greeks' delight in the human figure and the Romans' interest in baths and body cleanliness, that we should be somewhat shocked and repelled when we read a passage in a medieval manuscript which states that the pigsty, the well, and the privy should be four feet apart. Apparently medieval man was more interested in the cleanliness of his immortal soul than in that of his body.

To understand and appreciate Gothic art, the student will have to apply a new set of aesthetic values to the problem. He will have to give up some of his classical concepts and come to realize that there are other equally valid forms of art. He will have to accept that in the people he may have classified as crude and uncultured, lies an immense source of artistic wealth. These early people are much closer to nature's source than modern Europeans and Americans. They are intuitive rather than intellectual in their creative responses. They are highly imaginative and relatively uninhibited. They tend to blur the lines of demarcation between fact and fancy which in itself adds great conviction and reality to their flights of fantasy. They all have one quality in common: a vivid and vitalistic directness. They all emphasize the life of the piece rather than the life of the model.

It is the life of the piece that is the key to our understanding. If we are to seek the true source of artistic expression found among the Germanic tribes of northern Europe, it will not be found rising out of Graeco-Roman models but out of that other mainstream of European art, the Scytho-Iranian or Persian source. It has become an accepted possibility that the people who inhabited northern Europe and who overran Rome as early as 410 AD may originally have come from the Eurasian steppes by way of the Black Sea and the Danube. These migrating tribes had earlier developed a unique and recognizable style of animal sculpture executed in metal. It was called Scythian, the name of one of the several nomadic tribes inhabiting the area around the Black Sea which is now a part of the Soviet Union. Strange as it may seem, the style of the animals depicted has a most amazing resemblance to that of the Paleolithic wall-paintings done in the caves of Altamira and Lascaux some 10,000 to 20,000 years ago. It is altogether possible that the stylistic similarity may have resulted from similar nomadic living conditions, their closeness to nature, and their dependence upon animals for their survival.

The Celtic artists of Ireland, in their early manuscripts of the eighth century, notably the *Book of Kells*, the *Lindesfarne* and *Echternach* gospels, all reflect the influence of Scytho-Iranian vitalistic art. They have, however, added the human figure to the animals and geometric ornament of the earlier art. It is rather surprising that so little emphasis has been placed on the possible origin of these early northern Europeans and that so little attention has been given to the true character of their art, a type of art which indicates an atavistic return to a much earlier time in history when nomadic peoples had such empathy with the phenomena of nature. This empathy, in turn, created a belief in animism, a belief which made them feel that all things in nature—the sun and moon, thunder and lightning, wind and rain, trees and flowers, animals and birds, animate and inanimate alike—were imbued with an inner life and spirit of their own. It is this belief in the spirit of the inanimate object that has given rise to that dynamic living quality in both their representative and ornamental work. The attitude lingers on even in the classical cultures. The tree and water nymphs of the Greeks are brothers to the leprechauns of the Irish. Michelangelo has even gone so far as to suggest that this concept may well have been the real source of all art. He has stated that when he contemplated an irregular block of stone, he was aware that a figure was imprisoned within the block and was struggling to be released from his stony prison. He felt that it was his duty as an artist to bring this figure into the living world by chopping away the confining stone. If the reader has any doubt about the lasting depth of this concept of animism, he need only examine the views of such modern religious groups as the Unitarians or the Universalists to find that, even though they will probably never admit it, they are actually accepting and practicing a sophisticated form of animism. One might suggest that this is all very fine, but what does it have to do with medieval stained glass, or since it has existed for such a long time, why should it be so different now?

Early Period: Twelfth-Thirteenth Centuries

We have studied the very earliest known stained glass at some length and have designated the examples as prestyle because they had derived their design format from other existing arts. It is now time to take a closer look at England and France, the two countries most responsible for the best in early Gothic art. We need to examine first the twelfth century, then the thirteenth century, to see what changes took place in the social structure, what kinds of religious buildings were erected, and what kinds of windows were made. How did these two periods, the twelfth and thirteenth centuries, differ from the periods immediately preceding them?

Prior to the twelfth century, all culture, including art, religion, music and literature, was concentrated in the abbeys of France and England. The abbeys of both these

27

countries not only became the centers of culture, but also the repositories of much of the art and learning which had been dispersed or partially destroyed after the fall of Rome. As yet, no really significant urban centers had developed. The three most important abbeys in France were those at Vézelay and Cluny in Burgundy, and Saint-Denis located on the perimeter of present-day Paris.

Cluny, a Benedictine abbey, was founded in 910 by William the Pious, Duke of Aquitaine. During the eleventh and twelfth centuries, Cluny became the largest and most famous example of monastic culture.

The well-known Abbey of Saint-Denis is probably the most important of all, not for its size, but because it affords the best illustration of the transition period which took place in the twelfth century. Much of the fame of Saint-Denis is due to its illustrious Abbé Suger. It was Suger who visited Cluny in 1130, ten years before starting his own abbey church at Saint-Denis. During his extended visit he observed the use of several innovations. In their abbey church they had used buttresses and even flying buttresses upon occasion. They had also utilized a form of pointed arch. However, in general, they were still retaining most of the Romanesque ways of building. Suger, intrigued by these new ideas, developed them into an organized architectural style. It is hard to fully appreciate the magnitude of his perfecting and applying these innovations which gave to the world the Gothic style in architecture and made possible the ascending clerestories and the towering windows of the Gothic period. In addition to his work in developing these new architectural forms for his own abbey church at Saint-Denis, he was also instrumental in having windows designed and executed for the same church. Bits of these windows may still be seen in the crypt; some have been glazed into the windows in the main church. Unfortunately, the windows of the main church were extensively restored by Viollet-le-Duc sometime between 1845 and 1856. Le-Duc at that time was considered to be the great savior of Gothic art. Now, however, he is more often thought of as an inept and arrogant destroyer of Gothic art. Many serious critics feel that any church or abbey which has been lucky enough to have escaped the great restorer's hand was indeed fortunate.

Whatever viewpoint the present reader may have, one look at the Saint-Denis restorations in comparison with the west front windows in the Cathedral of Notre Dame at Chartres should make the sterility of the Saint-Denis restorations quite obvious. Among the original windows in Saint-Denis was a Jesse Tree depicting the human genealogy of Christ, beginning with Jesse, the original progenitor of Christ, and ending with Christ Himself. There is a similar window in the west front of Chartres Cathedral.

Abbé Suger was not only responsible for the execution of the windows in his own church but, by his expression of interest and enthusiasm, he also spread the gospel of the importance of stained glass throughout the land. The three west windows in Chartres Cathedral were made, if not actually under his direction, at least with his aid, advice, and encouragement. It is indeed fortunate for the world of art that Suger was such a discriminating and energetic person. The good Abbé was not only blessed with a dynamic interest in architecture and stained glass, but was also a confidant of King Louis IX, acting as his regent while Louis was away on the Crusades.

Previous to the abbey culture, the civilian population had been largely nomadic, headed by powerful chieftains; their political organization had been tribal. Following this nomadic tribal pattern, the feudal system arose where life collected around the castles of the feudal lords.

Abbé Suger had started building the abbey of Saint-Denis in 1140; by 1180, Philip Augustus had become king and was developing Paris as a northern capital. Paris became the home of Thomas Aquinas, among other notables.

With the twelfth century we come to a change. Interest is now centered in towns outside the abbeys; the guilds are being born, and the Gothic cathedral, with its pointed arches and its flying buttresses, soars upward toward the heavens. Something decidedly new and important has happened. No matter how we view these countries, one thing appears certain: some single tremendous driving force has been let loose; a new and exciting development has taken place. Never before, in these or any other countries, has a population so large moved forward with such singleness of purpose. Nor had there ever been such total participation of all the people in such a vast building program.

It is small wonder that this great force had been wrongly interpreted as the expression of the new Christian faith. True, this had contributed to the effect. But if it had even made a substantial contribution, why was the action so much more vivid, so much more spectacular and so much more universal here than in the Eastern areas of Christendom? This promise of total participation had appeared for a brief time in Ravenna under the Arian Christians; but, as we noted earlier in our explanation of the events leading up to the Iconoclast Edict, the Eastern Church at Constantinople and the Western Church at Rome had joined forces in order to eject the Arian Christians from Ravenna. Being native Ostrogoths, they returned to their northern homes. The descendants of these same Arians, with their inherent belief in humanism, formed the nucleus and rallying point for the Gothic Christians who now seem to cause us such surprise.

If this sensational new growth was not totally the result of

Christianity, what caused it? Gimpel, in his book *The Cathedral Builders*, opens up an entirely new point of view by suggesting that one of the major inspirations for this new dynamic movement was economic in origin. Before the expansion of the new Paris, the small towns such as Le Mans, Poitiers, and Châlons-sur-Marne had been Roman outposts and, as such, had been strategically located on rivers or on main Roman roads. They were now ideally situated for economic growth.

By the twelfth century, the town, not the abbey, was becoming the economic and artistic center, and the cathedral, now the seat of the particular bishop of the area, was emerging as the center of all activity, both economic and religious. The area around the choir and apse remained for religious services, but everything west of the transept was used for secular purposes. The main nave frequently served as a town meeting spot, while the individual bays were occupied by merchants, very similar to our modern farmers' market.

The guilds, representing new kinds of craft organizations, were being formed. A hydralike combination of capital and labor lodged in the same body, this sort of organization may seem strange to us at the present time, but apparently it worked very well then.

As the Gothic cathedral took its place as the center of the economic and religious life of the community, it rapidly became a status symbol. Each town strove to outdo the other to have the biggest and highest cathedral, the best and most sculpture and stained glass.

The vaulting of Chartres Cathedral rose to 122 feet—seven feet above that of Notre Dame in Paris. Amiens raised hers by twenty-five feet, while Beauvais, in an attempt to surpass all others, lifted her vaulting still another ten feet. The builders had overreached themselves—the roof fell in, not once, but twice. In operating these competitive enterprises, the towns called upon all of their members to give their full support, much as we do today when raising funds for our social services. The guilds donated many of the stained-glass windows for the various cathedrals which, by the way, turned out to be an excellent advertising project; a panel illustrating a particular product could be and was placed strategically at an eye-level position, a position which no one looking at the window could miss.

In summary, we might restate the question asked previously. Why should this Scytho-Iranian strain of vitalistic nomadic art be so important and different now? The answer is quite simple. It had always been important but had never been widespread in the West. The art of the pre-Han and Han dynasties in China evolved from it. The Luristan animal bronzes of Persia, made in the second millenium BC, were derived from this source. While these countries had developed their art slowly, adapting these strains to their own needs, the sudden large-scale economic and religious outburst in northern Europe demanded an immediate art form to fulfill its needs. They had a form ideally suited to their expressive requirements and they used it. They were not a literate people; Charlemagne himself could neither read nor write. So rich and poor alike were dependent upon an effective visual language.

While religion and culture were confined to the abbeys, a limited number of hand-lettered illuminated manuscripts were sufficient for the education and training of their literate monks. However, when religious faith spread to the urban areas and huge cathedrals were built, it became necessary to initiate some effective form of visual presentation which would act as an educational medium. The windows of the new cathedrals could be and were filled with stained-glass windows depicting the life of Christ, the Virgin Mary, and the many prophets, saints, and martyrs of the Christian faith.

The great difference between the Eastern Byzantine Church and the medieval Roman Catholic church of northern Europe was clearly defined. In the Eastern Church, the service and ritual were restricted to the clergy and the royal family. The general populace was forced to receive its religious training, experience, and enlightenment indirectly. On the other hand, the services in the medieval Roman Catholic churches were attended by the entire population. Cathedrals such as Notre Dame in Chartres would frequently have as many as 10,000 worshipers in attendance at a single service. Abbé Suger was the first to add radial chapels to the ambulatory of his church in Saint Denis. He did this to provide additional space, so that a number of Masses could be given simultaneously and thus take care of the thousands of parishioners filling the church.

Stained-glass windows became the textbooks for teaching the stories of the saints, the life of Christ and of the Virgin, as well as the steps in the Passion leading up to the Crucifixion. The clerestory windows were usually reserved for over life-size single figures, while those of the nave and ambulatory were filled with small-subject medallion windows. In the north and south transepts, the clergy usually placed a large multipanel subject window surmounted by a rose window. When one realizes that Chartres Cathedral was glazed with 176 windows averaging eight by twenty feet, and that these were designed, executed, and installed within thirty years, the accomplishment defies belief.

The attitude of medieval sculptors and stained-glass workers toward their creations was markedly different from that of present-day Europeans. The fact that the work of the medieval artists remained anonymous and that they never seemed to have talked or written about the aesthetics of their art has greatly puzzled modern man. It is true that there are a few pieces that have been accepted as having been signed by the artists who made them. There is, however, some question about whether these signatures have been correctly interpreted. For example, an inscription in a medallion window of the cathedral of Rouen says "Clement of Chartres made me." If one takes cognizance of the medieval practice which recognized that the donor (or the person who commissioned a work of art) was its creator, there is reason to believe that Clement may have been a lesser member of the ruling class rather than a stained-glass artist. The theory gains some credence when one considers a similar inscription above the head in the Alfred Jewel (Ashmolean Museum, Oxford) which is translated: "Alfred had me made." In this case it is clear that Alfred did not make the jewel himself.

Another interesting fact is that medieval workers did not consider themselves artists but simply as craftsmen and members of an integrated society. The reason that they never talked or wrote about their work was that they felt that a piece should stand on its own merit and that it was their duty when executing a commission to do the best job possible.

An excellent example of this integrity is in one of the clerestory windows in the Cathedral of Angers. In a section of the border there is, when viewed from the floor of the Cathedral, what appears to be an ormanent. It is not until you go up into the triforium gallery to look at the window close up that you find, not a piece of ornamental border, but a beautifully drawn and painted figure of a kneeling archer. Not one person in a million will ever see this figure, yet the greatest care has been lavished upon this obscure figure. When this kind of care is taken with every square inch of a window, it produces a subtle difference in the total effect.

The thirteenth-century Great Angel of Chartres Cathedral is an excellent example of the early period. Its location in the north choir clerestory demands that it be clearly presented to be well seen. Its style of drawing and painting, derived from the Byzantine mosaics, is bold, archaic in character, and quite legible. The figure, though dynamic in movement, reaffirms both its architectural framework and its horizontal barring. The swirl of the wings adds to the figure's movement without detracting from its horizontal or vertical stability. Its bright reds, blues, and yellows, relieved by the judicious introduction of well-placed whites, round out the general effectiveness of this justly famous window.

The type of painting used to delineate the drapery in this early period is particularly noteworthy. It serves a dual purpose: that of dividing the drapery into folds which

fig 13

A thirteenth-century archer from the Cathedral of Angers

display the underlying form of the figure, and that of breaking up the expanses of color into harmoniously related parts. In this period, not all of the drapery lines were made by painting. In some cases, as can be seen in the Great Angel at Chartres, the lines are partially defined by the leads. When this is done, it makes possible a color change as well as a pattern one. This, in turn, adds greatly to the variety and subtlety of the color.

The windows of the early period are architectonic. Borders are always geometric; even when they incorporate details such as the acanthus leaf, they still retain their abstract quality as well as affirmation of the architectural demands. The bars are used as design assets, never ignored or disguised. Every detail is subordinated to the one bold statement. The Great Angel of Chartres, then, is that typical example of artistic discipline, the work of an artist able to organize his material to eliminate trivia and to make that one bold statement which establishes his work as one with history; yet this work is anonymous.

Middle Period:
Fourteenth and Fifteenth Centuries

Unlike the early period where a piece from either the eleventh, twelfth or thirteenth century would serve equally well as an example, the middle period requires an example from both the fourteenth and fifteenth centuries to adequately cover the important transitional differences. The fourteenth century, plus or minus a few years, may be considered the turning point between early and late Gothic. In the latter part of the thirteenth century, there were indications that the first half of the Gothic period was slowly grinding to a halt. The fourteenth century opened with a promise of continuous economic expansion, the dynamic innovative and creative growth that made cathedral-building possible, as well as the religious singleness of idea and purpose which was such a part of the twelfth and thirteenth centuries' credo, were fading. Nevertheless, the century started with a degree of hope for the future.

True, the church had become complacent and increasingly more corrupt, and its followers acted more out of habit than faith. Reform was in the air; the intellectual elite had already begun to doubt even the efficacy of the Church.

In 1340, with the naval victory at Slys, the British gained control of the Channel, initiating the Hundred Years' War which lasted until 1453. In 1348, the Black Death swept over Europe. Beginning in Italy, it rapidly moved to France and then to England. Some estimates say that one-third of the population of Europe was wiped out. This devastation added to France's and England's financial problems and slowed the war down. The English continued to be successful until they were defeated at Orléans by Joan of Arc in 1429. If she had continued to receive the support of the weak and corrupt French monarch, the war may well have been decided then. As it was, it dragged on until the English were decisively beaten in 1449. By 1453, all that the English could save out of a hundred years of war was the French port of Calais.

No original creative changes in architecture, sculpture, or stained-glass windows were developed after the thirteenth century. Both France and England spent so much of their wealth fighting each other that little was left for developing the arts. The concept that history repeats itself has become such a cliché that when it does occur, we are quite surprised. But what happened 200 years later in Italy, at the peak of the Renaissance, may in a sense explain what happened earlier in the fourteenth century.

The Renaissance had spawned such a series of skilled artists, such as Raphael, Leonardo da Vinci, and Michelangelo, that those who followed were understandably frustrated. Their frustration had stripped them of the power to act creatively as artists; all that was left was to emulate their immediate predecessors. They superficially exaggerated the stylizations of the masters by distorting and elongating their forms or by introducing fantastic and irrelevant ornamental details. It took very nearly seventy-five years—until the beginning of the baroque period—for this mannerist movement to wear itself out. There certainly is a parallel between this post-Renaissance period and that of the fourteenth century that points to a recognizable cycle of artistic rise and fall.

After the tremendous creative outburst of the twelfth and thirteenth centuries, it is not difficult to see how, sooner or later, this drive would have to slow down. It is also easy to comprehend how the people of the fourteenth century would feel inadequate when faced with the tremendous accomplishments of the earlier glass artists, stonemasons, and sculptors. Contemporary critics, knowing that the budgets for cathedrals had been severely reduced in the fourteenth century, and that the spirit of great creative achievement had been exchanged by artists for one of problem-solving, assume falsely that all quality had disappeared from the windows of that century. This, however, was not the case. True, the artists of that century were faced with creating solutions for quite new and complex problems and in this they performed admirably. Let us enumerate a few of the changes and the problems which demanded new answers:

1) Change in architectural style and format of new window openings
2) Change in the type of color
3) Change in the type of subject material
4) Change in the type of figure drawing and painting
5) Combining figure work with white or grisaille
6) Origination and development of the canopy
7) Change in the character of ornament
8) Change in the iron work

Let us also not forget that these problems were predicated upon the desirability of cutting costs.

In this connection we must mention here a type of glass with the French name *"grisaille"* that appeared in the thirteenth century with the purpose of either cutting costs or introducing more light. It is mostly white glass. Some strips of color were used in the main part of the windows while color blocks were added to the borders. The basic patterns resemble those found in thirteenth-century medallion windows. The medallion shapes, however, were defined by lead rather than iron. An acanthus pattern, with its background darkened by crosshatching, provided a soft, pleasant, silver-gray effect. Examples of this glass may be found in France at Saint Serge in Angers, at Soissons, and in Chartres in both the cathedral and the church of Saint

fig 14
A grisaille panel (Westlake)

Pierre. There is a great deal of grisaille work in England. The best examples are in Salisbury and in York. By far the most famous are the five lancets in the north transept of York Minster, called the Five Sisters. These windows were not mentioned before in the remarks about windows of the early period because there is every indication that when originally made, they were considered as temporary glass to be later replaced by more colorful examples.

In the fourteenth century, however, when cost was a major item, they were revived, amplified, and varied into a new and useful style. In the church of Saint Pierre at Chartres may be found a veritable treasure house of windows showing the transition from thirteenth- to fourteenth-century glass: the windows of the very last of the thirteenth century display a rather clumsy use of figure with grisaille in combination, but in the later fourteenth-century examples in the same church, the bridge has been spanned so that these windows form excellent examples of smaller fourteenth-century window treatment.

While France and England had been locked in the intermittent but deadly and exhausting struggle of the Hundred Years' War, the Italians had been steadily moving forward into the artistic and cultural period of the early Renaissance. Within a period of less than twenty-five years, painting had moved from the Byzantine-inspired work of Cimabue to the rising humanistic painting of Giotto. By the time the war between England and France had ended in 1453, the Italian Renaissance was in full swing. This was the era of such masters of painting as Mantegna, Piero Della Francesca, Fra Angelico, Botticelli, and Leonardo, in Italy; and, in the north, the Van Eycks and Roger Van Der Weyden. It was evident that this new, more naturalistic style of painting would be bound to affect the art of glass painting. What was also becoming apparent was that stained-glass artists were adapting the new style of painting to their own craft. As long as the prevailing acceptable style retained its flat character, all would be well. Already, however, painters such as Masaccio were developing chiaroscuro painting, with deep light and shade as its most important characteristic. This style, when adopted, would spell the doom of the art of stained glass and usher in the sixteenth century and the later period.

Where the change from the thirteenth to the fourteenth century was abrupt, the transition from the fourteenth to the fifteenth century was gradual. All of the major characteristics of the fourteenth century were retained in the fifteenth century, namely, the extended use of white glass, less color as well as secondary color, larger pieces of glass, the use of the canopy, more naturalistic drawing, and the use of silver stain. The introduction of more white was not only repeated in the fifteenth century, but was carried to such an extreme as to present practically a screen of white with small areas of color retained for emphasis. Sometimes an entire figure appeared on one piece, frequently including heads, halos, hats, and crowns. Although silver stain originated in the early part of the middle period, it was not used extensively until the fifteenth century when it became one of the major materials used in glass painting, being employed for hair, crowns, halos, ornaments, flowers, and parts of border ornaments. It was also used regularly to decorate the finials and crockets of the canopies.

France has more than her share of superb eleventh-, twelfth-, thirteenth- and fourteenth-century glass. But if one wants to see fifteenth-century glass by far the most and best is in England. It is said that, although there are windows of this period in almost any of the large churches or cathedrals and in many of the small parish churches throughout the country, sixty per cent of all old glass from the eleventh through the fifteenth centuries will be found in the towns of York and Canterbury. Glass painting of the fifteenth century, particularly that of England, is without doubt the most skillfully done, the most subtle, and the most personalized of all glass painting. In the smaller churches of York, such as All Saints, Saint-Martin-le-grand, Coney Street, Saint Michael, Spurrier Gate, St. Martins cum Gregory and York Minster, what is so satisfying is that the viewer may approach the windows close enough to touch them.

Although the fourteenth-century style in France and England was quite similar, the parallel pattern of development ended with the beginning of the fifteenth century. While the French single figures or figure compositions were strictly contained within their canopied frames, the taller English perpendicular-type windows offered additional height for their ever-ascending canopies. In the portals and niches of these rising canopies many small figures began to appear. Their appearance added a rather charming informal whimsey to what otherwise might have become an endless array of architectural pinnacles, crockets, and finials. Unlike most large windows which were designed so that they could only be properly observed at a distance, the taller perpendicular types found in the larger English cathedrals were frequently so situated that they not only could be seen but carefully studied at a distance of a few feet.

In the English windows the figure compositions, as well as the larger single figures, are not restricted to their immediate canopy frames, but are allowed to wander in and out of their canopies, creating a much looser and more relaxed mood.

Compared to the superb fifteenth-century English glass painting, the French work, though expertly executed, seems dry and formal. There are, however, some fifteenth-century examples in France which do compare favorably with their English counterparts. There is one beautifully done Saint-Etienne window in the nave of Bourges Cathedral, and a very charming Saint Catherine in the now destroyed Saint Vincent Church of Rouen. Strange as it may seem, this dry formalism became a distinct asset in the early sixteenth-century French windows by helping to restrain a tendency to overpaint which coincided with the adoption of the new Renaissance style.

Late Period: Sixteenth Centuries

Early in the sixteenth century, all of the least desirable features of the late period began to appear. Windows which had previously shown some consideration for their architectural surroundings now sprawled their realistic figure subjects over four or five lancets without regard for architectonic values. Painters increasingly adopted chiaroscuro deep light and shade as a new technique for expression. It is a well-known fact that to achieve chiaroscuro form in easel painting, color must be sacrified. It is also equally true that color is the paramount asset of stained glass.

The fifteenth-century artists could increase their whites, mute their colors, and expertly flat paint their figures. But when the sixteenth-century artists tried to imitate the Renaissance easel painters by using chiaroscuro techniques, they succeeded in arresting the art of stained glass for a good three hundred years.

In the early and middle periods of the art of stained glass, the term "glazing" was used not so much to indicate a division of labor as it was to define a sequential process in the making of a window. Many critics, past and present, steeped in Renaissance culture, have repeated with monotonous regularity that the glazier found it expedient as well as mandatory to call in the fine artist to add the necessary artistic touch to his windows. This particular conceptual error led to the belief that the entire history of the art could be studied and understood as an evolutionary process beginning at the point where the glazier, assisted by the painter, dominated the scene to the point where the painter took over completely. Following this reasoning, they also added that the art was separated into two distinct operations: that of glazing and that of painting, automatically discriminating in favor of painting. On the surface, this would appear to be an excellent observation; but unfortunately, this idea is derived solely from a Renaissance concept—the separation between the fine artist and the craftsman—a distinction between fine and applied art. This is unquestionably what happens in the present-day stained-glass studio, but it is not what occurred in a medieval shop. Medieval artists would never have understood this attitude. They were trained to do every process of the craft. An artist of the medieval period considered himself to be a craftsman/artist and would have been equally able to cut, glaze, draw, or paint. He would never have thought of setting up a division of labor such as would entail one person being a painter and another a glazier. He left this compartmentalized thinking to the twentieth century's artistic insensitivity.

In medieval art there was no separation between the glazier, the cutter, the designer, or the painter. The iconography and symbolism were established and interpreted by the clergy. This material was in turn translated into the illuminated manuscripts of the time by the monks. The easel painters, the fresco painters, the stained-glass artists, as well as the sculptors, utilized these early manuscripts as design models for their various arts. In the fourteenth and fifteenth centuries, the painting style of the period was selected and adapted by the stained-glass artists for their own particular technique. Early in the sixteenth century a social distinction was made between fine and applied art, a distinction which established the painter as socially superior to the craftsman in all existing arts. From this point on, the art of stained glass began to decline. The anonymity which had been prevalent since the art's inception gave way to the creation and recognition of a whole series of famous and popular glass painters. The best known, of course, were the Italian artists already renowned as fresco or easel painters. Among them can be found such names as Ghiberti, Ghirlandajo, Perugino, Raphael, Castagna, and Uccello. Almost every European country claims to have a window made from a cartoon by Raphael. Castagna and Uccello were certainly two of the better Italian artists who made, or at least drew, the cartoons for windows. Uccello's angular compositional style lent itself well to the technique of stained glass, while Castagna himself was trained as a stained-glass artist. There were artists of distinction who were responsible for the design and painting of windows in Flanders, Germany, France, and England. It has been said that Albrecht Dürer designed windows for some German churches, but there is no existing evidence that he did so.

The best of the sixteenth-century windows were done in France and England. There are windows of high quality by Engrand le Prince in the church of Saint-Etienne at Beauvais. The Saint Eustace and the Jesse Tree are particularly noteworthy. There are also excellent sixteenth-century windows in the church at Montmorency on the northern outskirts of Paris. There are important windows of the same period in Winchester and York cathedrals, as well as at Malvern Abbey, Cambridge, and Oxford in England.

The high quality of the sixteenth-century windows done in both France and England was very likely due to the persistence of the traditional Gothic standards inherent in these two countries. However good a few of these sixteenth-century windows may have been, this "new style," as it was called, ushered in a series of practices inimical to the making of good windows. It represented a subsidence of the most effective Gothic features found in earlier windows while, at the same time, it emphasized the chiaroscuro technique of the easel painters, along with clever manipulative skills inappropriate to the medium.

By the middle of the eighteenth century, the art of stained glass had descended to an unbelievably low level. It was about this time that Joshua Reynolds made a window painted entirely upon large sheets of pure white glass, a window which showed neither taste nor an understanding of the medium.

Around 1850, the Industrial Revolution, which had begun in the middle of the previous century, had achieved its immediate goal in Europe and the United States. The world markets were now being flooded with their mass-produced goods of questionable quality. Like many incidents throughout history, there was now a series of occurrences arising which certainly seem to have been related; whether or not they were caused by the Industrial Revolution could be argued.

In 1848, a group of English painters, unhappy with the Royal Academy for rigidly following the Renaissance traditon of Raphael, decided to band together and form what they chose to call the Pre-Raphaelite Brotherhood. In selecting a period before Raphael which appealed to their romantic sense, they chose the Middle Ages as being sufficiently removed from their present environment. The group was composed of Dante Gabriel Rossetti, William Holman Hunt, John Millais, and several lesser personages.

In 1850, the Gothic Revival was started. Apparently it began as a kind of commercial venture; at the start, knowledge of Gothic art certainly was not one of its assets. In France, Voillet-le-Duc was one of its adherents. Later its influence was followed in the United States by architects such as Ralph Adams Cram and Bertram G. Goodhue.

In 1853, William Morris and Edward Burne-Jones entered Oxford. Burne-Jones was already an artist of some note, with an interest in medieval art. William Morris, a writer and craftsman, had previously developed an honest interest in medieval art and a healthy dislike for the direction which England was taking in the Industrial Revolution. It was inevitable that sooner or later these two would become friends and that, with their common interest in medieval art, they would ally themselves with both the Pre-Raphaelite Brotherhood and the Gothic Revival.

In 1862, William Morris organized a stained-glass studio and was joined in the venture by Burne-Jones. Morris was to select the glass and Burne-Jones was to do the designing and make the cartoons. In spite of the fact that Morris had an understanding of Gothic craftsmanship, he made the fatal mistake of suggesting and approving the separation of the artist and the craftsman which has been maintained as studio practice down to the present day.

Morris is frequently given credit for the discovery that the structural irregularities, striations, bubbles, and chemical differentiations were the secret of old glass. He undoubtedly recognized these facts; but Charles Winston, a barrister, hired a chemist so that he could carry out analyses and make reproductions of the old glass. As early as 1850, he had started his work and, by 1856, he relates in several letters written to a Mr. Wilson that he had successfully duplicated all of the colors used in twelfth-century glass, and describes his difficulties in getting the makers of glass for windows to produce his glass. He was forced to buy a furnace and make the glass himself. Winston had made facsimile twelfth-century glass two years before Morris had entered Oxford and six years before he had started his studio with Burne-Jones as designer.

There is little doubt that each one of these events played a part in creating a turning point in the art of stained glass. The Pre-Raphaelite Brotherhood, in attracting the interest and approval of the writer and art critic John Ruskin, was responsible for publicizing the growing interest in the art of the Middle Ages. The origin of the Gothic Revival certainly stimulated the rebirth of stained glass by providing a new demand for windows. Charles Winston, by discovering a way of duplicating the quality of twelfth-century glass, made possible the production of a most valuable glass for future windows. Windows designed by Burne-Jones and executed in the studio of William Morris, though inspired by the glass of the Middle Ages, were already showing a new freshness of approach destined to influence later modern glass. The Gothic Revival, with its original values somewhat in question, was destined to have the greatest impact upon future stained glass. For the results of this impact we will turn to the United States in the early 1900s and begin the contemporary period.

Contemporary Period

During the Gothic Revival, the English and French concentrated on the erection of new public buildings, while church-building was confined largely to the restoration of early churches and windows. On the other hand, before the Revival, the United States had practically no Gothic-type churches, which left this field wide open. Ralph Adams Cram and Bertram G. Goodhue were the leading exponents of this new style of building. They not only built many churches along the eastern seaboard, but acted as consultants to other regional architects. During their heyday, no local architect would have thought of doing a Gothic church without employing Ralph Adams Cram as a consultant.

At the same time that this phenomenon was taking place, two new persons entered the picture: John La Farge and Louis Comfort Tiffany. John La Farge, who was a mural painter of some ability, decided to transfer his efforts to the making of stained glass. It was he who invented opal glass, whose color could be seen through and was also reflected back from the surface of the glass. Louis Comfort Tiffany was an artist-craftsman who founded a studio in order to produce lamps, bottles, and other *objets d'art*. He set up a glass furnace in Corona, New York, where he proceeded to make a German type of glass called Favrile. Tiffany also executed windows as well as *objets d'art* from this glass. Eventually, he made use of La Farge's opal glass. He undoubtedly was a supersalesman, for it is Tiffany who

made a reputation in the making of opal glass windows and not La Farge, the inventor. Tiffany windows were installed in many of the new Gothic churches. Unfortunately, neither of these men had even a glimmer of what a good medieval window should look like. As a result, their windows are without doubt the worst examples of stained glass ever to be executed.

To fill the windows of the new Gothic-type churches being erected in the United States, new companies were formed here and old ones expanded in England and Germany. The English firms produced a type of pseudo-fifteenth-century glass with certain undesirable sixteenth-century types of painting. These windows were rather expertly done but very sterile.

In Germany, a Renaissance-type of window was fitted into a fifteenth-century canopy and sufficiently overpainted to give it the appearance of being covered on the back with light-gray paper. These windows were the famous Munich type which fill many of the Catholic churches of the early 1900s in this country.

The only really worthwhile windows done in the very early part of the twentieth century, either in Europe or the United States, were those made by Christopher Whall of England. Ralph Adams Cram, finding it impossible to procure suitable stained-glass windows for his newly erected churches, encouraged several American artists to try their hand at making acceptable thirteenth-century-type windows. Among those who became well known as well as successful were William Willet of Philadelphia, Charles Connick of Boston, and Henry Wynd Young of New York. John Gordon Guthrie, who worked for Henry Wynd Young and later started his own studio, was probably the most gifted and original glass artist of his time. These men all belonged to that period which came at the very end of the Gothic Revival. Their work was associated with the Gothic tradition—all, that is, save Guthrie who, though he lived to a ripe old age, would most certainly have become a modern had he been born a bit later.

It is only to be expected that when modern glass was made it would first be made in Europe. Since the European architects could not hope to surpass the old cathedrals of their native countries, they wisely began by designing and building ecclesiastical structures in a modern vein. This, in turn, provided both a place and a demand for a contemporary type of stained glass. Although there were some interesting windows made, it is disappointing to note that by and large these new contemporary windows were both affected and superficial rather than vital and inspiring.

Not everything that was done in the United States during this period followed the Gothic tradition or imitated Renaissance ideas. It was in the early part of the twentieth century that the architect Louis Sullivan coined the now-famous phrase, "form follows function," while, in 1919, at Weimar in Germany, the Bauhaus School of Design came into existence. The immediate purpose of the Bauhaus was to bring the fine artist, the artisan, and the craftsman together, with the hope of adding some aesthetic quality to the new industrial products which were flooding the markets of the world. Ultimately, the aim of the Bauhaus was to develop a synthesis of artist and craftsman capable of using new materials properly or old materials in new ways. To Sullivan's emphasis on function was added an additional one concerning material and its proper use. This design concept was accepted enthusiastically in Germany and the United States. Unfortunately, during Hitler's tenure, the movement was suppressed in Germany. A variation of the German Bauhaus was started in the United States by László Moholy-Nagy. It flourished for a time, but instead of fulfilling the early noble promise of promoting an understanding of material and its proper use, it degenerated into a clever superficial style now exploited extensively by commercial and industrial design artists.

What is true now, William Morris discovered in the latter part of the nineteenth century: namely, that a beautifully hand-crafted product will inevitably be more expensive and exclusive than a machine-made one. What has changed today is that mass production has become so automated that it has eliminated the crafts for utilitarian purposes and, because of their exclusiveness, has turned them into works of art. What is needed now is for more gifted artists to apply their creative talents to such crafts as stained glass, mosaic, and ceramics, so that these works may rightly take their proper place as works of art along with painting and sculpture.

Stained glass is primarily an architectural art which can best develop its potential as a handmaiden of architecture. But it can never do so as long as contemporary architects persist in seeing the art as either an essentially medieval ecclesiastical art or as a superficial decoration to be casually added to a structure after the fact. Contemporary architecture is particularly suitable for the use of stained glass, mosaic, and ceramics. In fact, without the use of one or all of these media, much modern architecture is downright barren in effect.

From time to time abortive attempts have been made to involve good modern artists in the designing of stained glass which was later executed in one of our existing studios. The results understandably have been surprisingly poor. You cannot, as can be seen in the case of Burne-Jones, take a good mural painter or easel painter and make a stained-glass artist of him overnight.

Sometime in the 1930s, the French experimented with what they termed "faceted" glass—a glass which was chipped along its edges in the fashion of a flint arrowhead. This chipping gave the piece a certain effective sparkle. This method of working was not continued for very long as interest in the new technique died out, but in the early 1960s it was again revived. This time the glass used was considerably thicker, varying from one-half to a full inch in thickness. This new glass was called *dalle* by the French. The pieces were cut to shape, faceted, and set in concrete. This type of glass has become popular in France, Germany, and the United States. In France and Germany the glass is set in concrete; in the United States it is set in a mixture of sand and an epoxy resin developed in this country. This glass is described in a later chapter on the various techniques in glass. A type of colored glass made by mounting small pieces upon a sheet of plate glass with a particular kind of epoxy resin is now being fabricated. This is also described in the same chapter. It is still doubtful whether any of these new methods are as effective or as structurally reliable as the time-tested use of antique glass and lead.

Modern glass is too new and in such a stage of experimentation that it does not warrant conclusive aesthetic judgment at this time.

36

GLASS AND GLASSMAKING

In the eleventh and twelfth centuries, when colored glass was first made for the new art of stained glass, the knowledge of color chemistry was in its infancy. The glassmakers knew how to produce certain colors, but their ability to maintain consistent results left something to be desired. There were certain impurities present in the base materials which caused unexpected variations in the colors. Far from hurting the glass, these imperfections were probably its greatest source of quality. For example, when the workers decided to make a pot of blue glass, they melted up a quantity of silica sand in an earthenware crucible, put in some alkali in the form of potash to reduce the melting point of the silica sand, and added cobalt oxide to produce a blue color. They were never quite sure whether the resultant glass would be pure blue, greenish blue, grayish blue, or purplish blue. Whatever the final product, it was far too expensive to be thrown away. A comparison between the cost of the material with that of the weekly wage scale will add some perspective to the problem. Records show that the average cost of glass was about $1.50 per square foot, while the average wage was about twenty-five cents a week. The best way to deal with the problem of color irregularities was to use the different color pieces variably in every panel. The glass artists were artistically intelligent enough to realize the value of this variation and to make it a part of their organized technique. The extremely high cost of making

glass may have had as much to do with the naming of their colors as their resemblance to rubies, sapphires, or gold.

The glass which is used for the making of stained-glass windows does not differ greatly from glass made for other purposes. The brown glass found in the common beer bottle, the green of the wine bottle, or the blue glass used as a container for poison can all be worked into a window if they are flattened out beforehand.

The basic material of glass is silica sand. In its raw state it requires such tremendous heat to melt it that it is impractical to use. As a matter of fact, it has only been within recent years that, by using electric furnaces, enough heat could be generated to melt it. With the discovery that the temperature for melting could be lowered by adding a flux of potash or some other alkali to the silica sand, the problem was solved. Without a flux it required a temperature of 3500° Fahrenheit to melt the sand. By adding the flux the temperature can be reduced to 1200°. The exact procedure which was used in the making of glass for windows was to build an earthenware crucible and fill it with silica sand; to this sand is added lead, potash, or some other alkali. It is also necessary to add lime to make the final product moistureproof. Glass has been recognized as a quickly solidified silica formation which is liquid when melted and which, upon being rapidly cooled, does not form crystals. In a sense it freezes when cooled—it has many of the characteristics of ice. Colors are made by introducing metallic oxides into the molten silica solution, either as solutions or as colloidal suspensions. The same oxides are capable of producing different colors with different glass mixtures. Different oxides of the same metal will also produce different colors.

Certain solutions such as those formed with cobalt, chromium, uranium, and manganese are fairly constant and produce a purplish blue from cobalt, a green or yellow from chromium, a yellow from uranium, and a violet or violet-red from manganese.

Ferrous oxide yields either an olive green or pale blue, according to the particular glass mixture.

Ferric oxide produces a yellow; lead a pale yellow; charcoal added to soda-lime glass also makes a yellow. (When the late Lawrence Saint was making his glass for the windows of the Washington Cathedral, it was a standing joke that some of his apprentices slyly trimmed off part of his famous red beard and tossed it into the crucible, thereby producing a beautiful yellow glass!)

There are several well-known types of glass which are composed of the following materials: English flint glass—of silica sand, carbonate of potash, and red lead; sheet or plate glass—of sand, carbonate of potash and carbonate of lime. Our always-informative Theophilus speaks of placing beech twigs in an earthenware pot and calcining these twigs to make a flux. One of the most fascinating means of producing color is by colloidal suspension. Solutions of one color in another occur often enough to be understood; the idea of suspending particles in the glass in order to produce color may be less well-known. The colloidal mixture produces color by reflection of light from particles, and as the reflected light varies, so will the color. A very easy and interesting way of illustrating this is by describing what can happen with the German liqueur known as *Goldwasser*. In this liqueur, gold flakes suspended in the liquid clearly appear as flakes; however, if these flakes are consistently decreased in size, the color of the liquid will change first to a pale pink and eventually to a strong pinkish red. This same process goes on in the making of gold ruby glass, only molten silica glass is substituted for the liquid. The result is a beautiful crimson red. The use of gold, though effective, causes the price to be almost prohibitive; most reds are made with copper or silenium, while some violet reds are made with manganese.

Nickel with a potash lead glass gives a violet color, while a brown color is achieved with soda-lime glass. Copper produces a peacock blue which becomes green as the amount of copper is increased. Copper oxide added to a glass mixture containing a strong reducing agent will produce a glass which, when first taken from the crucible,

fig 15
Placing the ingredients into the crucible

fig 16
Plunging the blowpipe into the crucible

is relatively colorless, but which when reheated becomes a beautiful ruby color. This is the mixture which is almost exclusively used as a red. Recently the Blenko Glass Company of Milton, West Virginia, has made some very beautiful reds from silenium, a nonmetallic material which is frequently found in copper ore. Besides certain mixtures, suspensions, and solutions, there are other ways to affect the color of glass. Heavy pigment in a thin sheet will give the color a bright thin look, whereas a small amount of pigment but an increase in the thickness of the sheet will produce a somewhat translucent density in the color. Most

fig 17
Centering, enlarging, and shaping the glass ball for the first time. This critical process determines the final uniform thickness of the sheet

fig 18
Centering and reshaping the glass ball after extra glass has been added in order to assure the proper sheet size

glass is transparent but may be made wholly or partially translucent by adding tin oxide to the pot. The accidental inclusion of tin oxide in the form of impurity in much of the old glass may account for its horny translucent quality.

Glass used for stained glass is usually more rubbery and less brittle than regular glass. This is important when complex curved shapes have to be cut; the glass will be tougher and less apt to fracture.

Silica sand mixed with an alkaline flux is placed in the crucible. When the mixture becomes molten the necessary metallic oxide is added to produce the desired color. To get

the glass from the crucible into workable sheets now becomes the job of the glass blower. To blow glass he uses a hollow metal tube approximately five feet long and one-half inch in diameter. One end of the tube is shaped for collecting the glass, the other is fitted with a mouthpiece and a handle. Three men usually comprise a working team. The first man plunges the preheated pipe into the crucible of molten glass. By deftly turning the pipe he gathers up a blob of glass about the size of a baseball upon the end of the tube. He passes the pipe with the red-hot glass to a second seated man. The second man's job is to center and properly shape the glass blob. When he has finished the shaping he returns it to the first man who again plunges the newly shaped ball into the crucible, gathering additional glass around the original ball. This he rests in a waist-high iron saddle. (Since the glass and pipe have now become quite heavy a support is necessary.) The new and enlarged blob is blown and rotated until it is the proper size. When it is removed from the saddle, it is then blown and swung, pendulum like, until long enough. The blower then places the elongated bubble into an iron cylinder, continuing to blow the bubble against the walls of the metal casting cylinder. A third man now enters the picture. He grips the two handles which are fastened to the top of the casting cylinder. By pulling the two handles together he is able to compress the top of the glass into a narrow neck. When he releases the handle and opens the hinged mold, the first glass blower is able to pull the glass out of the mold and onto a table where he breaks off the blow pipe. Before the glass has a chance to cool it is placed by the first worker in the annealing oven which is called a "lehr". Once this cycle is started, the process is continuous. After the glass has passed through the annealing oven where the temperature has been lowered over a period of five hours, the glass is again placed upon a small table where still another worker, equipped with a special tool, breaks off both ends of the glass cylinder, one at a time. This tool, made of quarter-inch copper wire in the form of a loop, has an insulated handle at either end of the wire. When the wire, heated by electricity, becomes red hot the workman draws the two handles together which tightens the hot wire around the base of the glass. The glass cylinder heated in this manner is easily broken by running a wet stick around the heated part and giving it a sharp tap with the stick. After both ends are broken off a cutting wheel is run down the side of the glass cylinder. Usually the inherent tension of the glass will cause it to break along the line of the cut. If it does not do so several sharp taps underneath the line will cause it to break. All that now remains to be done is to flatten the cut cylinder. To do so the glass is fed into a special furnace. In this furnace the cylinder is flattened, smoothed out and

fig 19
Placing the tube in the
saddle and blowing to
expand the ball

fig 20
Swinging the glass ball like
a pendulum to elongate it
so that it will properly fit
the metal mold

fig 21
Crimping the neck of the
cylinder

fig 22
Drawing out and breaking
off the cylinder

fig 20

fig 21

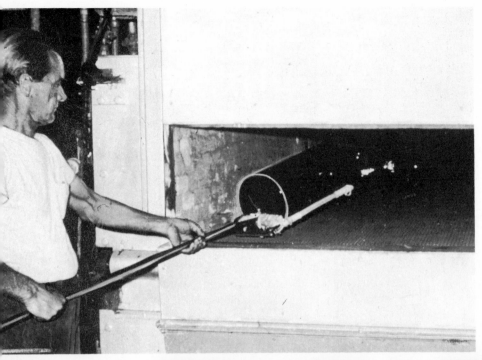

fig 23
Picking up the cylinder
with an asbestos fork and
placing it in the annealing
oven

fig 24
Scoring the cylinder with
a hot wire
fig 25
Breaking off the ends of
the cylinder

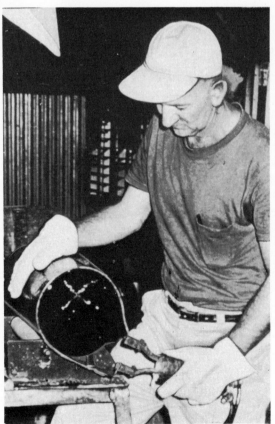

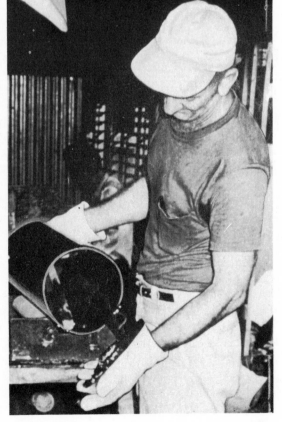

fig 24

fig 25

41

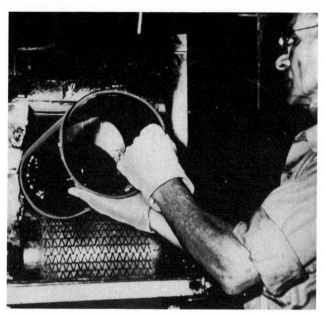

fig 26
Placing the cut cylinder into the flattening furnace

rubbed down with charcoal blocks. Following this the glass is fitted into another annealing oven where it gradually cools to room temperature over a period of seventy hours.

This is the process carried out by the Blenko Glass Company of Milton, West Virginia, and Marko of Mexico City, Mexico. Some notable improvements have been made by the Blenko Company in recent years. The glass has become more uniform and much easier to cut. Also the change in the sheet size is an improvement. Originally the Blenko glass, when opened out, was approximately 13″ by 21″. Now the sheets are 19″ by 25″. It is interesting to note that when a metal cylinder is used the glass will have a faceted surface, whereas when a wooden mold is used the surface will be smooth. This is because a wooden mold breathes, allowing the gases to escape, while a metal mold traps the gases which in turn causes surface irregularities.

The general name for all handblown glass is "antique" glass. English, German, and French antique glasses are made in a similar fashion, but differ in that when the balloon has been formed, certain variable treatments are utilized. The bottle-and-mold technique is not used in making English muff glass; when the balloon has reached the proper dimensions, the blower places his thumb over the mouthpiece while simultaneously heating the bottom end of the balloon. The combination of air pressure and the softening of the heated end causes the cylinder to burst open at the heated end; when the pipe is rotated the hole can be enlarged to parallel the rest of the cylinder.

42

With German and French glass the problem is somewhat different, since the cylinders are larger. For French antique glass they are 34″ long by 8″ in diameter; for French semi-antique glass, 47″ long and 13″ in diameter, and for German antique glass, 42″ long and 13″ in diameter. These cylinders are all too long to be blown while standing on the ground. For making this glass, the blower stands on a special raised platform located in front of the furnaces. The added length of the French and German cylinders makes several heatings necessary during the blowing process. The platform upon which the blower stands has what is known as a saddle mounted on one of its sides. The raised platform allows the blower to swing the larger balloon out over one side of the platform to shape it. When the overlarge balloon has reached its intended size, it is alternately reheated and worked in the process of eliminating its base which is done in the following manner: the glass blower rests the balloon in the saddle while the assistant applies a red-hot piece of glass to the bottom end. This hot piece causes the glass immediately surrounding it to soften, which in turn permits the assistant to cut a hole in the base with a pair of scissors. By heating and spinning, this hole may be made to parallel the rest of the cylinder. From this point on, the cylinder is treated in the same way as the other types of muff glass.

There is a second type of glass blown in the same manner as muff glass known as "Norman slab." This glass is made in exactly the same way as the bottle and mold glass first described. The only difference is that the balloon is no longer than 9″ and the mold is rectilinear. The final bottle shape is squarish rather than cylindrical. When this bottle is cut apart it produces four rectangles, 6″ by 9″, and one square piece, 6″ by 6″. Each of these slabs is thicker in the center and thinner on the edges, causing the glass to be darker in the center while shading to a lighter color on its edges.

There is a third method of making glass which starts with a smaller ball of material. Instead of swinging the inflated bubble to form an elongated balloon, the blow pipe rests on the table while it is being spun. A stick is pressed against the end of the bubble to form a disc of between 12″ and 14″ in diameter. Then the pipe is broken off and the disc is placed in the annealing oven. This glass is called "crown" or "spun rondel." Each different method of fabricating glass results in a glass which has its own peculiar qualities.

Muff glass, since it is swung in a vertical downward direction, tends to make streaks and imperfections follow the same vertical path. It also causes the color to shade from light at the top to dark at the bottom.

Norman slabs produce similar characteristics as far as the direction of the drift is concerned, but the light-dark

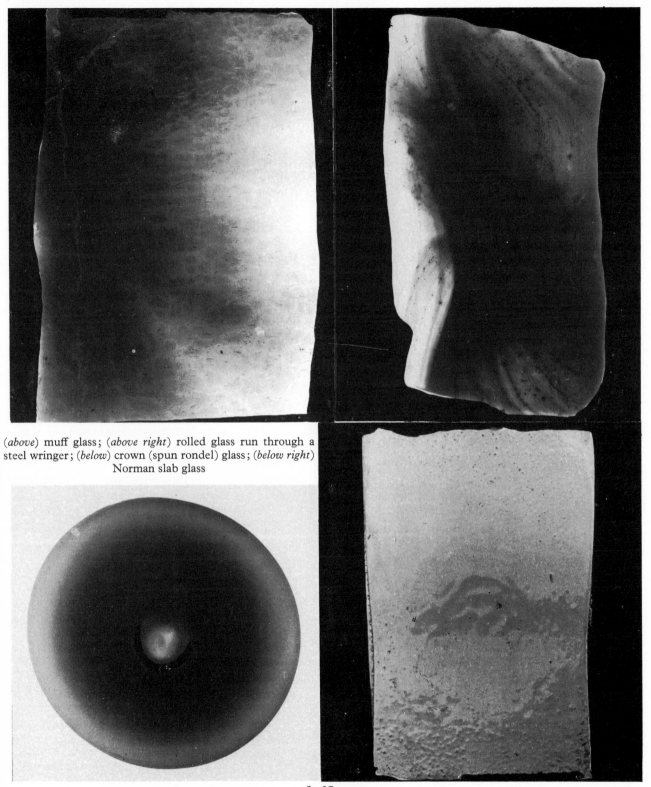

(*above*) muff glass; (*above right*) rolled glass run through a steel wringer; (*below*) crown (spun rondel) glass; (*below right*) Norman slab glass

fig 27
TYPES OF ANTIQUE GLASS

character is varied by being dark in the center, with light toward the top and dark toward the bottom of the piece.

In the spun rondel or crown glass, textures and color form spiral configurations.

These various types of glass all have one thing in common: they develop a great deal of color and texture change within a very small area. This all adds to the variety and quality of the window in which they are used.

There is, finally, one type of sheet which does not call for the glass blower and does not seem to have a name. This glass is made by taking a blob of glass from the pot and running it through a steel wringer to produce slabs of roughly 6″ by 9″. This is the way Larsen Company made the glass for Bryn Athyn Cathedral at Beth Ayres, Pa., and also the way Lawrence Saint made the glass for his windows in the Washington cathedral. This glass is particularly effective, partly because every effort is made to imitate the exact formulae and textures of medieval glass.

There is a type of glass called "flashed" which can be made by all of the previous methods. It arises out of the fact that copper used as a red for glass is so dense that a solid color would be completely opaque. The solution is simple: first a blob of white glass is gathered upon the blower's pipe, but before blowing it out, the bubble is dunked into a pot of ruby. The result is something like the dipping of chocolates. The main ball is white covered with a thin coat of ruby. When blown out and formed into a cylinder, the red has thinned out enough to produce a deep red glass.

It took the glassmakers a very short time to realize that they could make an infinite number of different kinds of red by varying the original ball of color from white to pale yellow to pale green or pale blue. Each different base produced a different kind of red.

Flashing had a dual purpose. By grinding away the red, a red on white combination could be made on the same piece. By flashing blue on white or green on white it was possible to get two colors on one piece; but flashed glass was used almost entirely to make different hues and shades of red or for heraldic shields where it was not considered correct to use a color on a color or a metal on a metal in any one section of a shield. Heraldic white is silver and heraldic yellow is gold. Flashed glass made possible a color and a metal on one piece of glass.

There are some indications coming from the study of microphotographs of pieces of medieval glass that some of the early glass had been almost entirely composed of built-up flashings. Some show a total of twelve laminations. One account suggests that as many as fifty were used. If this is true, the glass blower must have started with a piece no larger than a peanut. These variable flashings, plus their natural tendency to drift during the blowing process, would produce a piece of glass with an almost infinite number of variations. They were extremely beautiful but prohibitive in cost.

In addition to the colors and textures found in antique glass which are caused more or less by the methods of blowing, there are some special effects made by other means. One of these is a bubbly glass which is made by sprinkling oil into the crucible of molten glass. The oil reacts in much the same fashion as it does in water, creating small bubbles which in turn fracture the light rays and produce a most interesting effect. As a matter of fact, it is to these same bubbles, which usually break out and fill with dirt when exposed to the elements, that we owe a debt of gratitude for the interesting texture which is found in old glass.

LEAD

The second member of the material triumvirate, and by no means the most glamorous, is lead. This drab, lackluster, blue-gray material is certainly not impressive to look at but let no one be fooled by appearances. In the form of grooved rods called cames it has been used extensively since the eleventh century to fasten pieces of glass together in the fabricating of stained glass and for other windows. In spite of all the advertising of and clamor for new materials, nothing has been discovered which can even vaguely equal its usefulness. It is pliable and flexible. It can be easily opened out or pressed together, wound around the most complicated glass shapes, cut with a knife, scissors, or block plane, and easily soldered. A window fastened together with lead cames and soldered at its joints is an unbelievably tough and durable structure. Much of the thirteenth-century glass extant still has its original leading. This is due largely to the fact that early lead cames were made quite thick and that the material itself contained impurities. It is no secret that lead oxidizes very quickly and that certain impurities such as antimony and tin often found in lead inhibit its oxidation. Unlike some other metals, in lead the oxidation takes the form of a thin covering layer which protects the underlying metal from further action.

The very earliest leads were formed in a most ingenious way. The bottom and sides of a shallow wooden box were covered with an inch of sand. Upon the level bottom surface of the sand, willow twigs or reeds approximately $\frac{1}{4}''$ in diameter and a scant $22''$ long were placed parallel. These twigs were propped up above the sand on small wooden pins to a height of $\frac{1}{32}''$. The distance between the willow twigs or reeds was a scant $\frac{1}{16}''$. Lead heated to a molten state in a large ladle was poured over the willow twigs, so that the final level of the lead in the box was $\frac{1}{32}''$ above the

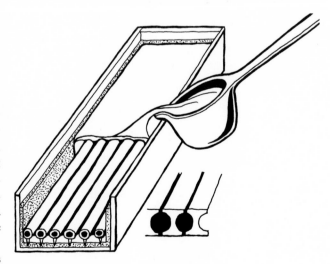

fig 28
A very early method of making lead cames by using reads

45

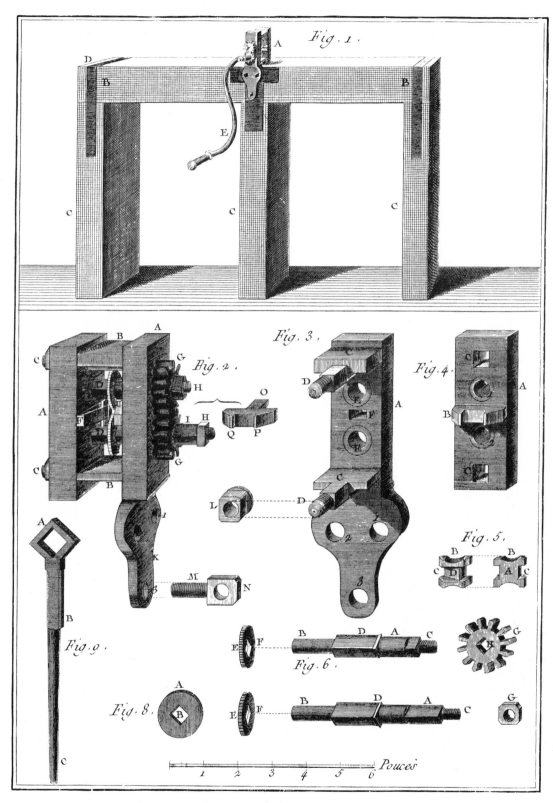

fig 29
German mill used in 1774

fig 30
Contemporary lead mold

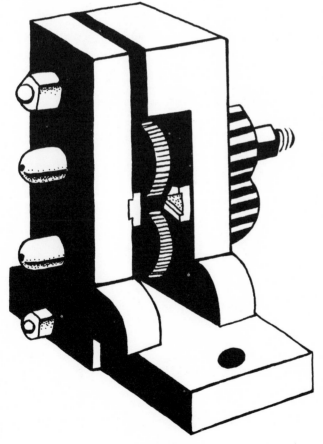

fig 31
Contemporary lead mill

twigs or reeds. The molten lead, which charred out the willow twigs, cooled rapidly enough to allow the twigs to be replaced by hollow tubes; what now remained was a thin sheet of lead 22″ square and $\frac{5}{16}$″ thick with hollow tubes. A cut was made directly through the center of each tube. The strips formed in this manner of cutting made crude but quite usable lead cames. The height and width of these leads could be changed by varying the diameter of the willow twigs or reeds. This method of making cames was quickly replaced by casting them in wooden or iron molds.

Modern molds are much shorter than the medieval mold and make three heavy castings to be drawn through a lead mill. To describe a lead mill and its use is fairly complicated. To demonstrate its use takes but a few minutes. If a studio is going to purchase one, the dealer will demonstrate its use and will furnish the buyer with detailed instruction. A lead mill is in reality a mechanized draw plate—the cheeks act as dies while the spindles and milling wheels serve the same purpose as heavy-duty draw pliers do for a draw plate, namely, to alter the size and shape of the wire drawn through the dies. The illustrations show a German mill used in 1774, and a contemporary one sold by James Hetley & Co., Ltd. of London.

Lead mills are used extensively in European studios but rarely in American ones. Presently, in the United States, lead cames are made by extrusion in very much the same way as spaghetti. The hydraulic presses used for this purpose are fitted with a die which has a series of identical openings. A pig of lead weighing 100 pounds is placed in the machine, pressure is exerted, and 100 pounds of identical lead cames are extruded. Cames made in this way cost very little more than the price of lead by weight. There are, however, certain disadvantages to lead cames made in this manner. Each different size or shape requires the purchase of 100 pounds of that particular lead. This might seem unfair, but rapid oxidation makes lead difficult to solder, so that it really should be made fresh and used immediately.

For small studios a lead mill is almost a must. Cheeks for the mill which determine the size of the lead may be purchased in $\frac{1}{8}$″, $\frac{1}{4}$″, $\frac{3}{8}$″, and $\frac{1}{2}$″ sizes, and even larger if necessary. Also high and low hearth spindles and milling wheels may be bought. By simply changing cheeks one may run off one strand or a dozen as needed. In this way the cames are always bright and clean. Another advantage is that all the scrap which gathers in the glazing process can be melted and recast. Any kind of lead scrap is usable. Frequently, when old houses are torn down, the lead plumbing can be bought cheaply. This kind of lead scrap contains a large percentage of tin which makes the lead cames a bit stiffer but also much more resistant to oxidation.

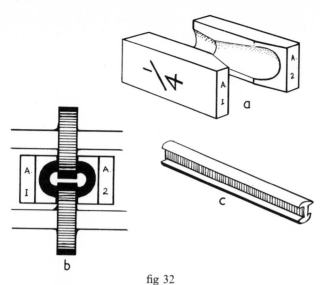

fig 32
CHEEKS AND SPINDLES FOR LEAD MILL
a) cheeks   b) end view of milling wheels   c) lead came showing milling-wheel marks

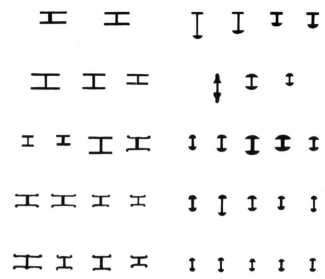

fig 33
Various types and sizes of lead cames that are available commercially

In addition, a stiff lead is somewhat easier to cut. The accompanying illustration shows a catalog page of the sizes and shapes made by one lead manufacturer. There is a type of lead which has not been mentioned but is shown in the catalog page. This is a lead with a steel heart and it is sometimes used to avoid reinforcement bars. However, it is difficult to work with because it must be cut with a hacksaw and, by and large, is hardly worth the trouble involved.

48

IRON

When the layman thinks of glass, his overriding interest understandably is color. It is quite difficult to convince him that painting has a great deal to do with the effect of the color. He will even insist that the twelfth- and thirteenth-century glass was not painted at all. He is indifferent, if not downright contemptuous, of the iron and lead work in a window. No one will deny that color is a window's crowning glory, but without iron bars to support the structure and leads to help form its fabric, the world would still be looking for its first stained-glass window.

A leaded glass window is able to support its own downward thrust weight in a section no more than three feet high. Much more height will increase the weight and cause the section to buckle. A section should be no more than three feet wide, preferably narrower. To support the weight of the sections, the early window makers devised a system of ironwork consisting of bars $1'' \times 1'' \times \frac{1}{8}''$ in the form of a "T" placed on its side. The glass section rested upon the horizontal ledge and the $1''$ band faced inward so that the window section could press against it. These bars are called saddle bars by the English and T bars by the Americans. The bars were set into the stonework to a depth of at least $\frac{3}{4}''$ to securely anchor them. An inch on either end was removed from the horizontal sections of the T bar so that only the narrow vertical section of the T remained to insert into the stonework.

Since there is such a tremendous inward pressure from the wind, which acts upon the window in the same manner as it does upon a sail, it is necessary to place $\frac{1}{2}''$ round bars every $12''$ to counter this thrust. The last $\frac{1}{2}''$ of the round bars is flattened so that both the bars and the window section will fit into the same rabbet. The bars are placed on the inside of the window. Originally, lead strips, and later copper wires, were soldered to the leads of the window and were twisted around the reinforcement bars in order to hold the section tightly against the bars, preventing the window from vibrating or flapping in a strong wind. In the eleventh and twelfth centuries those windows that were not more than three feet wide were barred in the manner described; as they became larger and wider, additional vertical bars were added. These took the form of dividers for their fairly wide borders. As the windows grew still wider, first two sections and finally three plus the borders were used. This division of the sections into blocks lent itself to the presentation of a series of related incidents in the lives of saints or martyrs. At first, these sections were made in the form of squares; later they were changed to alternating squares and circles, the circles being defined within the square blocks by the lead cames and emphasized by the color. The next inevitable step was to turn the simple circles and squares into a complex iron armature. Once started in this direction it can easily be seen that there is no

49

fig 34

Medallion window armatures from Trinity Chapel, Canterbury Cathedral

limit to the variety of pattern possibilities which can be created. The accompanying illustrations from Trinity Chapel in Canterbury Cathedral show just a few of these possibilities.

By dividing the window into many relatively small patterned sections, the armatures provided excellent space for serial subjects but were not suitable in their medallion form for the division of large single figures. For this reason the medallion windows were used mostly in the lower nave and apsidal chapels where they were more easily seen. The windows in the west front, the nave clerestory, the choir clerestory, and the transepts retained the original horizontal and vertical T-bar construction.

For years it had puzzled us that if one or more large-scale figures were used in most west front windows, why were the three most famous west front ones, namely those in the Cathedral of Notre Dame at Chartres, made in medallion

form? Robert Sowers, in the Winter issue of *Art Journal*, 1968–69, published by the College Art Association, has a most interesting explanation. The three west windows in question are twelfth-century works saved from the 1194 fire and later adapted to the newer thirteenth-century cathedral. But Sowers explains that these three windows were originally in a second-story position above the narthex and were visible at very close range. That they are so visually effective in their present position is a tribute to the imagination of the architect of the thirteenth-century cathedral for his skill in adapting these earlier windows to the newer cathedral.

The iron work, besides serving as an aesthetic, decorative and educational medium, was effective in acting as an architectural handmaiden. The total weight of a window area made of glass fastened together with lead cames and fixed in place with iron armatures was less than a tenth of the weight of a cathedral's stone masonry walls. This meant that the windows could be indefinitely enlarged to produce both illumination and decoration. In fact, Louis IX, when he came to build Sainte Chapelle in Paris, was so impressed with the glass which his regent mother, Blanche of Castile, had put in the north transept of Chartres Cathedral that he decided to fill every available space in the chapel with windows separated only by the narrow standard dividing bars known as mullions. Instead of creating a greater aesthetic impact, he managed to produce an excellent illustration of a stained-glass greenhouse. Stained glass needs large areas of dark wall space to bring out the windows' greatest color effects.

It might be interesting, while still on the subject of iron work, to tell something of the iron used in the armatures of these early windows. It was known as charcoal iron and was made by placing chunks of iron ore in a charcoal fire. This was done on relatively small hearths. The iron which was made this way had a very small carbon content which made it quite malleable and, even more important, it was practically rustproof. Very nearly all of the iron work put in the thirteenth-century cathedrals still remains intact, while much work done in the 19th century had to be replaced as it had completely rusted away.

But there was one disastrous consequence of charcoal ironmaking. Almost every citizen of the thirteenth through the fifteenth centuries made his own charcoal iron, and the drain on the local forests for charcoal was catastrophic. Queen Elizabeth finally brought the manufacture of iron under the Crown, and France seems to have been able to replace the rape of her forests. But not so with Spain and Greece; they have never recovered from the almost total destruction of their forests. Their little remaining topsoil is still being eroded.

THE STUDIO

For the first time since the Renaissance, the class distinction between artist and craftsman has been shaken. Men able to do things with their hands have become so scarce that they are now being elevated to the status of artists, certainly a very healthy change for the future of the arts.

In our present-day studios, we should make every effort to break down the barriers promoting specialization if we are ever again to produce windows that can match those of the medieval period. This, then, is the major difference between the studio of today and that of the past—not one of methodology or procedure.

In the light of our present technological knowledge, it may come as a surprise to find that the way of making a stained-glass window today does not vary greatly from the way it was done in the Middle Ages. Everyone knows that good working conditions and adequate space are mandatory for the proper and efficient execution of a product; stained glass is no exception. Glass studios, like photographic laboratories, may occupy a space which is just barely usable or they may be expanded into an almost perfect facility. Many excellent photographs have been developed and printed in the family bathroom and it is equally possible to make good windows in just as makeshift quarters. Most stained-glass artists have worked in several studios before starting their own. They have all planned their ideal workshop but, unfortunately, when the time has come for them to strike out for themselves they have been forced by circumstances beyond their control to accept many compromises. In the end, these restrictions may all have been for the best, for no matter how grandiose the ideas or how perfect the plans, circumstances continue to occur which prove the most perfect studio inadequate in a surprisingly short time.

A satisfactory plan for a studio will, of course, grow out of the steps required in the making of a window. They will control the type and size of areas and will also determine what equipment can be grouped together.

Anyone setting up a large commercial studio will or should know what he is doing, so will have little use for the following descriptions and illustrations which are planned for a minimal studio space, just large enough to accommodate a group of four workers.

In the perfect studio there are many pieces of equipment, large and small, which could be housed ideally in separate rooms. Since certain practical considerations must be tolerated, one might start by listing the step-by-step procedure followed by most reliable studios in making a window.

1) Making the sketch
2) Making the template or pattern
3) Making the cartoon
4) Making the cut line

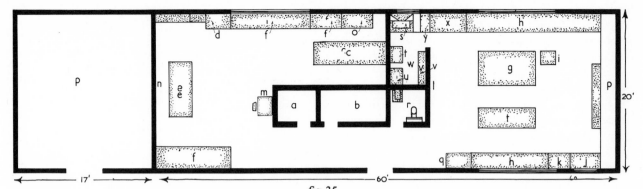

fig 35
PLAN FOR A STUDIO

a) private office
b) office
c) laying-out table
d) cartoon storage
e) platform for drawing
   cartoons
f) cabinets

g) glazing table
h) glass racks
i) fluorescent lights
j) cutting table
k) choosing table
l) rack on wall for small
   tools

m) designing desk
n) drawing wall
o) paper rack
p) storage
q) bookcase for sketches
r) lavatory
s) sink

t) table
u) kiln
v) kiln plates
w) kiln room
x) shelves
y) plate glass rack

5) Cutting the patterns
6) Selecting and cutting the glass
7) Painting the glass
8) Firing the glass
9) Glazing—fixing the glass in its lead
10) Cementing and setting

Office

In a studio, two small offices are needed—one in which to take care of business correspondence, bookkeeping, and other office work; the other a private office where clients can be interviewed. Both of these offices should precede the other studio rooms.

Drawing

All operations which in any way utilize drawing may be carried out in one large room. This would include the making of a design or sketch, working on the template after it has been made from the window opening, laying out the cartoon from the templates, drawing the cartoon, making the cut line from the cartoon, and tracing the false lead lines over the cut line.

Glass Work

All work upon the glass itself may be done in a separate room—the cutting of the patterns, waxing them to the plates which have been painted with false lead lines, selecting and cutting the glass, and tracing and painting the glass, even laying out the glass in special trays preparatory to firing.

Firing

The firing of glass should be carried out in a small room separate from the others. Even an electric kiln generates some undesirable heat. The kiln room should be large enough to hold at least two medium-sized kilns, a rack for storing kiln plates, a table upon which to lay out the plates preparatory to firing, a set of shelves for the storage of whiting, a flour sieve, plate spacers, and other tools required for firing preparations.

Etching

A small room is needed for acid work such as etching. This room should include a sink with running water which has available work space on either side of it. A set of shelves for storing acid, etching materials, and other related tools should be added. A vent hood with an exhaust fan must be placed above the sink to eliminate acid fumes. It is also advisable to equip both this and the kiln room with special dry-type fire extinguishers.

Packing and Storage

A large storage and packing room is almost mandatory. It will be invaluable for storing extra cases of glass, boxes of lead, extra pieces of plate glass, and an almost endless series of small tools; other pieces of equipment and materials which are only used occasionally can also be stored in this room.

Glazing and Cementing

Glazing can be done in the room used for glass cutting,

53

but if space is scarce, it is much better to put glazing with cementing. Glazing takes much longer to do than cementing, which means that a room used for both purposes can be used most of the time for glazing. It is better, however, to use a separate room for each operation. In case the room is used for both purposes, it should have two large tables: one for glazing, the other for cementing. The glazing table should have at least one half of its underneath area reserved for a tier of sliding trays. These trays will be loaded with sections of windows laid out ready for firing or glazing. Since cementing is an extremely dusty and dirty operation, it is well to keep it separately housed when space is not a problem.

The Drawing Wall and Other Heavy Equipment

The walls of this room should be constructed of a material with a surface which is smooth for the drawing of the cartoons. The wall upon which the cartoons are to be drawn should be at least 12′ high by 12′ wide. It is more important to be able to put up the entire cartoon of a window for examination than it is to set up the entire window. Once the window is drawn correctly the glass will take care of itself. Above all else, the cartoon wall should be smooth. There is nothing more exasperating than to have a ridge or a dent appear right where critical detail comes in the drawing. When working on a large drawing it is necessary to have some means of changing your working level. The simplest solution is to build a short flight of stairs and put it on casters. The steps themselves ought to be fairly broad and the stairs should have a platform at the top with a sturdy railing around it. Many an artist deeply engrossed in his work has stepped back to take a better look at his drawing only to find himself sprawled out on his studio floor.

Shelves for books can be mounted on the walls wherever space is available; the more shelves the better. Two tilt-type drafting tables are needed—a small one for general sketching and a reasonably large one to take care of work on oversize sketches. One, preferably two, large layout tables will prove invaluable for an endless variety of uses. A large rack for holding four heavy rolls of paper will be needed. Space and cupboards will have to be provided for the storage of paints, paper, and other drawing materials. A fairly large closet will be required to house the ever-mounting number of sketches and cartoons as they are completed. It is not advisable to belabor the reader with an endless string of minutiæ—details of useful or desirable materials and tools. Only the larger pieces of equipment or the more esoteric tools will be mentioned hereafter.

54

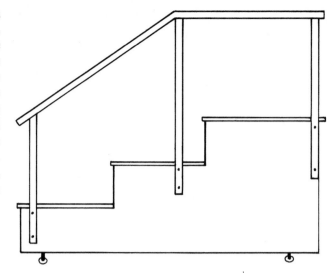

fig 36
Flight of steps used in drawing a cartoon or painting a window

Fluorescent Lights

Because proper light is such a basic necessity for the selection of colors as well as the painting of the glass, there is no single item of equipment more useful for the present-day glass artist than the fluorescent light. Before these lights were available, the selecting, cutting, and painting of glass presented a constant problem. In the late spring, summer, or early fall, the difficulties could be coped with; but from the middle of fall to the latter part of spring, six months in all, gray days and short days used to make window making a nightmare. In the winter, whether the days were clear or gray, no painting could be done before 9:00 A.M. nor after 3:00 P.M. In the south, or south of the border, the situation was better, but then there were very few studios located in these areas.

There is a strange dichotomy which seems to occur in most arts, but which is particularly apparent in the art of stained glass. Artists in most crafts have a penchant for guarding their most trivial tricks of the trade as vital to their artistic survival. When they happen to be presented with a technique which is new, different, or really worthwhile, there is no way that you can get them even to try it—the use of fluorescent light, for example. Most studios continue to resist its use. When one considers that the light is cool, diffused, and constant, it is difficult to understand why the studios react in such a manner. Ours was one of the earliest (if not the earliest) studios to use fluorescent lights for window making. By experimenting with these new lights we discovered that glass placed six inches away from 40-watt fluorescent bulbs set five inches on center, would read the same on an exposure meter as bright north daylight. From the moment of this discovery, neither day nor night nor summer nor winter created any more difficulty for us. Glass could be cut or painted as easily at midnight as at noon.

In the past, one objection to the use of fluorescent lights was the striping caused by the separated tubes. Industrial-type fixtures, called "box-type strip fluorescents," are now available in two lengths, 48″ and 96″ respectively. They are mounted two tubes to a fixture on white enameled metal boxes. When placed side by side, they make a continuous bank of lights $2\frac{1}{4}″$ on center. This bank can be extended as needed. Placing the lights $2\frac{1}{4}″$ rather than 5″ on center greatly increases the available light and decreases the

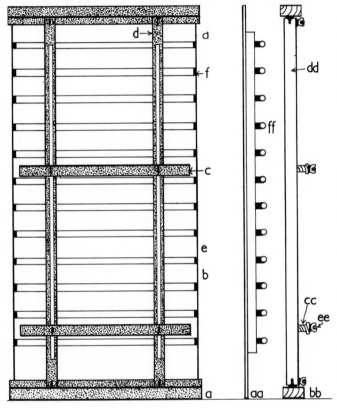

fig 37
FLUORESCENT LIGHT WALL

a) front view
aa) profile view
b) $\frac{3}{8}″$ plywood back wall, front view
bb) $\frac{3}{8}″$ plywood back wall, profile view
c) cross member, front view
cc) cross member, profile view

d) upright member, front view
dd) upright member, profile view
e) butterfly screw, front view
ee) butterfly screw, profile view
f) fluorescent light bulbs, front view
ff) fluorescent light bulbs, profile view

striping effect. Most new fluorescent fixtures come in what is called "instant start"; a rheostat can be used with this new type of fixture. It will permit the user to lower his light power to suit the light source of the window he may be executing. An additional diffusing material such as alsynite can be placed between the lights and the glass if the user still objects to whatever striping may remain.

To make proper use of the lights, a wall should be built out of $\frac{3}{8}″$ plywood mounted on two-by-fours, twelve feet long. For ease in handling, as well as for mounting the fluorescent fixtures, it is better to make the plywood in sections of 48″ × 48″. A wall can then easily be made in 48″ modules; a good overall size will then be 144″ × 144″. You will need six beams, 2″ × 4″ × 144″—two for the horizontal members and four for the vertical ones. This will permit you to fasten the plywood panels 48″ on center on the vertical beams. This wall must be fastened securely to the floor and ceiling. A wall of this size will handle almost any normal three-paneled window up to 144″, not including the ornamental peak or "tracery". If you have a larger window than this to set up for examination, you will need either a church or an auditorium to be able to get far enough away to look at it.

When working on the cutting or painting of a window, all you will ever need to set up at the same time are two sections. If this should seem to inhibit your working methods, remember that the medieval artist did not have any plate glass upon which to wax up his work. The only time he saw his handiwork all together was when it was finally set in place.

For a small studio, a single panel section 4′ × 4′ × 4′ will do very nicely—extra modules can be added whenever the need arises. When the wall has been mounted on the frame, the entire surface should be covered with a matte white paint to act as a reflector for this wall.

The fluorescent fixtures should be mounted horizontally, as has been mentioned before, and the bulbs placed five inches apart on center. Fasten the transformers and starters to the back of the panel. The new instant-start fixtures may be substituted for the older type, in which case it will not be necessary to paint the board white, as the fixtures themselves constitute the reflector base.

It is extremely important that this new wall with its fixtures be set at least 24″ forward from the regular studio wall. This will allow a small stepladder to be used behind the new wall when it becomes necessary to replace starters or electrical wiring. The fluorescent wall should have the fixtures wired in sequence with a separate switch for each 48″ section of lights. They can begin at the left-hand base section, proceeding upward to the top of the panel. This same procedure can be carried out in each of the other two

55

panels. It is advisable to place a switchboard alongside the battery of lights to contain the separate switches. There are several different types of white bulbs available, but the "cool white" ones are by far the best. If you wish to photograph your work, these bulbs can be used together with Kodachrome II daylight film with an electric flash to make the same exposure. This should clearly demonstrate that the color rendition is excellent.

The Glass Easel

No stained-glass artist would deny the value of a good easel, but the one which appears periodically in every new book on the technique of stained glass is a machine of the devil. The first illustration of this easel appeared in the book *Stained Glass Work,* by Christopher Whall, published in 1905; and each new book on the subject repeats the same illustration of the same easel with slight variations and shows its construction and its counterbalancing mechanism. On the surface, it would appear to be a very excellent piece of equipment. It can be raised or lowered with ease. There are $\frac{1}{2}''$ holes drilled on either side of the stationary frame at $6''$ intervals, with a similar size hole on either side of the base of the movable inside frame. A short $\frac{1}{2}''$ round bar can be inserted when the holes match to secure the easel in its raised or lowered position. The mobile portion is fitted with a series of removable plates of glass. The glass to be painted is waxed up on the various plates and the plates set into the easel. At this point the fun begins. If the easel is balanced for three plates and if the plates are no larger than three feet high, all will be well. The difficulty is that windows can vary from $37''$ to $35''$; when they do, your lovely $36''$ plates are either too long or too short to link up and so you end up with but two plates, placing the pieces of glass at the top of one plate and at the bottom of the other. This makes your counterbalanced easel one third too light; your operational performance to raise or lower the window in order to get the pin into the matched holes begins to resemble a comedy act. If, by any chance, you happen to let go of the window, it will rush up to the top of the easel and crash, knocking plates and glass pieces into a pile of rubble on the studio floor. This can occur any time you happen to be just a bit relaxed or careless. But this is nothing compared to what invariably happens every two or three years when the sashcord holding the weights snaps. The shambles in this case is beyond belief. A much simpler and far safer, though less romantic easel can be made for a much lower cost. The flight of steps used in drawing the cartoons will work equally well for raising or lowering the painter's working position.

The easel which can be used against the wall of fluorescent

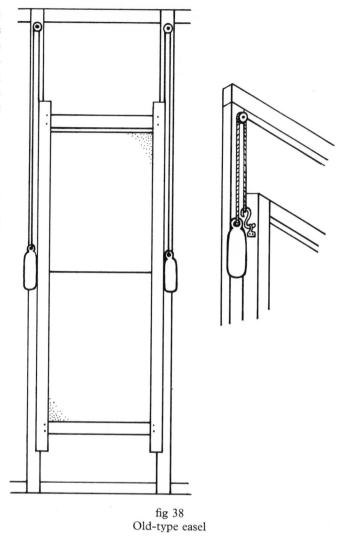

fig 38
Old-type easel

lights is relatively simple to construct, as can be seen in the accompanying illustration. Four beams $2'' \times 4'' \times 144''$ will be needed to make the outside frame. One is securely fastened to the studio rafters, another to the floor. The other two are fastened to the top and bottom to complete a rectangular frame $12' \times 12'$. Two more two-by-fours are used for the uprights. A third additional upright may be added if two wide and two narrow openings are desirable. It is possible with this arrangement to have space for four painters. The top and bottom beams are fitted with T bars extending their full length. The T bars must be drilled and securely fastened with screws to the top and bottom two-by-fours. The two or three remaining beams are fitted with U-irons drilled and securely screwed to both ends of each beam, as illustrated. These beams, plus their fittings, should fit snugly between the top and bottom beams. It

56

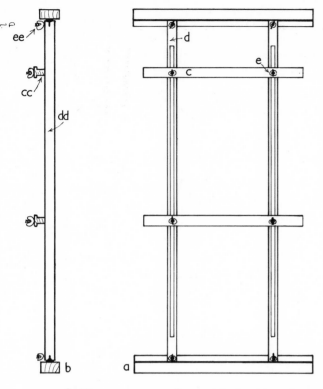

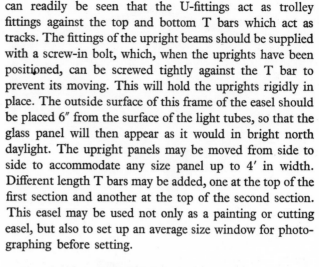

can readily be seen that the U-fittings act as trolley fittings against the top and bottom T bars which act as tracks. The fittings of the upright beams should be supplied with a screw-in bolt, which, when the uprights have been positioned, can be screwed tightly against the T bar to prevent its moving. This will hold the uprights rigidly in place. The outside surface of this frame of the easel should be placed 6″ from the surface of the light tubes, so that the glass panel will then appear as it would in bright north daylight. The upright panels may be moved from side to side to accommodate any size panel up to 4′ in width. Different length T bars may be added, one at the top of the first section and another at the top of the second section. This easel may be used not only as a painting or cutting easel, but also to set up an average size window for photographing before setting.

The Selecting Table

In practically every stained-glass studio, one of the major problems is to determine what to do with those pieces of glass which are too large to throw away yet too small to put in the glass racks. The problem has been partially solved in many studios by placing a series of shelves one above the other in one of the studio windows. These shelves are backed with double-weight sheetglass. The small pieces of antique glass are set up on the shelves and leaned against the window glass. Like many suggested solutions to a problem, this one sounds good at first. In use, the rack turns out to be a bit small, takes up too much window space and since most of the pieces are irregular in shape, it requires a good deal of time to place the glass on the shelves.

fig 39
NEW-TYPE EASEL
a) front view
b) profile view
c) cross member, front view
cc) cross member, profile view

d) upright 2 × 4 bar, front view
dd) upright 2 × 4 bar, profile view
e) butterfly screw, front view
ee) butterfly screw, profile view

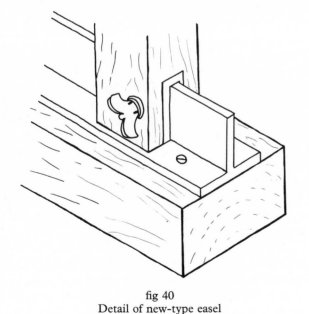

fig 40
Detail of new-type easel

fig 41
Traditional glass rack

57

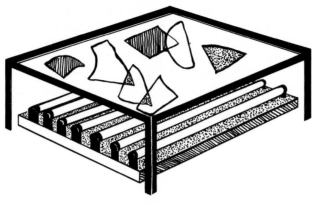

fig 42
Selecting table

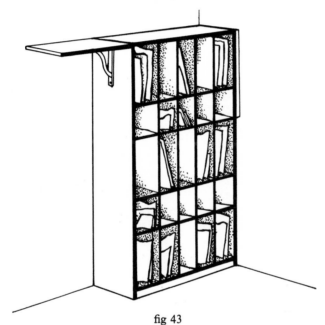

fig 43
A small glass rack for storing sheet glass. The tip has hinged ends for additional cutting space

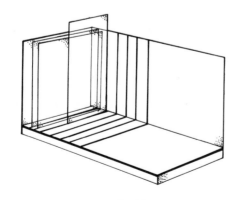

fig 44
Plate-glass rack

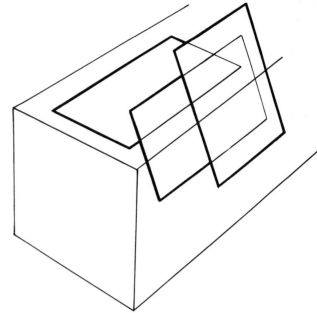

fig 45
How to handle a sheet of plate glass, or a cemented or uncemented section

In use it becomes more of a burden than an asset. But it invariably passes through a series of retrogressive transitions —at first it is eagerly received as a new tool; as enthusiasm for its practical value wanes, it becomes an attractive decorative addition to the studio; ultimately it gathers dust and is finally discarded. The workman cutting glass returns to his habit of tossing his smaller pieces into a general scrap bin where they lie for years under six inches of other scrap.

A much better solution is a fluorescent light table. One can be made very easily with 4′ fluorescent instant-light fixtures mounted upon a plywood board, 48″ × 48″ and ¾″ thick. Around the board a frame 8″ high must be fastened. The frame should be rabbeted to hold a series of four ¼″ sheets of plate glass 24″ × 48″. The unit may be placed on two or three sawhorses, or a table can be made to support it. This type of selecting table, because it is flat, provides instant space for much more glass than any upright rack. Its easy visual accessibility causes it to be used much more than any other type of rack. When pieces get too small for easy cutting, they can be placed in the usual scrap boxes.

Even in a small studio, you will need several sheets of ¼″ plate glass to hold sections which have been cut and waxed up for painting. You can start with six sheets, 36″ × 36″, and two or three longer ones, 36″ × 48″. Second-hand plate glass can be purchased for half the cost of new plate and will be just as good. Sooner or later, one of the local

58

storefronts will get broken and the owner will be only too happy to give it to you just to get rid of the pieces. It will not be long before you have quite a collection of odd size but very useful pieces.

We have illustrated a very simple and easily made rack which will hold a number of plates in a vertical position.

A large sheet of ¼″ plate glass can be dangerous if improperly handled. The safe way to pick up a piece of plate from the rack is to grip it on either side slightly above center and carry it this way to its destination. If it is to be put on a table, first rest it against the edge of the table top, rotate it to a horizontal position with its middle against the table's edge, tip it forward quickly and push it onto the table top. To remove the same plate, simply reverse the procedure. A similar method is used when handling a section of a window.

Take flexible rods, fixing them in the earth in an angle of the house at both ends equally in the form of arches, which arches may have the height of a foot and a half, and also a similar breadth and a length of a little more than two feet. You then will beat up clay strongly with water and horse litter, so that three parts may be clay and a fourth dung. With which, being well beaten together, you will mix dry hay, making of it long flat pieces, and you will cover the arch of rods, inside and outside, to the thickness of a fist, and in the middle above you leave a round opening through which you can put your hand; make for yourself also three iron bars of the thickness of a finger, and of such length that they may traverse the breadth of the furnace, in which, on both sides, make three holes, so that you can place and withdraw them when you wish. Then place fire and wood in the furnace until it is dried.

Theophilus
The Various Arts, Chapter **XXII**
Of the Furnace in which Glass is Burnt

THE KILN

It is clear, from this account, that the early glass kilns were wood fired. What Theophilus has described above is known today as a flash kiln. Fire burning kilns have passed through an evolutionary series from wood to coal, to gas, and to oil. But all of these operate on the same general principle—they all use flame heat which requires oxygen in order to burn.

There are two kinds of flame firing kilns: the flash kiln which has just been mentioned, and the muffle kiln. Both kinds can be used for glass, but only the muffle kiln can be used for ceramics. In a flash kiln the glass is exposed to the open flame which rises up the sides of the kiln until it meets on the arched ceiling of the firing chamber. This type of kiln is very fast firing. In the muffle type, the heat source is much smaller and takes much longer to fire. The firing chamber is separated from the fire by a wall, so that the heat rises and encircles the enclosed chamber but does not touch the material being fired. This type of kiln is ideal for firing pieces of glass which vary greatly in thickness from the center to the edges. The slow firing and slow cooling are assets instead of liabilities in this case.

A flash kiln operates on the radiant heat principle, whereas the muffle type utilizes the convection method. Until the lower-priced electric kilns came on the market, most glass was fired in a gas kiln. Where gas was not available, oil was used instead.

There are certain pieces of equipment which even a small studio must acquire in order to produce windows. A

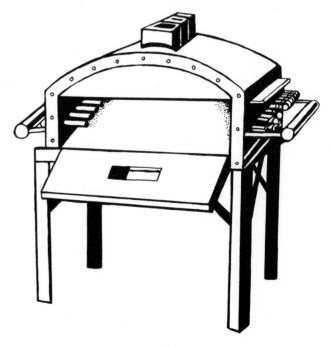

fig 46
Gas-kiln section

60

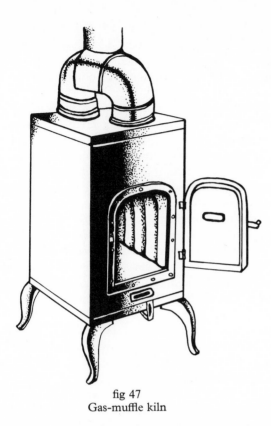

fig 47
Gas-muffle kiln

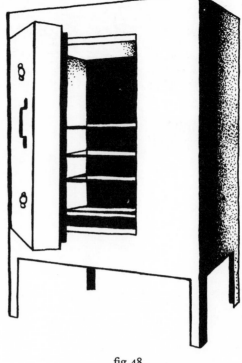

fig 48
Electric-kiln-front loader

kiln is a case in point—a small studio should have at least one medium and one small-sized kiln. For firing glass, electric kilns made for ceramic work are excellent and quite efficient. There are a number of companies which make ceramic kilns—the particular model which we have in mind is a top loader made to be fired at a maximum temperature of 2300° Fahrenheit. It is rated as 220/110 volts, which means that if it is going to be fired at a maximum of 1200° Fahrenheit for stained glass use only, it can be operated on a 110-volt standard house circuit. If, however, it is going to be used as an alternate glass and ceramic ·kiln, it will be necessary to wire it for 220 volts. The small kiln has an octagonal inside chamber $14\frac{3}{8}''$ in diameter and a depth of $13\frac{1}{4}''$, which will accommodate three round ceramic plates $13''$ in diameter. Twelve $3''$ separator posts will be needed to support the kiln plates. The medium-size model has an inside chamber $17\frac{1}{2}''$ in diameter and a depth of $18''$, which will accommodate four hexagonal plates $16\frac{1}{2}''$ in diameter. Four more $3''$ separator posts will be needed for this model. This kiln is also rated 220/110. The smaller kiln is capable of firing approximately three square feet of glass at one time while the medium one will take care of nine square feet. The cost of these economy-type hexagonal kilns is about half the cost of the standard square-type kilns, and are just as good.

fig 49
Electric kiln-top loader

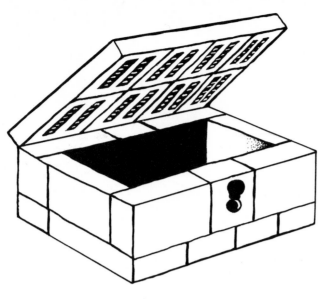

fig 50
Electric flash kiln designed by the authors to accommodate a single tray of glass. Since the heating elements are in the ceiling of the kiln, it will fire the single tray of glass very rapidly

A studio can operate with one kiln, but there are several good reasons why one or more additional ones are desirable. Electric kilns have a most annoying habit of burning out elements just when they are needed most. It is also advantageous to have an additional kiln when work to be fired begins to pile up. When the studio has two, one can be loaded while the other is firing, or one can be emptied while the other is cooling.

Since the electric ceramic kiln has its heating elements exposed to the materials being fired, it produces both radiant and convection heat. One of the manufacturers of these new electric kilns has developed a ceramic mount for the heating elements which takes full advantage of their radiant properties—it directs the heat outward so that when the elements are mounted the correct distance apart the entire area of the kiln is covered. We have designed and developed a flash kiln using these radiant-type elements. The elements are placed in the top of the kiln so that the radiant heat is directed downward on the plate containing the glass to be fired. This kiln measures $54'' \times 18'' \times 4''$ inside. The design is based upon multiples of $18'' \times 18'' \times 4''$ to accommodate standard $16'' \times 16''$ ceramic firing plates. One measuring $18'' \times 18'' \times 4''$ can be fired on a 110-volt circuit. The larger size requires a 220-volt circuit. More about these electric and other type kilns is explained under the chapter on firing.

It can easily be demonstrated that if these kilns are fired in a continuous cycle, they will be able to service a much larger studio staff than the four persons we have been considering.

THE SKETCH

In this country at the present time, the subjects and their interpretation for church windows are determined by a committee, composed of minister, architect, donor, artist, and laity. In the Middle Ages, it was the responsibility of the clergy, the authorities upon liturgical matters, to define the subjects and to determine the symbolic interpretations for all forms of religious art. The iconographical and symbolic data were in turn translated into illuminated illustrations by the monks; when a certain subject was to be depicted, their manuscripts were used as models. This was equally true for sculpture, fresco, and stained glass. As a result, the sketch could be bypassed and the artist could proceed directly to his full-sized drawing or cartoon. In the present-day studio it is customary for the artist, after getting some kind of a subject suggestion or approval, to make a sketch of the proposed window. A $1\frac{1}{2}''$-$1'0''$ scale works best for normal sized windows no higher than ten feet; this scale is large enough to represent the smaller details but does not make a sketch whose overall length is so large that it becomes cumbersome to handle or mail. If the window happens to be higher, it may be necessary to go to a scale of $1''$-$1'0''$. Any smaller size is too small to give more than an impression of the window. A window no higher than two feet may be drawn full size at once.

All studios do not make sketches in the same manner. Some do quite impressionistic ones giving only general proportions, composition, and some suggestion of the proposed color, while others make sketches which are very detailed. We have found that there is less chance of disappointment on the part of the client if he is given a reasonably accurate picture of what his window will look like when finished.

Our experience in making scaled full-color reproductions of famous old windows has led us to prefer making sketches for new windows that really look like glass. A good sketch should show the general composition, the shape, size, and color of the glass pieces, the heads, hands, and ornamental details, the leads, the round bars, and the T bars. A window, to be structurally sound, must have $1''$ iron T bars placed horizontally every three feet, and $\frac{1}{4}''$ round bars every twelve inches. The T bars are needed to carry the downward thrust caused by the weight of glass and lead; the round bars are to counter the thrust of the wind pressure from outside, so that the window will not flap in the breeze like a sheet on a clothesline. By now it should be abundantly clear that the stained-glass designer must start with a preset format: an opening with a ladder of horizontal black lines, $\frac{1}{2}''$ and $1''$ in width at measured intervals. If he were foolish enough to ignore this imposed requirement when making his design, he would indeed be making a serious mistake, for this imposed structure serves the window designer in the same way as the sonata form serves the composer of a symphony—it provides both artists with an architectonic form upon which to build their creative pieces. More extensive descriptions of T bars and reinforcement bars are given in the sections on iron work, glazing, and setting.

At one time we used regular transparent watercolors for making sketches, but we found that, since they remained permanently water soluble, they caused us trouble. The only white which is available in transparent watercolor seems to be Chinese white. When this is built up over colors to heighten them, the white remains sticky indefinitely. We now do our sketches with casein colors. They are insoluble when dry and can be used opaquely or transparently. They can be built up into many color layers which can be fixed again and again.

For rendering the bars, leads, and details, use negro lead pencils which come in various degrees, from very hard to very soft. They are made by L. C. Hardmuth and can be obtained at any good art supply store. Some studios use pens with India ink for this purpose, but we have found that the India ink is too uniformly black to represent the details, bars, and leads properly. Casein colors have enough abrasive quality so that when they are drawn on with a negro pencil, the line comes out bright and sharp. One of the secrets of effective sketching is to heighten the original color with white. Add a transparent wash over the entire piece, including the heightened area. Either spray or brush on a coat of alcohol fixative. Repeat the process again and again. Each time the process is repeated, the sketch will take on greater depth and will look more like real glass. It is quite surprising to see how closely a sketch done in this manner will resemble the finished window. The sketch should be finished off by outlining the window part with a black band, $\frac{1}{2}''$ wide—this will help give contrast to the color and make it appear brighter. Black India ink is the best material for this purpose. The sketch may then be left as is or matted. It may seem like a bit of gratuitous effrontery to suggest that a sketch should be neatly executed before it is presented, but many a commission has been lost by submitting a sloppy sample of work which in other respects was excellent. Much more could be written about making the design, but this is a creative process which develops much more effectively when the actual production methods have been assimilated.

THE TEMPLATE

Before a full-size drawing is executed, it is imperative that a template the exact size and shape of the window opening be made. There are two terms used in speaking of a template: the sight size and the full size: The sight size is the exact frame size as seen by the viewer as he looks through the window from the inside. The full size is the sight size plus whatever the depth of the rabbet or groove may be. Any window will have either a rabbet or a groove. A rabbet is made by cutting out a right-angle section from the edge of a stone or wooden frame, on the outside of the window frame. The cut, of course, does not go all the way through but stops about $\frac{1}{2}''$ from the inside. The rabbet is the same as that found in a picture frame or the frame of a standard double-hung sash. A groove is just what the name implies—a shallow groove cut in either a stone or wooden window frame. Both rabbets and grooves are generally cut to a depth of $\frac{1}{4}''$. This, in turn, calls for an addition of $\frac{1}{4}''$ on every edge to the sight size or $\frac{1}{2}''$ overall in both the length and width to make the full size. Both the sight size and the full size should be clearly marked on the template for future reference. The full size is easy to determine by sight examination if the frame is rabbeted. If it has a groove, it will be necessary to determine the depth of the groove by pushing a nail into the groove alongside of the temporary glass in several places.

Where the window is rectilinear, making a template is easy; it can simply be measured. However, when the top is arched or cusped, the problem is more difficult. In the days before drafting tape was available, one could do nothing

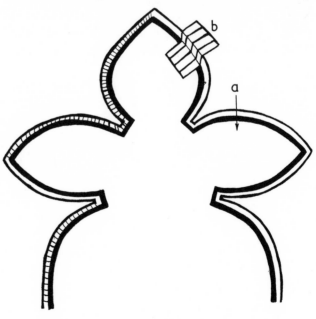

fig 51
TAPING AND MAKING A TEMPLATE
a) rough cut paper   b) drafting paper

but cut and fit while perched perilously on the top of a 20′ extension ladder, a ladder which invariably rested on a slippery floor. Now the solution is much simpler. The shape of the top may be cut scant of the actual sight size; to this, strips of drafting tape 1″ wide and 4″ long may be applied; two or three overlapping thicknesses of tape should be used to build up a sufficient body of tape. The tapes should extend at least 2″ past the rough-cut template top. This can all be carried out in complete safety on the ground. When finished, the person about to make the template can grasp the top with its attached tapes, sticky side toward the window, and gingerly mount the ever-treacherous ladder. The template for the top may then be attached to the window. The template, being cut slightly scant, will stick to the window in many places. The tapes should be pressed against the frame to form a sharp angle. In making the template for a shaped top, the spring line must be located and marked. The spring line is the exact point where the window changes from a rectilinear form to a curved one. This entire process is not as difficult as it may at first sound, for in almost all cases the window will have glass of some sort in the opening; so the template maker will have a firm base upon which to press the template. With a sharp knife he should cut the template along the angle where the tapes now join the stone or wooden frame, in other words, along the sight size of the template top. The newly made template should be traced on a heavy sheet of cardboard. It would be wise, at this time, for the template maker to remount the ladder and give the new template a final check. It can be embarrassing if the window turns out to be scant or oversize when it is finally completed. There are other distressing errors that can occur in template making. One

of the most amusing after-the-fact examples happened while we were working in the Henry Wynd Young studio in New York. We received a letter offering us a commission to design and execute a two-paneled window depicting Saint James mounted upon his traditional white charger. We promptly accepted and sent one of our workmen from the studio to make the necessary template. He returned in good time with the template and the window was made. We placed the forefront of the horse in the left panel and Saint James along with the rear of the horse in the right panel. The two panels when finished were set up in the studio 4″ apart. They appeared quite handsome but, alas, when we came to set the window, the two panels, instead of containing the usual 4″ narrow mullion between them, turned out to be over 4′ apart with a doorway between. Our horse, instead of looking like a spirited white charger, resembled a rather strange-looking dachshund. Needless to say, we had made, not one, but several errors. We should have questioned our template maker or we should have sent either the sketch or cartoon to the donor for approval before making the window.

It is not known for certain how early window workers made their templates, although Theophilus does mention paper as being used in his time. It was, however, very scarce, and used very infrequently until the thirteenth century in Western Europe. It is just possible that the templates might have been made by using cloths stiffened with glue. On the other hand, the tops of window openings in the first part of the thirteenth century were either square or half round. If square, they could have been measured at the bottom of the opening and, if round, they could have been inscribed with a compass.

When you wish to compose glass windows, first make for yourself a flat wooden table, of such breadth and length that you can work upon it two portions of the same window; and taking chalk, and scraping it with a knife over all the table, sprinkle water everywhere, and rub it with a cloth over the whole. And when it is dry, take the dimensions of one portion of the window in length and breadth, marking it upon the table with rule and compass with the lead or tin; and if you wish to have a border in it, portray it with the breadth which may please you, and in the pattern you may wish. Which done, draw out whatever figures you will, first with the lead or tin, then with a red or black color, making all outlines with study, because it will be necessary, when you have painted the glass, that you join together the shadows and lights according to the drawing on the table. Then arranging the different tints of draperies, note down the color of each one in its place; and of any other thing which you may wish to paint you will mark the color with a letter.

Theophilus
The Various Arts, Chapter XVII
Of Composing Windows

THE CARTOON

MATERIALS AND TOOLS

1) A smooth topped table, 48″ × 72″
2) One roll of a good quality white paper with a slight tooth, 36″ wide, preferably 100 per cent rag stock; unsensitized blueprint paper is excellent if procurable.
3) An HB drawing pencil.
4) One 72″ metal straight-edge
5) Two rulers, one a yardstick, the other a 10′ inside steel retractable tape ruler
6) One large carpenter's metal right-angle
7) One beam compass, if the window is round topped
8) Erasers—one kneaded, one or more hard erasers, such as Blaisdell NuWay 536T
9) Several sticks of Koh-I-Noor compressed charcoal No. 2
10) Several 2B charcoal pencils
11) One set of hard pastels
12) Fixative
13) Tortillon stumps (blotting paper or chamois)
14) Small chamois skin
15) One roll of 1″-wide drafting tape
16) One roll of 1″-wide black drafting tape

In the fine arts, the word "cartoon" refers to the full-size working drawing for frescoes, tapestries, mosaics, stained glass, and even large easel painting.

It must be remembered that when windows were made in the eleventh and twelfth centuries, drawing paper was not readily available. To make a cartoon at that time the medieval artist must have followed some form of the method which Theophilus has described. It could well be that they may have used charcoal in place of the lead or tin to draw in their figures and ornaments. The lack of paper must have challenged the inventiveness of the medieval artist. When he was commissioned to do a number of clerestory windows and the scheme called for a series of single figures to fill these windows, he would frequently turn the figures over. When this was done, there was a certain repetitive quality achieved. It is remarkable how difficult it is to discover this device when studying a row of such figures, particularly when the position of the hands was changed or the color of the garments was altered. A still greater difference in the figures could be achieved by making one head young and clean-shaven and another old and bearded. Today we are fortunate in having paper to save us from some of the trials and tribulations which beset the medieval artists.

To lay out the cartoon, first roll out enough cartoon paper to provide at least 8″ more than the length of the window to be drawn. The 36″ paper will be more than wide enough for the average single-paneled window or for any single lancet of a normal multi-paneled window.

If the window is to be wider than 33″, the cartoon paper

can be placed sideways on the layout table. If the section is to be more than 36″ wide, its height should, under no conditions, exceed 36″, in which case your cartoon paper will be sufficiently wide to accommodate the acceptable height of the section.

In order to proceed with the layout, you must determine the center line of your panel. An extremely easy way to do this is to measure in 18″ from one edge of the paper. Do this in several places along the edge and place points. Then using your 72″ straight-edge, connect these points. This center line is certain to be correct, as the cartoon paper could not be satisfactorily rolled initially if the two edges of the paper had not been parallel. In order to get a straight line at the bottom of the paper, fold over approximately 3″ of the bottom so that the sides of this fold-over exactly cover the edge of the paper underneath the fold; crease this fold firmly and cut it with a knife. You can now check the accuracy of the base by placing one side of your large metal right-angle along the edge about 2″ up from the cut, rule a line along the bottom of the metal angle, place your straight edge accurately along this line and continue it across to the other edge. Now place one side of your metal angle on the opposite edge with its base on the continued line. Note if this rests accurately along the line; the chances are good that it will if each step which you have followed has been properly executed. A 1″ black drafting tape can be used to substitute for a 1″ T bar. Using this tape will permit you to join additional pieces of cartoon paper on the center line of the T bar.

To proceed with the layout of the cartoon, first measure the full size of the height from the base up along both edges of the paper. Rule a line across at the top; obviously, if the window is more than 6′ high you will have to make intermediate measurements along the edges. Recheck to make sure that the $\frac{1}{4}$″ has been added to the top of the template, then place the template on the center line and trace the top correctly on the layout. What happens next may at first strike the reader as incomprehensible. Experience has proven that the full-size measurement of the window cannot be used without modification. The reason is quite simple: in the process of cutting the groove or rabbet, as well as in fabricating and setting the stone pieces used to make the window frame, certain variations are bound to occur in the depth of the groove or rabbet.

It has been found expedient to reduce the full size by $\frac{1}{16}$″ on both sides, top, and bottom to compensate for the depth differentials. In the past, churches in this country have had some trouble with windows imported from France, England, and Germany. The heat and temperature variations are not as great in those countries as in the United States. Because of this, the European firms have a

fig 52
Robert M. Metcalf drawing a cartoon from the sketch

habit of making their windows practically full size. When set in this country, expansion from heat causes them to buckle. This again will serve to illustrate another reason for modifying the full size of the window.

The finished window should have a $\frac{3}{8}$″ binder lead. This will allow coverage over and above the depth of the rabbet or groove which will make certain that the outside of the window will be defined by lead and not by a possible irregular line in the stonework. Add this second line $\frac{3}{8}$″ inside and parallel to the present modified full-size line. Before starting the execution of the cartoon, draw in the 1″ T bars in their proper places; position and mark the centers of the $\frac{1}{2}$″ round reinforcement bars along the outside edges. There is no point in drawing these in at the present time as they will get erased or covered during the drawing of the cartoon.

It might seem that the following account of the effects of age should have been included in the section on glass painting. However, since the cartoon is the place where the particular treatment of glass painting originates, it appears reasonable to include it here.

It is no secret that age mellows our objects of veneration and that it also adds its measure of wear and tear. But anyone who has tried to add imaginary arms to the Venus de Milo will have to admit that no possible arms are quite as satisfactory as Venus sans arms. In the passing years stained glass has received its full complement of good and bad from the aging processes of time. That the windows of Chartres Cathedral have gained immeasurably from the effect of patina and corrosion cannot be denied. Winds blowing sand and rain against these windows for centuries have succeeded in breaking out bubbles and other soft portions in the imperfect old glass. The pitted areas later fill with dirt and rust to produce a vibrating texture. A certain lichen which attaches itself to the outside surface of the glass causes the colors to become diffused and jewel-like. The artist of today who does not make use of the accidents of time is passing up one of history's gratuitous offerings. On the other hand, the artist who slavishly imitates the misplaced dirt of the past is just another victim of bad judgment. While some artists have correctly read the beneficial effects of patina and corrosion on old glass, many have misinterpreted their observations by covering their windows with a heavy coat of glass paint and rubbing lights out of the center of the individual pieces. What happens when this is done? First of all, the dark left around the edges of the pieces thickens up the appearance of the leads while the lights taken out of the center of the pieces gives the entire window an unpleasant bulbous effect. All of the desirable flat quality which is so charming and so architecturally fitting in the old glass is destroyed.

Why is it that the old windows, with all of their patina and corrosion, look flat while many modern windows appear bulbous? Close examination of any window will show that the flange or thin rib of each lead is raised about $\frac{1}{8}''$ above the surface of the glass. This protects the edges from the angular blasts of wind, rain, and sand. In the old glass, as a result of this shielding, about $\frac{1}{16}''$ around the pieces is void of corrosion. This clearer area next to the leads creates the flattening effect so noticeable in the old windows. This same effect can easily be duplicated in modern windows by clearing out areas $\frac{1}{16}''$ wide on the edges of a number of the glass pieces.

Some of the arts of today have been considerably altered throughout the centuries by accidents and aging. A notable example of this has occurred in the field of sculpture. When pieces of early Greek sculpture were unearthed in the

Renaissance period and transported to Italy, their earlier polychroming had disappeared as well as their heads, arms and legs. Headless, armless, pure marble sculpture became a Renaissance style which has carried down to the present time. Other arts have been affected to a lesser degree by patina and corrosion. Stained glass in particular has been modified and enriched by this phenomenon. Present-day artists in stained glass have imitated this effect caused by patina and corrosion with varying degrees of success and understanding. There is, however, one accident caused by breakage during the passing of time which seems to have been passed over. This is the rhythmic quality created by breakage. Even a casual examination of early glass will reveal that when a piece cracked, the line of breakage would continue into the background passing through one, two, and sometimes three pieces. This breakage is more noticeable in the lighter fourteenth-century windows where its effect adds greatly to the quality of the windows. The continuation of the lines through many of the pieces helps to relate one area to another. The only present-day stained-glass artists who seem to be aware of this phenomenon and use it are those who have had the good fortune to have worked under John Gordon Guthrie or Ernest Lakeman. The use of this lead rhythm is a dominant characteristic of their work and is also used by us in designing and executing windows. Conscious application of this newly discovered lead rhythm opens up a whole new dimension in stained-glass design. It dispels the narrow concept that leads are used only to define forms and separate pieces of glass. It suggests that there can also be an added aesthetic quality in the manner in which this division and definition takes place. A stained-glass window organizes color in much the same way that a symphony organizes sound. New instruments added to either medium have an enriching effect.

Planning the organization of this type of lead structure will need to be done on the cartoon. If a 12" strip of $\frac{1}{4}''$ lead is kept close at hand during the drawing of the cartoon, it can be bent into different curved shapes and placed upon the cartoon to test for proper line direction. One final suggestion: use some of the $\frac{1}{8}''$ lead occasionally to relieve the monotony which results from using all $\frac{1}{4}''$ lead.

Today, when making a window, the cartoon should be reasonably complete. All of the glass pieces should be drawn in their correct size and shape. This does not mean that later, when the window is being cut, that some of the larger pieces may not be divided into several smaller ones, or that several small pieces may not be consolidated into one larger piece for the sake of a better color distribution. You ought never to freeze a sketch or a cartoon to such an extent that no changes are possible. What is important is to strike a happy medium between an accurate, workable cartoon and a drawing which retains some flexibility. From the time a sketch is started until the window is completed, each new process should add a new dimension to the window. The sketch must not be copied in the cartoon, nor the cartoon be literally reproduced in the painting. T bars and round bars must be properly placed. In the sketch their placement should be considered as a design adjunct. Now their placement will determine the exact size of the sections and may well decide whether or not the window can be set.

The way a cartoon is drawn ought to be the prerogative of the particular studio. There is no right way to do it. Some artists make their full-size drawings in line only, others in line and tone. Rarely do they make them in color. We have found that cartoons done in line, tone, and color represent the final appearance of the window more effectively and, in addition, help to produce a richer plastic effect. When color is used, it presents some technical problems to the novice; but, after a short time, the technique can be mastered and when it is, it actually speeds up the process.

The artist who is drawing the cartoon must think in terms of glass as he works. A drawing for a window is not just a figure composition to be later broken up into cuttable pieces, but a tightly composed fabric of lead and glass. It has become all too prevalent for some commercial studios to hire a facile figure draftsman to rapidly execute compositions and then for the owner of the studio to hand over these drawings to his good glass men to convert into a window. This sort of operation is not only an insult to a good glass man, but also guarantees inferior windows.

It must always be kept in mind that the cartoon is being made for a window, that the pieces indicated should be simple in shape to avoid difficulties in cutting, and that the lines and tones which are being suggested are made with the full knowledge of their being readily and easily interpreted into good glass painting.

In making a cartoon Koh-I-Noor No. 2 compressed charcoal is excellent for lines and tones. For very precise drawing a 2B charcoal pencil best serves the purpose. There are many good charcoal pencils on the market. We have found the Eagle charcoal pencil to be the best. Pastels of any kind work well for color. We prefer hard pastels, but soft ones do quite well. In using them, work the colors in the same way as charcoal, rubbing them out and picking out the highlights with erasers. Kneaded erasers are good for large areas, but for sharp precise lights we find sharpened hard rubber erasers better; a popular one is the Blaisdell NuWay 536-T.

When finished, these cartoons are fixed by spraying with an alcohol and white shellac fixative. You can make your own fixative for considerably less than you can buy it in an art store. To make fixative, fill a jar with one part white shellac and four parts denatured alcohol; shake up the mixture and let it stand, preferably overnight. The shellac will settle to the bottom. You will then have a quantity of clear amber liquid above the shellac. Pour this into a separate jar, trying not to stir up the shellac. Put this aside—this is your fixative. This same process can be repeated three times. After the third time, throw away the remaining shellac—it will be exhausted.

Having suggested at the outset that the way a cartoon is drawn is or should be the prerogative of the individual or the individual studio, we have gone on to suggest the proper way to do a cartoon—our way. The authors have tried, if not all the ways to do a cartoon, at least most of them. We have scraped the bottom of the barrel by using flat lettering pens with India ink to draw the leads. We have not as yet followed the Theophilus technique of drawing upon white-washed boards but, who knows, we may even try that some day. What has become clearly evident to us is that one thing and one thing alone is imperative in drawing first a sketch and then a cartoon, and that is to permit the knowledge and use of the material to dominate the solution. How to design and then properly draw the cartoon is best studied and learned by cutting, painting, and glazing windows. What you draw on the cartoon is what you will or should inevitably paint on the glass. Therefore, two factors remain important: first, that the medium used in the drawing of cartoons should closely duplicate the appearance of the glass painting; and second, that it should be the most flexible medium possible. Compressed charcoal when rubbed out simulates the glass painting matte, while the fairly hard charcoal pencils used to draw the more definitive parts approximate the effect of the tracing brush. In addition, the soft kneaded eraser and the sharper hard ones will pick lights out of the charcoal-toned surfaces in much the same manner as scrubs and sharpened sticks will do to the glass matte. The rubbed-out color areas made with the soft or hard pastels and lightened with the erasers, of course, will not in any way equal the brilliance of the glass, but they will help to define and establish important parallel relationships between the lead, the bars, the trace lines, and the matte tones of the actual window. What is equally important is that the drawing materials which have just been suggested are tremendously flexible, making needed changes merely a matter of rubbing down an offending area. Before final fixing, the T bars, round reinforcement bars, and the outside binders should be blacked in solidly with compressed charcoal and any charcoal or pastel smudges removed.

THE CUT LINE

For this operation you will need:

1) A smooth-topped layout table for making a full-sized window—if only a small panel is involved, a smooth drawing board 2″ larger in each dimension than the size of the panel you are about to do will be excellent.

2) Several sheets or two rolls of kraft paper, 40″ wide; one should be 30-lb. weight, the other 80-lb. weight; any available paper can be used for a small panel so long as one piece is thin and the other thick.

3) A roll of drafting tape.

4) A 6H drawing pencil or a mimeograph stylus; an HB drawing pencil.

5) Twelve large sheets or a roll of carbon paper, 24″ wide; regular $8\frac{1}{2}″ \times 11″$ typewriting carbon paper can be used for small panels.

6) A six-foot metal straightedge.

7) Two rulers, one a yardstick, the other a 10′ inside steel retractable tape ruler.

8) A large carpenter's right angle.

9) A beam compass if the window is to be round-topped.

In laying out the various strips of paper, make certain that they are placed so that the edges curve downward. If they are placed the other way, you will have a great deal of trouble making your drawings lie flat. When you come to cut the glass over the patterns, you will find that it will be very nearly impossible to do if the edges curve upward. An effective correction can be made by dragging either the section or the individual patterns over the edge of a table. This causes the pieces to reverse their curvature. It will solve the problem, but it is still preferable to place the paper so that the curved edges face downward.

On the layout table, place a piece of 80-lb.-weight kraft paper about 4″ larger in all dimensions than the window you are about to work on; cover this with carbon paper placed face down, first along one side and then along the other. Be sure that the carbon paper is overlapped in the center. When the entire surface of the first piece of kraft paper has been covered with overlapping carbon paper, tear off short lengths of drafting tape in order to fasten both the kraft paper and the carbon paper to the layout table. On top of these place a 30-lb.-weight piece of kraft paper and again fasten this to the table with pieces of drafting tape; add more carbon paper, topping the lot with the cartoon. Again fasten the cartoon to the table with drafting tape. There is always a temptation to use either staples or thumb tacks for the fastening process. Don't do it. Using staples or thumb tacks only a few times will ruin the smooth surface of your table. It is also a great deal easier to draw over tapes when using either a straightedge or a right angle. This is now the time to recheck the measurements on the cartoon against those on the template. If the instructions given under the making of the cartoon have been followed

71

fig 53
Making a carbon of the cartoon for the "Tree of Jesse"

correctly, the modified full size presently shown on the cartoon should be $\frac{1}{8}''$ less in both the height and width than that shown on the template. If this proves to be true on your recheck, begin by ruling lines on either side of the cartoon to establish the full modified size of the window width. Do the same at the top and bottom. The modified full size of the entire window will now have been established. The cartoon already has the 1″ T bars and the $\frac{1}{2}''$ round reinforcement bars drawn in. Rule the outside lines of the T bars and indicate the center of the round reinforcement bars along the outside edge. Do not draw them across the cut line. If you do, someone may interpret them as lead lines. No glass pieces should be divided along the center of the reinforcement bars.

With either the 6H pencil or the mimeograph stylus, using a reasonable amount of firm pressure, draw over the center of each lead line. When you think you have covered every lead line, carefully remove the tape from one corner, lift the cartoon and first sheet of carbon paper by the corner; you will be amazed at how many lines you have missed! Do not let this discourage you. No matter how many times one goes through this layout process, he will always miss some lines. Add the missed lines and follow the same procedure with the other corner. Now carefully turn the cartoon and carbon paper back halfway to check the remaining lines. When satisfied that all lines have been carboned, return that half of the cartoon and retape it. The same process may be duplicated on the other end. You may now remove the cartoon and the first layer of carbon paper, but do not remove the tapes from the other layers.

Beginning at the top, number each pattern; starting at the left-hand side, number to the right; return from right to left, repeating the process until all patterns are numbered. Do not be surprised when you find that you have numbered

72

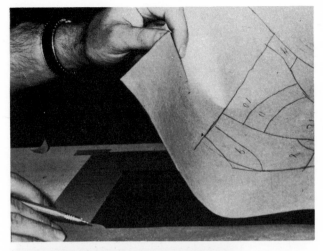

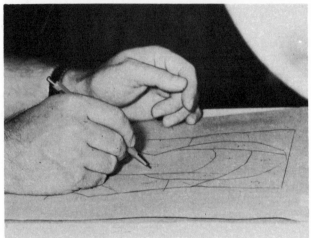

figs 54 and 55
(*above*) Lifting the corner of the cartoon; (*below*) Numbering the patterns

paper. If you have pressed hard enough while making the carbons, the lines on the bottom piece of paper should be clearly visible though somewhat faint. This does not matter too much as this carbon is going to be cut up into glass patterns. The other cut line on the thinner paper is put aside for the glazing after it has been used as a guide for tracing the false lead lines on the plate glass.

To trace the cut lines, select a sheet of $\frac{1}{4}''$ plate glass two inches larger in all dimensions than the section you are about to work on. Place your cut line on the layout table with the plate glass on top. Almost any reasonably dense water-bound black paint will do. The cheapest and by far the densest pigment is lamp black. It is, however, sometimes difficult to obtain and must be ground up in gum arabic or casein in order to use. Black casein or one of the acrylic paints can be purchased in studio-size tubes. If you are not going to use large amounts of black paint, these tubes are more convenient. The best brush to use for tracing the lead lines on the plate is an extra-long-haired square-ended oxhair or sable about $\frac{3}{16}''$ wide and $1''$ long; second best is a long pointed camelhair brush, something like the old-fashioned striping brush; as a matter of fact, a No. 5 pointed oxhair tracing brush will work very well. Enough water should be added to the color so that it will flow, but not so much that the color will be transparent. Use an arm rest, the same one you will use for glass painting; the use of an arm rest allows you to relax in tracing your lines and also makes it possible for your brush tip to be directly above the line. Fill your brush as full as you can without having the paint run off it; use a slow but steady stroke. If you work too rapidly, the line will dwindle out; if too slowly, the line

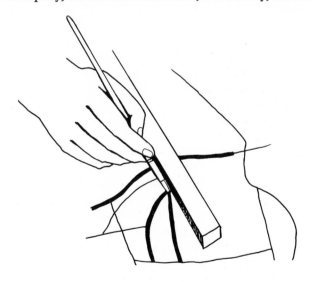

fig 56
Tracing false lead lines by using a guide

yourself into a corner. To keep from doing so becomes quite a game. There are three reasons for numbering the patterns; one is that while making a window, the glass must be laid out several times; second, numbering helps to locate the pieces; and third, since the numbers are drawn upright, they clearly indicate the tops of the pieces.

Now that the cartoon and the first set of carbons have been removed, a line should be drawn in the exact center of these outside binders. These lines will correspond to the center of the other leads in the window. Through the center of the $1''$ T bars running horizontally a $\frac{1}{8}''$ band should be indicated to account for the heart of the bars. On the sections above and below each of the T bars, $\frac{3}{8}''$ binder leads should be drawn. As in the top, bottom, and sides, a line must be drawn exactly in the center of these leads.

You may now remove the remaining cut lines and carbon

is apt to turn into a puddle. Always keep in mind that you must be constantly filling your brush.

If you have difficulty in tracing a straight line, a small strip of wood about 2″ wide, 1″ high, and 12″ long, can be placed $\frac{1}{2}$″ from the line. If the second finger of the tracing hand is pressed against it while the tracing is being done, it will act as a guide.

Preparatory to cutting the glass itself, the heavier of the two sheets of paper must be cut into patterns. Patterns were previously made by using a two-bladed stencil knife. The two blades of this knife were placed $\frac{1}{16}$″ apart which allowed for the heart of the lead plus a bit more to take care of certain inevitable inaccuracies made in the glass cutting. Today patterns are cut with a three-bladed pair of scissors. The center blade of these is made $\frac{1}{16}$″ thick; the two thin blades are fastened on either side of the center blade. When used, they cut a line on either side of the center blade which in turn takes out a strip $\frac{1}{16}$″ wide. The scissors are certainly unique but also very expensive. A studio making a number of large windows can scarcely afford not to own a pair. To make patterns with these scissors it is necessary to cut with a very short stroke which should start at the point where the blades are joined together with a screw. This short stroke makes it possible to cut around sharp corners. If this suggestion is ignored and a long stroke is attempted, the scissors will act like a gyroscope by refusing to change direction. In both the two-bladed knife and the three-bladed scissors, $\frac{1}{32}$″ is taken off of each pattern. For small panels, except for the pride of ownership, neither is necessary. The problem can easily be solved by using a speedball No. B4 pen point in a standard penholder; all that has to be done is to draw over the lead lines on the pattern paper with this pen. When finished, a cut can be made on either side of this heavy black line with a regular pair of scissors. The center of the outside binder lead should be similarly covered with the same heavy line. When cuts are made on either side of this black line, each pattern will be $\frac{1}{32}$″ smaller, the same as with both the two-bladed knife and the three-bladed scissors.

The patterns, after being cut, should be waxed to the plate which has already been prepared with false lead lines. This is done by pinching off a small bit of thumb wax, rolling it into a ball about $\frac{1}{8}$″ in diameter, placing this on the center of the back side of the pattern and in turn pressing the pattern against the plate or window glass. The thumb wax or soft wax is made as follows:

1 lb. Beeswax (by weight)	453 grams
1 lb. Cornstarch (by weight)	453 grams
4 oz. Resin (by weight)	113 grams
7 oz. Venice turpentine (by weight)	198 grams
1$\frac{3}{4}$ oz. Sweet oil (olive oil) (by measure)	35 cc's

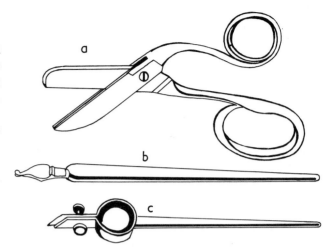

fig 57
DIFFERENT TOOLS USED FOR CUTTING PATTERNS
a) three-bladed shears   b) B5 speed-ball pen   c) two-bladed knife

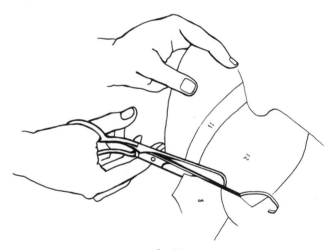

fig 58
Cutting patterns with three-bladed shears

Beeswax alone is somewhat greasy. The cornstarch helps eliminate this. To modify the effect of the cornstarch, Venice turpentine is added. This makes the mixture stickier. In warm weather the wax may become too soft; the resin will make it harder and more brittle. Finally, the olive oil seems to make the mixture generally better.

To mix the ingredients, place the wax in the top of a double boiler. Fill the bottom of the double boiler with water. Never place the wax or any other of the ingredients over an open flame to mix. When the wax is melted, add the cornstarch, a tablespoon at a time. Stir the mixture thoroughly after each spoonful is added. You will note that the wax will boil up immediately upon adding the cornstarch and will subside after a few minutes. If you do not heed this warning and dump all of the cornstarch in at one time, you will think that you are the Sorcerer's Apprentice, for the wax and cornstarch mixture will boil up out of the boiler in a truly alarming fashion. You will be fortunate if you do not set the studio afire. After all of the cornstarch has been added and the boiling-up stops, add the resin, Venice turpentine, and sweet oil (olive oil), in that order. While mixing and stirring, be very careful as each item in the formula is highly inflammable. After all of the materials have melted, the mixture can be poured into a muffin pan and allowed to cool. When you wish to use the wax, the muffin pan can be placed over a fire for a short time. This will cause the wax next to the pan to melt. By pushing a table knife into the wax, it is possible to rotate the wax muffins and lift them out of the pan. These wax muffins will be a convenient size to work with.

A wax which is used by sculptors to make small models can now be purchased. This wax is very much cheaper than beeswax. It can be worked without modification, but resin will have to be added as the weather becomes warmer. It is unbelievable that practically no studios know about thumb wax. A recent writer on glass has suggested using plasticine for this purpose. Plasticine is abominable—it is greasy, and when employed, allows the glass to slide off the plate if the heat in the studio rises the slightest bit.

The great value of soft wax lies in the fact that it softens when held in the hand but hardens immediately upon contact with the cooler plate glass. For this reason it can be used to wax up individual pieces as they are cut.

. . . Afterwards heat in the fire the dividing iron, which should be thin throughout, but thicker at the end. When it glows in the thick part apply it to the glass which you wish to divide and presently the commencement of a small fissure will appear. If, however, the glass be hard, wet it with saliva, with your finger, in the spot where you place the iron; being instantly cracked, draw the iron along where you wish to divide, and it is followed by the fissure. All the portions being thus divided, take the riesel iron, which is a palm in length, curved at each extremity, with which you will equalize and join all parts together, each one in its place. These things being thus arranged, take the color with which you should paint the glass, which you compose in this manner.

Theophilus
The Various Arts, Chapter XVIII

GLASS CUTTING

TOOLS AND MATERIALS NEEDED:
1) At least one ball-ended cutting wheel
2) One pair of unbreakable goggles
3) A pair of cheap pliers for grozing
4) A pair of level-breaking pliers
5) A pair of cheap pliers with jaws filed to a curved shape
6) A half-pint jar of kerosene
7) A small ball peen hammer
8) A first-aid kit
9) A medium-sized India stone, 6″ × 2″
10) Half a pound of petroleum wax or beeswax
11) One medium fine file
12) One gauge cutter

Cutting glass in the medieval period was no simple matter and there is no doubt that it was done the way Theophilus has described. But just try cutting a piece of glass with a red-hot iron! Only straight or slightly curved lines can be done in this way. Deeper curves and irregular shapes must be chewed away with the grozing iron, which makes their edges look like a Mayan obsidian knife or arrowhead. It is this appearance of the edges that makes it possible to recognize authentic medieval glass when its glazing lead is removed.

Before explaining anything more about glass cutting, it might prove helpful to explain some of the dangers which can arise in the handling of glass. Just a few admonitions will be given now; others will be mentioned as the occasion demands.

If you wear glasses regularly, keep them on when working with glass. If you don't, a pair of goggles is not a bad idea. In either case, keep your head a reasonable distance away from the glass while you are cutting. Splinters can get into your eyes even with glasses or goggles on. All glass splinters are flat and disc-shaped and will lie flat upon the iris of your eye. Do not rub your eyes—tears will wash out the discs. If you are handling fairly large pieces of glass, hold them by both sides above the center of gravity or by the top. Large sheets of glass have a way of containing the start of a hidden fracture. If you hold them in any other way than has been suggested, the piece of glass may break diagonally. Since the edge will be razor sharp, either one of the pieces may swing downward like a guillotine resulting in a severe and painful cut. As difficult as this advice may be to follow, when a piece starts to fall under no conditions make a grab for it. Jump away and let it fall. The most you will lose is two or three dollars' worth of your choice glass, but you will still have your hand. What has just been said is not an attempt to frighten you away from working with glass— it is simply to warn you of some of the dangers and how to avoid them. Very few people have been seriously hurt while working with glass. It is surprising how quickly a glassworker becomes sensitive to the dangers of handling

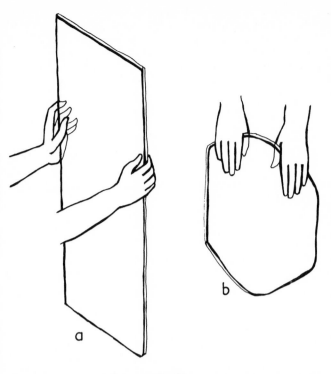

fig 59
HOW TO HANDLE LARGE PIECES OF GLASS
a) piece held by sides   b) piece held at top

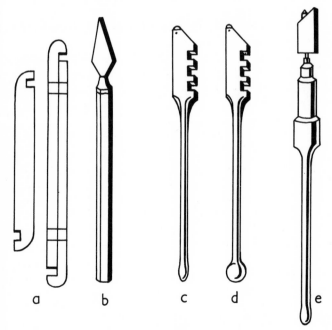

fig 60
GLASS-CUTTING TOOLS

a) early grozing irons   d) ball-tipped cutter
b) early dividing iron   e) diamond cutter
c) plate-glass cutter

the material and how casually he is able to operate while still retaining a healthy respect for its cutting edges.

It is not known for certain when a diamond was first used for glass cutting. The diamond point was an improvement over the hot iron, but unfortunately it suffered from many of the same defects. Slightly curved or straight lines were relatively easy to cut, but deep or more complex curves were almost impossible.

The real breakthrough came with the invention of the wheel. It is called a cutter but actually it is a revolving ice pick or, more correctly, a glass pick. A glass cutter does not cut glass, it splits it just as an ice pick splits ice. It has been mentioned previously that glass has many of the properties of ice. Like ice it has no grain or laminations. A fracture in either material can be started in any direction; once started it will continue in that direction unless a new fracture is begun in another direction. The wheel acts as a continuous fracturing or splitting instrument. Every newly designed tool retains some obsolete detail. In examining the cutter, you will observe the three slots located directly behind the cutting wheel. These slots make up an improved thirteenth-century grozing iron or, as this Theophilus translation calls it, "a riesel iron." The original grozing iron, as you can see, had a slot on either end of the tool, one large and one small, to be used on glass of various thicknesses. The teeth on the glass cutter are much the same except that there are three of them of different sizes. Both tools were designed for the same purpose—to chew off pieces of projecting glass in order to perfect the final shape of the piece. Although no longer used for grozing, these instruments have a tendency to bite off semi-circular chunks, which makes them useful for specialized breakers when cutting small deep curves. Rounding the forward

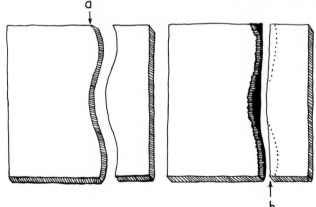

fig 61
a) cut made with a diamond or wheel
b) cut made with a dividing iron and grozed

77

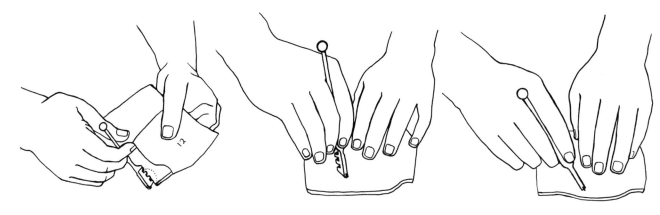

fig 62
How to use the rounded teeth of the cutter to break out small deep curves

fig 63
A right way to use the cutting wheel

fig 64
A wrong way to use the cutting wheel

edges of the teeth will greatly improve their performance. However, pliers are more effective and have largely supplanted the grozing iron.

As with most tools there is a right and wrong way to use a glass cutter. The right way will feel awkward at first but so will the wrong way. The cutter should be held between the first and second finger of the right hand with the first finger resting upon the broad flat surface directly above the grozing section. The teeth of the grozing section should be facing downward. Cutting can be practised at first without using a pattern. Later, when you have gained some experience, you can place the pattern over a selected piece and cut it. Cutting wheels are made in two styles: one with a narrow tip used mostly for cutting plate glass, the other with a large ball tip for cutting antique glass, which requires a considerable amount of tapping.

When the first glass cutters were made someone erred. Instead of being made so that the first finger could rest upon the flat surface provided on the shaft of the cutter, the casting had been executed so that the thin, instead of the flat, side would face up. In cutting, the first finger now would not have only to rest upon the thin edge, but would, in addition, require considerable pressure while cutting.

A number of these incorrectly made wheels were sold to the English glass firms before the error was discovered. The English were so delighted with the new wheel's superior performance that they did not complain about the error, but taped the thin edges so that they could be used. Some time later when the English reordered wheels, the corrected models were sent. The English firms promptly returned them, demanding the incorrect models instead. For many years the American wheel companies continued to make and furnish the incorrect models for English firms and they, in turn, continued to tape and use them.

Let us now return to our cutting. We have already spoken of the proper way to grasp the cutting tool. Now in making the cut, place the rotating wheel upon the glass with the tool at right angles to the glass and as near perpendicular as possible. Stiffen your arm all the way to your shoulder and use your body weight directed through your shoulder. A steady pressure can be increased or lessened at will. Draw the cutter toward yourself, not allowing it to wobble from

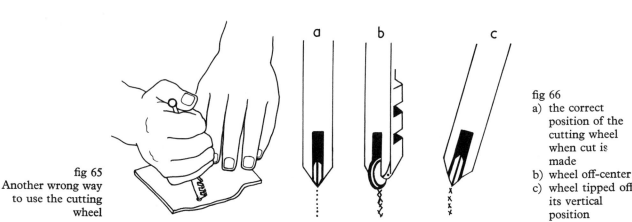

fig 65
Another wrong way to use the cutting wheel

fig 66
a) the correct position of the cutting wheel when cut is made
b) wheel off-center
c) wheel tipped off its vertical position

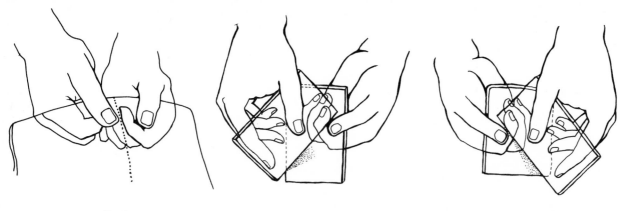

fig 67
The thumb break

fig 68
How to remove the razor-sharp edge from a newly cut piece

fig 69
How to complete this removal by reversing the process. See text for more complete description

left to right. When making the actual cut, pivot your body, not your arm. When you draw the cutter toward you, a line which is just barely visible should appear on the surface of the glass. There are times when a better cut can be made by pushing the wheel away rather than drawing it toward you, but these occasions are rare.

All glass is not of uniform hardness; soft glass cuts with the slightest pressure, very hard glass is almost impossible to cut; 95 per cent of all glass made for stained-glass windows will cut with modest pressure. A little practice will enable you almost instantly to tell the required pressure to use. Many beginners think that they have not made a proper cut unless glass splinters fly in all directions. As a matter of fact, when this happens either too much pressure has been exerted, or the wheel has been allowed to stray too far to the left or right of the vertical position; a fracture has not been started, only a deep furrow has been plowed through the surface of the glass which, when tapped, will almost certainly break in some other direction than the one intended. A proper cut produces a barely audible crackling sound as it is being made.

All cuts are made in the same manner. Only the way of breaking the glass varies. These differences are caused by three changing conditions: (1) the variable thickness of the glass; (2) the depth and complexity of the curves described; (3) how close the cut is to the edge of the piece of glass. The first example, known as the thumb break, is the easiest to execute and always produces the cleanest break. For this reason it should always be tried first. If the cut is short and straight the piece can easily be broken in the following manner: grasp the piece of glass by its nearest edge. Do this by placing your right thumb on the top at the right side of the newly cut line with your first finger closed underneath the glass. Repeat this with your left thumb and first finger.

Be sure that your thumbs are placed parallel to the cut. Do not hold the piece with your thumbs facing each other. If you do, the pressure when exerted will be inward and correspondingly the pieces will be driven toward the thumbs instead of away from them. Sooner or later you are bound to get a severe cut if you persist in breaking pieces in this way. To break the glass, press upward with your two first fingers and outward and down with your two thumbs. The action is very much the same as you would follow in breaking a saltine. On glass of normal thickness, where the cut is short and straight, it is seldom necessary to tap under the cut line in order to break the piece.

When the two pieces are broken apart, hold one piece in the left hand and the other in the right hand. Hold the one in the left hand firmly and horizontally, tip the right-hand piece slightly downward, and scrape its top edge against the bottom edge of the other. As you scrape, drag the two pieces in opposite directions. By placing the bottom piece on top and repeating the scraping process in opposite directions, you will be able to remove the razor-sharp edges from both pieces. It takes only a split second to do this scraping and in time it becomes almost a reflex action. Leaving the edges unscraped can cause a severe cut as well as ruining a good badger blender or matting brush during the painting of a window.

If the glass happens to be thicker than normal or the cut longer, it may be necessary to start a fracture before breaking. To do this, reverse the cutter so that the ball end is forward. Place your thumb upon the top flat side of the tool in the same place where you had previously rested your first finger when making the cut. With your first finger underneath the cutter and the ball end directly underneath the cut line, flip the ball upward, hitting the spot under the cut line sharply; use your fingers to make the stroke.

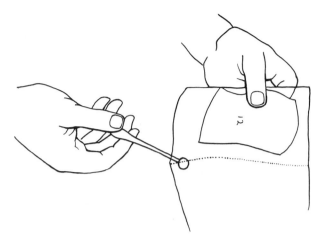

fig 70
How to tap the thumb break when the piece resists breaking

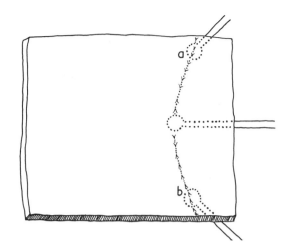

fig 71
How to cut and tap a fairly long curve

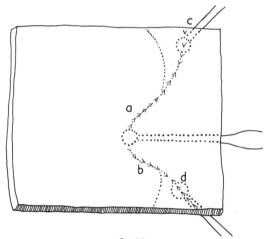

fig 72
How to cut and tap a compound curve

Swinging from the shoulders will not improve the result. The chances are that you will miss the line altogether. A short sharp finger-activated tap will work much better. A very thick piece can be tapped with the round end of a small ball peen hammer. After starting the fracture, you can break the piece by the thumb-breaking technique.

Curved pieces, obviously, are more difficult to cut than straight ones—for one thing, even the shallower curves must be tapped. To do this, one should start the fracture at one end, then go to the other end, and finally to the center until the fracture points join. If the fracture is started at one end and the cutter continues to extend this line, it will have a strong tendency not to follow the curve but to go straight ahead. As the curve is made deeper, this tendency becomes a certainty. Even if the pieces are properly tapped, frequent breakage results. If you have two compound curves and they are relatively shallow, one way to solve the problem is to extend the first curve straight ahead. This can then be tapped and broken out. The second curve will then be easy to cut and tap for breaking. The illustration will explain this better than words.

In rare cases it may become necessary to cut very deep curves. When this is the case, a series of shallow curves are cut and these curved pieces in turn are cut across. Again, study the illustration. When these cuts have been made, they are broken out a piece at a time, preferably with the grozing pliers. If a special pair of pliers have their square jaws ground in a curve, the curve will better fit the deep cuts and facilitate the breaking of the glass. Even though it is possible to make this kind of cut, it is still a better idea to stay away from deep curves. An inside right-angle cut is impossible to make, so don't try it.

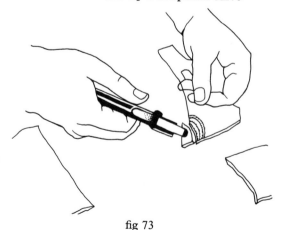

fig 73
How to make a series of curved cuts and break out the narrow curved pieces

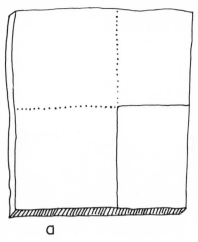
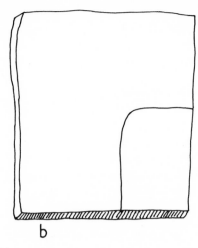

fig 74

a) an exact right-angle cut is impossible   b) the correct way to make an approximate right-angle cut

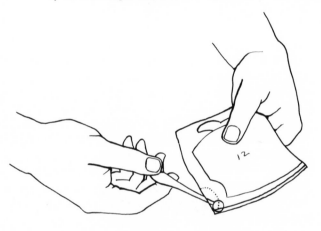

fig 75
How to cut and tap a small deep curve

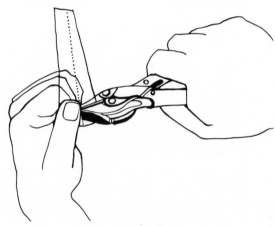

fig 77
How to position the breakers

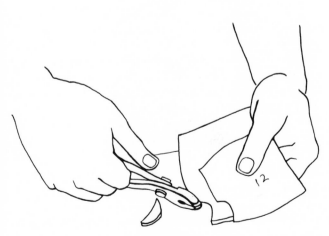

fig 76
How to break out and groze a small deep cut with the rounded grozing pliers

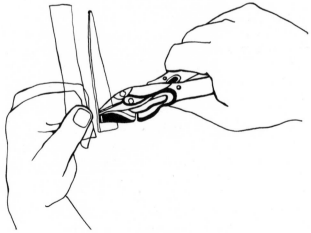

fig 78
How to break a piece with the breakers

When the piece to be broken off is very narrow, too narrow for the thumbs to be used, it will have to be tapped with the ball end of the cutter. When the piece gets narrower still, it will be necessary to utilize the breaking pliers.

The jaws of breaking pliers remain parallel as they are opened and closed. Also, the jaws of these pliers are generally wider than most. Because they are much more expensive than regular pliers, it is advisable to protect them from excessive wear by placing drafting tape on the inside of their jaws. This will also keep them from crunching the glass, thereby making a cleaner break.

To break the piece, the tips of the jaws are placed exactly on the line of the cut and bent downward to break the pieces apart. Frequently, due to the irregularity of antique glass, the breaks are uneven, presenting the cutter with small projections which must be removed. Grozing irons and the grozing section of the wheels are no longer used for removing these irregularities. Glassworkers now use a small pair of cheap pliers for grozing. These pliers work better if the temper is removed from them by heating. In use, they are rolled over the edges of the pieces to remove the projections so that the pieces will fit better.

Before starting the cutting of a window, you should cut some glass over a pattern. This is not quite as easy as freehand cutting. The cutting wheel will follow along the edge of the pattern. You will now see why the heavier kraft paper was used for patterns. If thinner paper had been used, the wheel would be continually riding up over the pattern. The most difficult cuts should be made first. The reason is simple; if the piece does not break properly, the pattern can be moved over and another cut made. It can be terribly exasperating if the difficult part is saved till last only to have it break in the wrong place. The accompanying illustration shows what sequence of cuts should be made in order to avoid this problem.

Selecting

Assuming that the reader is familiar with the cutting process, he should now proceed with the fabrication of the window.

Make certain that a sufficient number of pieces of glass of all sizes and colors have been placed upon the selecting table. The plate glass with its artificial lead lines traced and its patterns in their proper places is also awaiting the next step. Turn on the correct battery of fluorescent lights. With the cartoon and sketch before you, decide upon a key color spot. Suppose that the background is to be blue: peel off one of the patterns which is to be cut in blue; decide what hue, shade, or intensity of blue is desired. When the

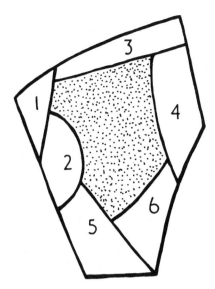

fig 79
The proper sequence of cuts

decision has been made, place the pattern over the particular piece of glass to cut it. When it is certain that the glass fits the pattern correctly, pick up a small piece of thumb wax, the same wax that was used on both the black paper and the patterns; allow it to warm in the closed palm of your hand; when it is soft enough, roll out a small cone with a rounded end. On the side of the glass which is to be mounted against the plate, wipe off a small pellet about an eighth of an inch in diameter onto each corner of the piece. When wax has been put on all four corners of the piece, position it so that all sides are in the center of the lead lines and press it against the plate. The wax will hold the piece firmly in place. You have now made your first creative choice in the color of your window.

The brown paper patterns block out much of the light, so that the first piece of color will jump forward from the rest of the panel. After examining your sketch and cartoon to determine the hue, shade, and intensity suggested for the adjacent pieces, peel off the next pattern and try several different pieces of glass in the exposed area. When satisfied, cut this piece and wax it in place. Continue this process; as more pieces are added, the window will grow before your very eyes and become more and more exciting. Vary the color in certain parts from light to dark and from bright to dull. Do not make all of the color of a large area darker or lighter than, say, a figure which stands against the background. Make some pieces in the figure lighter than the background, some darker. This effect of counterchanging allows your eye to pass back and forth and to make transitions between the various areas. Remember, you cannot soften an edge by smudging as you can in painting.

When you are selecting glass for the pieces which are on the outside binder sections, be sure that they are of normal, or slightly thinner than normal, thickness. If they are too thick, you will have difficulty later in setting the window. A note of warning might be in order at this point—the suggestions for varying the color and value of each piece of glass in a given area should not be taken too literally; a large percentage of the color in an area may be cut from the same sheet of glass, using the suggested variations for what they are—subtle relief from what might have become a monotonous regularity. When a number of pieces are cut from the same sheet, it makes it possible to save a great deal of glass. The irregular patterns may be turned one way or the other until the pieces are placed so close together that very little glass is wasted.

Most studios accept the fact that for every square foot of window made, an equal amount of glass goes into the scrap bin. Some place the waste as high as two-thirds. Any method of working which will save material should be looked on with favor.

The proper cutting side for antique glass is the smooth side. In the case of flashed glass, the smooth side is the flashed. If an attempt is made to cut it on this side, the cut will only penetrate the thin layer of flashed glass. As a result it will not break. If the glass is cut on the reverse side, it will automatically put the thin color on the outside where it will easily be worn away by the action of the elements. The answer is quite simple; turn the pattern over and cut the piece on the back side. This will then put the flashed surface on the inside of the window.

Waxing up

Most studios, instead of using thumb wax, cut their glass down on the table, waxing up the entire section at one time when the cutting is completed. To do this they melt beeswax in a small saucepan over an electric hot plate. The tool used for waxing up has a copper tip which closely resembles that of a large pen point. The tip is first dipped into the hot wax and then touched to the glass where several pieces intersect. Since there is a $\frac{1}{16}''$ gap between the pieces, a drop of hot wax deposited at the intersection will fall to the plate and hold the pieces securely in place. This process is repeated until all pieces have been firmly attached to the plate. Though cutting and waxing can be accomplished more rapidly in this manner, the artist is unable to see the color he has chosen until the section has been completely cut and waxed up. Before the section is lifted upright make certain that none of the pieces have been left unwaxed. Tapping your fingers over the surface of the glass will immediately disclose any unwaxed ones.

Glass Selecting

The racks built to hold the English and American glass in the studio are made to hold the full sheets. To make it possible to store and handle German antique and French semi-antique glass, the sheets need to be quartered. Regular French antique must be cut in half. To cut one of the large sheets, make the cut on the narrow dimension first. After the cut is made, place a $\frac{3}{8}''$ round bar directly under the cut line. Hold the left side of the glass down on the table and press down on the right-hand side. The glass should split along the cut. If it does not split, start a fracture with the ball end of your cutter by tapping, and repeat the process. This should do it.

It is possible to buy French, German, or English antique glass directly from the makers in the various countries. But hiring your own customs broker, plus the other red tape

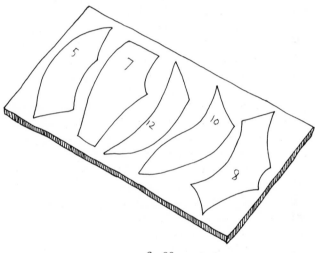

fig 80
How to arrange patterns on a large piece of glass to avoid waste

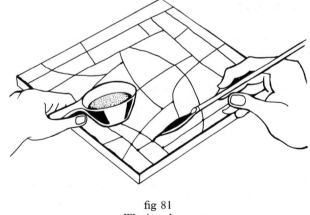

fig 81
Waxing down

83

involved, would make the glass more, not less, expensive.

Care of Your Wheel

A cutting wheel will last a long time if it is cared for properly. To keep a wheel in top condition, certain rules should be followed:
1) Do not let any other person use your wheel. As with pens, everyone uses them in a different manner.
2) Keep your wheel well lubricated at all times. It is a very good idea to partially fill a jar or can with kerosene. When not in use, the wheel can be placed in the container so that the cutting edge is covered by the kerosene. While you are cutting, swish it frequently in the kerosene. This will wash out the glass splinters, which cling to the wheel's axle; prevent rust; and lubricate. Splinters and rust cause the wheel to tighten up and jam.
3) Do not run your wheel back and forth over the same cut. All this does is plow a deep scratch which will not break. It also dulls your wheel. When a wheel gets dull, it can easily be sharpened but make sure that it really is dull. It could be that the glass which you are cutting is harder than that to which you have been accustomed.
4) Be sure that you remember the proper way to hold and use a cutter.

Sharpening the Wheel

In order to sharpen the wheel, first take a close look at the cutting wheel itself and notice how it is mounted in a narrow slot, the edges of which are very nearly square. Before the wheel can be sharpened, the section containing the small wheel must be filed down, as shown in the drawing. Care must be taken not to file away too much. If you do, the wheel's axle will fall out or be seriously weakened. To sharpen the wheel, an India stone $6'' \times 2'' \times 1''$ will be needed. Before starting, place several drops of oil on the stone and spread the oil with your fingers. Now pick up the cutter, hold it as if you were about to cut a piece of glass; tip it to the right of vertical position and place it on the lower left corner of the stone at the same angle as the bevel of the cutting wheel. Raise the wheel to a slightly more vertical position, and sweep the cutter in an arc, as shown in the diagram. Turn the cutter over and follow the same arc; this will sharpen it on both sides. The wheel will be partly rolled and partly ground against the surface of the stone. After a few tries you will get the feel of it. The action is very much like that which occurs when one drives the front wheels of an auto diagonally against the curb. If the wheel just rolls over the stone, no sharpening action

will take place; and if it does not roll at all, a flat place will be worn on the wheel which will make it useless. You can always tell when a wheel has a flat place: it alternately cuts and skips when you try to use it on a piece of glass. There are many workmen in the trade who prefer a well-sharpened, used cutter to a new one. The new ones are too sharp for the average antique glass.

One of the employees taking a short cut down the alley on his way to work at the old Henry Wynd Young Studio in New York, discovered a plate-glass firm. It is well known that cutters of plate glass use wheels only a few times and then discard them. Having discovered the particular trash can where they were thrown, he made a point of stopping each day to collect the discarded wheels. The amusing outcome was that the Young firm never bought a single new wheel in ten years.

Gauge Cutting and Temporary Glass

When windows are made just to close out the weather, the buildings are often filled with what is called temporary glass. This glass is replaced later with more important work. In this case the stained-glass artist will attempt to simplify the windows involved by making a design which can be gauge cut. The gauge is a tool made for cutting straight or diagonal lines. It is really a metal straightedge fastened at a right angle to a large drawing board. It is usually made large enough to handle sheets of glass up to

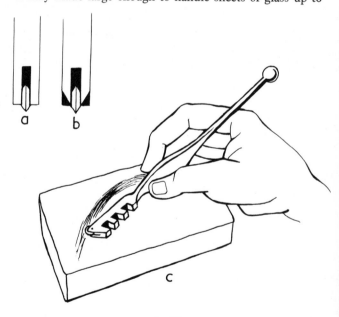

fig 82
SHARPENING WHEEL
a) tip of wheel b) tip after filing c) angle of wheel for sharpening and arc traversed

84

Plate 5
Peonies Blown in the Wind
Window by John La Farge, from the house of Henry P. Marquand, Newport, R.I.
The Metropolitan Museum of Art, Gift of Miss Susan Dwight Bliss

a) by Donald Viterelli

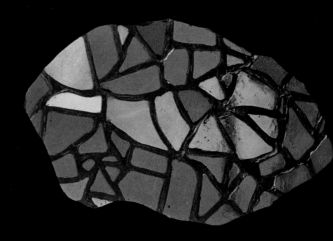

b) by Thelma Gaillardo

Plate 6
EXAMPLES OF WORKS BY STUDENTS USING THE EVOCATIVE TECHNIQUE

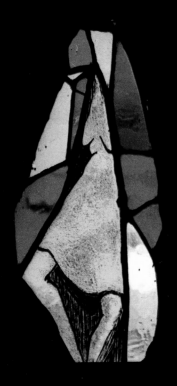

c) by Jennie Read

d) by Diane Sonen

a) Glass abstraction by Robert R. Metcalf

b) Glass sculpture by James D. Metcalf

c) Applique panel by Gertrude A. Metcalf

Plate 7
NEW AND RELATED TECHNIQUES

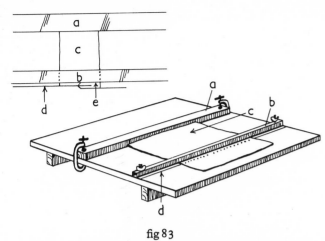

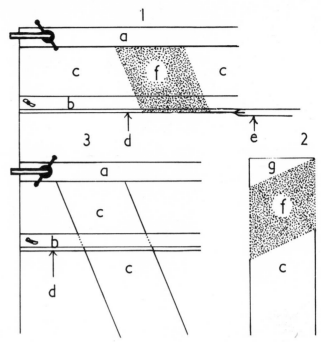

fig 83

GAUGE CUTTER SET UP TO CUT STRIPS FOR MAKING SIMPLE SQUARES OR OBLONGS

a) top strip of gauge
b) bottom strip of gauge
c) glass
d) cut line to center of e
e) glass cutter

fig 84

HOW TO CUT STRIPS AND DIAMONDS

1) Shows gauge cutter set for cutting strips for a diamond shape
2) Shows where strip with end g is cut off
3) Shows gauge cutter with strip g cut off for diamond and correctly placed for making diamonds

a) top strip of gauge cutter
b) bottom strip of gauge cutter
c) glass
d) cut line
e) tip of cutting wheel
f) pattern
g) piece to be cut away

30″ in their smaller dimension. The top of the board has a raised square bead. To this the top of the gauge is securely anchored. The bottom of the gauge has a set screw which can be tightened down to hold the glass firmly during the cutting process. To cut, the glass is butted against the top bead and slid underneath the gauge. Prepared patterns are used to determine the size and shape of the pieces. When it is cut along the straight edge, the center of the wheel is forced a scant eighth of an inch to the right of the gauge. This distance must always be taken into account when placing your pattern on the gauge.

To do this properly, first put the cutting wheel against the gauge, butt the pattern snug against the wheel, and draw a light pencil line along the right side of the pattern. The pattern may now be removed. Push the sheet of glass forward until it touches the pencil line; when it is exactly on the line, let your cutting wheel follow along the gauge. As the strips are cut, they may be stacked in trays. When a sufficient number of strips have been cut, they should be returned to the gauge to be cut into their final shapes. Patterns can be made as guides for cutting oblongs, squares, or diamonds, either large or small. Borders are just thinner strips. If the pieces are to be square or oblong, all that has to be done is to follow the same procedure as in the cutting of the original strip. The original strips should always be cut so that the narrow dimension will be the narrow dimension of any piece which is to be cut from them. Large as well as small pieces of glass may be effectively cut with the gauge.

When cutting a diamond-shaped piece, a different procedure must be followed. First, lay out the exact pattern for the diamond. Butt the upper left side of the diamond pattern (f) against the underside of the top (a) of the gauge cutter. Put the small cutting wheel of your glass cutter against the lower right-hand side of the diamond. This will provide the correct position for the line upon which to gauge cut. Rule this line d and remove the pattern. When the cutting wheel is placed on line d and the straightedge b is butted against the cutter e, a line should be ruled against the underneath base edge of b. Slide a sheet of glass under straightedge b, butt it against a, tighten the set screws on b and run the cutter along the straightedge to cut. Release the tension by loosening the set screws of b. Draw the glass forward and break off a strip. Continue cutting strips as needed. To finish the cuts for the individual diamonds, replace the diamond pattern on the right end of each horizontal strip, cut away area g as indicated. Now turn the strip over and butt it in a vertical position as shown in 3c. Slide the strip under the gauge cutter b and

93

follow the same procedure as in cutting the horizontal strips. The result will be a perfect diamond.

Most temporary glass is made in the form of oblong or diamond panes. Sometimes the glass is painted to cut down the glare. Frequently borders are added. At this point, let the stained-glass artist beware—one more step in this direction and he will become a large volume commercial manufacturer. All pieces of the same color cut over the same identical pattern will fill tray after tray a foot deep. This will be the end of an art and the beginning of a business. Do not prostitute the potential quality of your future work for a small bag of silver.

Take copper beaten thinly, burning it in a small iron cup until it is quite a powder, and take particles of green glass and of Greek sapphire, grinding them singly between two porphyry stones, and, mixing these three things together, so that a third part may be powder, a third green, and a third sapphire, grind them together upon the same stone, very carefully, with wine or urine, and putting it into an iron or leaden vessel, paint the glass, with great care, according to the lines which are upon the table. But if you wish to make letters upon the glass, cover the parts all over with this same color, writing them with the handle of the pencil.

Theophilus
The Various Arts, Chapter XIX
Of the Colour with which Glass is Painted

GLASS PAINTING

In reading the complete book *The Various Arts* by Theophilus, it becomes quite clear that he was not only a learned man but a fine craftsman as well. Most writers of his time were given to the compilation of other men's skills, but not so with Theophilus; most of his writings on art or the crafts were gained by first-hand experience. Only occasionally does he quote secondhand knowledge and when he does, his writing is noticeably unconvincing. However, when he is describing how glass paint is made of copper oxide with the addition of ground glass as a flux he is unquestionably both accurate and knowledgeable.

Theophilus is certainly on safe enough ground when he speaks of mixing glass paint with wine or urine, for every account of paint mixing from his time through the Renaissance has used this traditional formula. Whether or not it has any real value is somewhat doubtful. On the other hand, when he fails to mention any binder used in the glass color, his knowledge is somewhat questionable. These analytical criticisms should not be construed as in any way damning to Theophilus. There is little doubt that his contribution to the knowledge of early techniques was truly monumental.

If color is the glory of a stained-glass window, painting is its *raison d'être*. It must be remembered that colored glass existed long before the stained-glass window and that the stained-glass window itself only came into being when the use of enamel as a painting medium was introduced.

Glass painting is not like easel painting or, in fact, any other method of painting. Oil, watercolor, egg or casein tempera, encaustic, and fresco are all applied to a flat surface, depending for their effect upon the images and color being reflected back to the viewer. Glass painting, on the other hand, is painting done with colored light. The only pigment used is a monochrome brown. True, this paint is applied to the surface of the glass; but both the purpose and its effect upon the surface of the glass are diametrically opposite from those of easel painting. Its major and most important reason for being placed there is to block out all or parts of the colored glass. This in turn produces images, patterns, and textures which reach the viewer on beams of pure and direct colored light. Today we perceive and enjoy stained and painted windows for their color and brilliance. To medieval man light itself was a part of the spiritual universe. There is little wonder then that he saw in his cathedral windows the light and bodyless representations of the pure spirit. Of all the monastic orders the Cistercian was most noted for its consistent opposition to ostentatious display in the decoration of their abbey churches, yet no less a person than the twelfth-century Saint Bernard of Clairvaux both accepted and praised the stained-glass windows of his time for their divine content and expression.

The description of glass painting by Theophilus has given rise to the term "smear shading" now commonly used by historians and archaeologists when referring to the twelfth- and thirteenth-centuries' technique of glass painting. The description goes something like this: the trace lines were made over the cartoon and, when dry, a brush loaded with a similar, but more transparent, matt color was smeared alongside the trace lines. A close examination of the eleventh-century Christ head from Wissembourg, the little twelfth-century archer from the clerestory in Angers, or almost any thirteenth-century piece of glass painting will indicate to the experienced glass painter that the glass was not painted in this manner. First of all in the account by Theophilus there is no mention of any binder having been used in either the tracing color or the matt. Present-day experience will demonstrate that if no binder is used in the color, the matt will streak badly. Yet the matt used on the early glass is remarkably even and smooth. Secondly, the character and pace of the stroke in the trace lines indicate that the binder used was quite viscous. The trace lines show every indication that the binder compelled a slow dragging stroke which produced a gradual minute taper and point to the tracing stroke. As a matter of fact, it has greatly puzzled many contemporary glass artists as to just what binder the early glass painters did use.

There are three ways the painting could have been done:
1) They could have fired the trace lines first and then have placed a smooth matt next to the already fired lines.
2) They could have used some kind of varnish binder. When this was dry, they could have placed a smooth matt alongside the unfired trace lines. (There is only one drawback to this solution: the oil in the varnish will repel a water matt to a certain extent where the two join, causing the matt to be considerably lighter next to the trace lines; this phenomenon is not indicated in examples of early painting.)
3) The piece could have been smoothly matted with a matt light enough so that the cartoon could be seen through it. The lines could then have been traced and, when dry, all of the matt except that part next to the trace lines brushed away.

The brown enamel which was used by the early enamelers, and which is still used at the present time, was in reality a very low-fire glaze such as is used in some pottery. The paint was originally composed of copper oxide which was mixed with a frit—glass ground to a fine powder. Since copper oxide makes a black pigment, it is often found too cold in color for certain pieces of glass. In addition, it was found that iron oxide could also serve as a glass paint. The trouble with iron oxide is that it is red and often too hot in color for certain pieces of glass. A happy medium can be reached by mixing iron and copper oxide with the frit. The resulting color is a very charming neutral brown, suitable for any color of glass.

There was a time in the early 1900s when glass paint was made with a great amount of soft flux. When fired, the pieces had a beautiful glossy appearance but, alas, the resulting paint was extremely impermanent. Glass painted at this time with this color can easily be scratched away with your fingernail. The closer the melting point of the glass paint is to the melting point of the glass itself, the longer it will last. A test for permanence can be made easily by placing a fired piece in a saucer of hydrochloric acid overnight. In the morning, if any of the paint can be scratched off easily, change your brand of paint.

The major qualification of any glass pigment is that it will not fire away at 1100° Fahrenheit and that it can be ground fine enough to make smooth-flowing pigment. The color of glass paint can easily be changed by varying the proportion of black to brown or by adding differing amounts of white to make the color grayer or lighter. A variety of white pigments may be used: gypsum, whiting, lime, or kaolin. Variations of black or brown colors can be purchased by the pound. They have different names such as ancient brown, bistre brown, umber brown, tracing brown, and tracing black. A good brown for matting can be made by mixing together equal quantities of ancient brown and tracing black. The tracing black can and should be used for the tracing of all line work. Any shade of brown can be made from red to black with these two colors. If white is added to any of the mixtures, any degree from white to brown can be made. Of all the white pigments suitable for glass paint, the easiest to purchase is whiting from a drug or paint store. White can be purchased in one pound packages under the name of obscuring white or matting white, but these are no better, and considerably more expensive, than those which you can make for yourself with whiting. Any white used alone will give the glass a frosted effect. If any of these homemade whites are used, it will be necessary to add some English flux No. 75. This flux is really a ground-glass frit. If a lot of flux is added, the paint will fire slick. If a little bit is used, the paint will just barely adhere to the glass. This same flux can be used to fuse glass. The only valid reason to mix white in any proportion to your brown is for back painting, which will be discussed later.

The glass painting of the eleventh, twelfth, and thirteenth centuries was limited to the painting of details—heads, hands, draperies, trees, flowers, leaves, birds, animals, and any one of a dozen representative forms necessary to tell the story depicted. The thin matt which was placed alongside the drapery trace lines around the eyes, mouth, and nose of the heads, as well as the many other forms, did tend to suggest a turn of form and to give the figures an appearance of low relief; but the main purpose of this matt was to protect the trace lines from obliteration by halation. Halation may be illustrated by what happens to the filament of an electric lightbulb. The light created by the threadlike filament spreads to such an extent that it is capable of lighting a whole room. The principle of halation is one of the basic phenomena affecting the painting of glass. The narrow strip of thin matt used on the early glass protected the trace lines from halating and thereby disappearing completely. An interesting experiment may be tried to illustrate the effects of halation. Trace a series of lines approximately two or three inches apart and a quarter of an inch broad on a sheet of white glass. Do the same thing on a medium shade of blue glass and also upon a similar value of red glass. Place black paper completely around each piece of traced glass. Now set these pieces in a window so that they are fully illuminated, and walk slowly backward away from the glass. Notice how the lines disappear in the bright light: first those upon the white piece, then the blue, and finally the red. You have witnessed your first demonstration not only of halation but how halation acts upon different colors and values.

If you will, now place a very thin matt about a half inch wide along either side of each line on each piece; the matt used can be barely more than dirty water. Step back again and see how strong the lines hold no matter how far you walk away from the pieces. You now will have witnessed your second demonstration of halation—of how a very thin matt stops halation from eating away the trace lines. If you continue to increase the density of the matt, at a certain point both matt and trace line will begin to suffer from halation. This is your third demonstration.

Now take three new pieces of glass: white, blue, and red; cover each piece with a matt of medium weight. When the pieces are dry, use the pointed end of your brush to scratch a line through the matt upon each piece. Walk backward again and see how the scratched line gets broader and broader the farther away you are from the pieces. This is your fourth demonstration. This last demonstration was one that used to occur periodically in one of our country's larger cathedrals. The choir boys on occasion were accustomed to taking potshots with a .22 caliber rifle at the hundreds of pigeons who lived in the niches of the cathedral. Stray shots were continually hitting the clerestory windows. When this happened, that little quarter of an inch hole appeared from the floor to be as large as a dinner plate.

All of the aforementioned examples refer to halation as it is displayed in painting. There is another important and similar phenomenon which occurs in relation to the glass itself. It is, of course, closely related to the action displayed in the painting. If a light piece of glass is surrounded by a relatively large area of dark glass, halation will react as it does with the paint. The light piece will spread out of all proportion to its actual size. Besides spreading, it will cause the color around it to appear much darker than it is. In extreme cases it will cause the color to seem almost black. As can be seen, the action will vary with the degree of lightness of the surrounded piece, or the lightness or darkness of the area surrounding the smaller light piece. In both the painting and in the glass itself, the effects of halation increase with the distance the viewer is from the window. Windows seen from no more than ten feet are not noticeably affected by halation. No other painting art is so rigidly controlled by a single phenomenon such as halation. The examples which have been given, though helpful in understanding the principle involved, will not provide the ultimate solution. Only the empirical experience of trial and error will enable a glass artist to judge in the studio how a window is going to appear when viewed from a hundred feet away in its clerestory position.

The early glass workers of the twelfth and thirteenth centuries were interested in two things—color and the delineation of forms necessary to tell their story. These they accomplished with consummate skill. They solved the problem of halation both as to color and painting. They had learned by trial and error that no large isolated areas of color could be successfully used. It is one of the great accomplishments of these early artists that they were able to give the effect of sustained color without really doing so. To achieve this, color areas were broken up by the use of lighter colored scrolls, hands, drapery, plants, and all manner of forms which could be made with lighter colored pieces of glass. Study carefully any good piece of thirteenth-century glass and you will discover bridges of light-colored pieces between the dark ones placed at exactly the right intervals. One error in judgment which began in the Gothic revival and which has persisted to the present time is that in following the successes of the early glass techniques, it is necessary to imitate their esoteric medieval mannerisms. It is perfectly possible to paint glass in the manner of the thirteenth century without, in any way, imitating the archaisms of the period. What immediate conclusions can we draw from our newly acquired knowledge of halation:

1) That the glass selected is affected in much the same manner as the painting
2) That the edges of all trace lines must be reinforced by a light semi-transparent matt, and that if the matt is made too dark, it will defeat its purpose
3) That sustained areas of color must be interspersed with white

If this is the first time you have attempted to paint glass, it would be best to do some serious practicing. It will be much better to start with a simple form such as a leaf, flower, or bird. Do not begin with a head; heads require too much drawing skill to execute successfully.

Christopher Whall has suggested transcribing a head by Botticelli, Holbein, or Dürer as an advanced *tour de force*. He is quite correct when he states that if you can execute any one of these heads successfully, you can paint anything on glass.

Before making your first sally into glass painting, it will be worth while for you to examine the pigment with which glass is painted and the various binders which can be, and are, used to hold the pigment together and which cause it to adhere when it is applied to the glass. Glass paint may be purchased from either of the two British ceramic companies of James Hancock or Heatons. L. Reusche of Newark, New Jersey, is the sole agent for Hancock's paint, and Leo Popper of New York is the agent for Heatons in the United States.

English glass paint is somewhat coarse, requiring considerable grinding before it can be used. The Hommel Ceramic Company of Pittsburgh makes excellent glass color in both tracing black and ancient brown—similar to the English colors. Hommel's color requires almost no grinding before using.

Binders for Tracing Color

There are innumerable binders which can be used in glass paint. The most common binder is gum arabic. Color bound with this gum can be remixed again and again. It is insoluble enough to allow careful matting over the trace lines when they are dry. To be sure, one cannot brush back and forth over tracing done with this binder without washing away the lines. If a few drops of vinegar are added to the paint, it will become much less soluble as well as thinner-bodied. What is gained in insolubility by this addition is lost in reworkability after it is dry. Whichever company's color you choose to use, it will have to be worked with a palette knife to some extent. To grind color you will need a palette knife and a piece of $\frac{1}{4}''$ plate glass about 14″ square. A smaller palette will not have room enough on which to work the color properly. On this palette place a level dessert spoon of tracing black dry pigment; add a small quantity of gum-arabic solution, an amount that will make a pool about the size of a quarter; to this add sufficient water to make a fairly thick paste. Grind the color with the palette knife, gradually spreading out the color; then scoop it back into a pile. Repeat the process again and again. From time to time you will have to add water as the

mixture will continue to dry out. If the color is coarse and granular, you will have to repeat the grinding process at least twenty-five or thirty times. If it is not so coarse, repeating the process half a dozen times should be sufficient. Since the most conventional binder in general use is gum arabic, the grinding of the pigment in this binder is being described first.

When the color is properly ground so that the mixture is no longer gritty, fill your tracing brush with pigment. To do this properly, add enough water to a small amount of this newly ground mixture so that when the brush is filled, the color will just barely run off the tip of the brush. The oxhair, or sable, tracing brush which you are about to try is called a "rigger." It will almost certainly frustrate you in your first attempt to use it. You will find it, or so you will think, too long and too limber. Accept your tracing brush with resignation and learn to use it. You cannot, no matter what you may think, trace successfully with any other kind of brush. Remember that you must always trace with a fully loaded brush. This means that with a line of any length or width you will have to load the brush several times. Different binders affect the colors differently. For one thing, gum arabic is a solution which may vary in its binding strength. It will have to be tested this time and every time a new batch is made up. To test the color, trace some lines upon a piece of glass. Make some of the lines with thick paint and some with thin. When dry, test them by rubbing the various lines vigorously. If they just rub off, they are all right. If modest rubbing lifts them, you will

fig 85
A palette knife and palette

98

need to add more gum. If, however, they polish up no matter how hard you rub, add more color. When the binder for this tracing color is just right, put it in a jar with a lid covering it. Label it properly and set it aside for use later. This color lends itself well to a fast, articulated brush stroke. It works well under a sharp stick, coming off clean when scratched. It is very easy to fall into the error of piling up your trace line when using this type of binder. Piling up causes frizzling when fired, which ruins the lines. Frizzling can also be caused by adding too much gum arabic to the color.

It is strange that very few American or European glass painters, other than ourselves, ever have used casein emulsion as a binder. It is more viscous than gum arabic, lending itself well to a slower, more controlled stroke. It scratches as sharply and as easily as gum-arabic tracing color. Hommel glass paint and casein binder work beautifully together. Of course, any other glass paint ground so that it is smooth will work equally well. Any given quantity of color can be mixed with casein binder. All that has to be done is to add enough casein to the dry pigment to produce a thick paste; then add sufficient water to make the mixture thin enough to pour into a jar. When you are ready to use the paint, place a small amount of this color in a glass caster saucer; keep adding water a bit at a time until the paint is thin enough to use. The caster cups can be purchased at any hardware store. They are excellent to use, as a second cup can be placed on top of the one with color; this will keep the color from drying out for several days.

The two binders most used in the trade are the previously described gum arabic, which, of course, is water soluble, and Venice turpentine, which is a fat oil of turpentine that is not water soluble. Venice turpentine is as thick as molasses. It is thinned to a usable consistency by adding ordinary turpentine. To test the right amount of binder needed, grind up some color with a small amount of Venice turpentine and thin this to a workable consistency with regular turpentine. After grinding, test the mixture by making lines with your tracing brush. If the brush strokes dry within ten minutes, rub them with your finger. If the lines rub off, more Venice turpentine must be added. If the color does not dry within a relatively short time, say, half an hour, and continues to remain dark and tacky, more color must be added. When dry, this color can be overlaid with a water matt. Even this tracing color cannot be brushed over indefinitely without lifting the tracing. Incidentally, this is a most disagreeable color to work with. Being sticky, it gathers dust even though you keep it covered most of the time. For some reason or other, this combination causes the hairs of the tracing brush to separate. Also, the oil in the binder causes the water matt to crawl away from the trace line. All in all, its major value is that a water matt can be put over it. This, however, seems to be an excessive price to pay for the advantage when it is possible to solve the difficulty in another way.

Another binder which has been used in the past is what the English call treacle. This is nothing more than sugar. Variants of sugar, such as molasses and Karo syrup, all act in the same manner. They are very viscous and tacky. They will fail to dry if too much binder is used. The stroke has a slow drag, is very precise, but cannot be speeded up. Unlike Venice turpentine, it does not cause the hairs of the tracing brush to separate. It cannot be overmatted with a water matt. If traced upon the bare glass, the lines are hard to scratch. These difficulties have all been solved by being able to work over a fluorescent light which allows you to put on and stipple a light matt which can then be traced over. Since the treacle-bound tracing color is placed over the matt, the problem of clean scratching is solved. This binder is now excellent if the painter wants a very precise tracing color.

There is a new gum made of methyl cellulose which makes an excellent binder. One of its unique qualities is that by a slight modification it can be changed from a binder with no flowing qualities to one as viscous as treacle or Venice turpentine. It, of course, would have a serious drawback; when tracing color is bound with it and allowed to dry out, when remixed it tends to bubble up. This does not seriously bother a matt, but it does make tracing a bit difficult.

Before fluorescent lights were used, overmatting a trace line was important. Now with these lights it is possible to place a water matt upon the glass, and stipple it out enough so that the trace lines upon the cartoon can be seen through the matt. Lines made with any binder can be traced on top of this matt. The under matt helps greatly to strengthen the lines which in turn keeps them from firing away.

Binders for Matt

Having discussed at some length the various binders used for tracing color, how do these same binders work when used for the making of matting color? Gum arabic and casein work in much the same manner. The binder is added to the dry pigment. To this, sufficient water is added to make a paint thin enough for a transparent matt. The proper amount of binder is more critical in the matt than in the tracing color. With the matting brush, place a thin matt upon a clean piece of glass, smooth the matt with your badger brush, and stipple it lightly, just enough to make the surface slightly mottled. Allow to dry and rub lightly. Your rubbing should be in a rotary motion, not as though you are trying to wipe off the paint from the piece. If the color wipes off, you need more binder. If, on the other hand, it tends to polish without coming off at all, add more color.

There is no absolute rule for how hard the color should be. Some glass painters prefer a soft, others a hard, color. Depending upon the particular type of painting to be done, a harder- or softer-than-normal color may be desirable.

Casein-bound tracing color cannot be overmatted like gum arabic-bound paint. Sugar, molasses, and Karo syrup are unsatisfactory 'for matt binders, and cannot be over-matted with any paint made with water-soluble binders.

Methyl cellulose makes a very fine matt, but tracing color made with the same binder cannot be overmatted with this or any other water-bound matt color. There is yet another binder which can be used for making matt color and that is white shellac. We had tried this binder a number of times without success. When thinned with denatured alcohol, the matt dried so fast that it was impossible to get it over even a small surface of glass, let alone badger or stipple it smooth. Not until we happened to be working with textile printing did we find the answer. To dissolve dyestuffs, a solvent called "Cellosolve" was recommended. This material is a fatty alcohol similar to di-ethylene glycol or ordinary glycerol alcohol such as is used for an antifreeze in your car radiator. We recognized certain characteristics of Cellosolve; first that it was soluble in both water and alcohol, and second that when left in an open saucer it would sit for weeks without evaporating. By experimenting, we discovered that if one mixed alcohol and Cellosolve half and half, it dried at the same speed as water. Glass paint made with the proper amount of white shellac thinned with the half and half mixture of alcohol and Cellosolve made not only a perfect rubbing matt but, what was more important, one which could be put on over any water-bound color including sugar, molasses, or Karo syrup. Use of this matt can revolutionize glass painting. More than half of all painted pieces can be done in one painting with one firing. This not only saves the time of repainting, but saves all of the in-between steps of removing the glass from the plates a second time and of firing everything at least twice. Besides being so useful, it is very easy to work with. It can be stored in a jar and will keep indefinitely.

The reader must be warned that when a polymer binder is used, the color must never be allowed to dry out. A polymer color once dry has lost its adhesive quality, though of course, gum arabic can be used again by adding water.

To carry out all glass-painting projects and techniques, the following materials will be needed:

1) A fluorescent light fixture, preferably 48" long, fitted with two 40-watt cool-white or Verda-Ray color-corrected bulbs
2) Two sheets of double-weight clear window glass, 14" × 20"
3) A jar of water
4) Three glass caster saucers
5) Tracing color (tracing black)
6) Matting color (half ancient brown, half tracing black)
7) Gum arabic
8) Casein medium (Permanent Pigment)
9) Methyl cellulose (Tepping Studio)
10) Venice turpentine
11) Gum spirits of turpentine
12) White shellac
13) Denatured alcohol
14) Cellosolve
15) One no. 1 oxhair and one no. 1 red sable (rigger type) tracing brushes
16) Bristle brushes: one round no. 24; two flat no. 4; one small oxhair round no. 5
17) One 3" flat badger blender
18) One round 1" badger blender
19) Several different types of small nylon house-painting brushes
20) One Japanese round pointed brush size 0 for silver stain
21) One 2" camel's hair brush, flat
22) One ¾" camel's hair or oxhair flat brush
23) One hardwood pointed stick
24) Needles set in soft-wood handles in sizes fine, medium, and heavy
25) A turkey quill sharpened like a square nibbed pen
26) Silver stain
27) Medium-sized palette knife
28) One arm rest
29) One mahlstick

Practice

The casual observer watching a stained-glass artist cut, trace, and paint glass is struck by how easy it looks. But when he tries to do the same thing himself, how different! The wheel is awkward to use. "Maybe it would work better backwards," or "Why can't they find something better than this with which to cut glass?" When he tries to trace, he is outraged by the long-haired mop he is supposed to use for tracing. He cannot see why he has to use an arm rest. "What's wrong with resting your hand on the glass?" When he uses a matting brush of any size and bears down on it, he is unable to put the color on evenly. When he tries to use the badger brush to smooth out the color and again bears down upon the brush, he succeeds in producing a surface that looks as if a rake had been dragged through it.

You can paint with a standard length sable water-color brush to obtain certain effects, but it runs out of color so fast that it is not practical. You can put your hand on the glass, but if you do, the grease from your skin will keep the tracing from being smooth; and finally, you can bear down on a badger brush when you want the matt to be streaky. But under ordinary conditions, when the badger is pressed down, the short tip hairs are flattened and the badger's greatest asset is lost. The trouble is not with the tools but with the observer's experience. It brings to mind the old story about the young man who was given a walk-on part in an amateur play. He was to walk on stage and when shot at by the villain, was to say his only line: "My God, I'm shot!" Through an error, on the night of the play the gun was inadvertently loaded with a live bullet instead of a blank. When the gun was fired, the young man yelled, "My God, I *am* shot!" In other words, before trying to paint upon a regular window, try some serious practicing with the various tools. The experimentally-minded reader may wish to try, at his own convenience, each and every binder for both tracing and matting. But for the present time, in order to simplify matters a bit, it might be better to select one particular binder for both tracing and matting.

Tracing

Tracing is really not the most appropriate word to use, since it suggests an attempt to duplicate exactly the drawing of the cartoon without any variation. A tracing should be a kind of freehand painting, using the cartoon as a guide, but never a slavish copy of the cartoon itself. The aim of the artist should be to express the spirit of the original, other-

wise the painting may resemble the work of a skillful sign painter, very perfect but lifeless. No person about to try glass painting should attempt to do so without practicing tracing and matting. Good glass painting, particularly tracing, can be learned by studying Persian ceramics or, for that matter, any good ceramic decoration from almost any culture. Chinese brush painting is an excellent source for study. Put a piece of glass over any of these examples and try making a glass tracing. You will discover almost immediately that the lines cannot be copied exactly because the strokes have a life and pace which can only be made with a freehand approach. They are, however, excellent examples to emulate when painting glass.

When a tracing is to be made, that section of the cartoon which is to be traced is placed over the fluorescent light box. The matted or unmatted piece is positioned over the cartoon and the arm rest arranged so that it spans the particular piece. If the arm rest is made approximately 2″ high × 2″ wide × 1″ long, it will span any normal sized piece of glass.

Before starting the tracing operation, make certain that the tracing color is thoroughly mixed. Place a small amount of color in a caster saucer and add water to give the color the proper consistency. Fill the tracing brush by first splaying it out in the color and then twirling it back to a point. This will get paint into all of the hairs of the brush. To trace, rest the under part of the palm of the hand on top of the arm rest; the fingers holding the tracing brush should hang over the arm rest directly above the spot where the trace line is to be made. A tracing line is not made by using the shoulder as the pivotal action point as is done in most easel painting or in drawing the cartoon. The action does

fig 86
How to splay out a tracing brush and then bring it back to a point

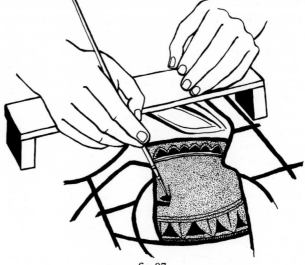

fig 87
How to trace with the arm rest

not even originate in the wrist but in the fingers. Before making the actual line, aim the top of the brush at the starting spot and make a practice stroke, just above the glass. Now make the stroke. Refill your brush and continue until the piece is completely traced. Pick up your newly traced piece but do not be discouraged by what you see. What looked good with the cartoon backing it up now appears with all its weaknesses. The pointed hardwood stick is used to remedy this problem; at least it is one of its purposes. If your tracing color is not too hard, it will be easy to correct some of your mistakes by scratching away the parts which seem sloppy. It is surprising what improvement is attained by a little judicious scratching. One difficulty, which will present itself almost immediately, is found in trying to trace a line upon a piece of glass which is in most cases at least an eighth of an inch above the line on the cartoon. If the piece is matted first, this problem will be greatly reduced.

Only the heads, hands, and minutely drawn ornamental details are traced down over the light table. All drapery lines as well as simple ornamental details are traced and painted upright upon the easel.

Matting

The accepted brush for matting has always been a 2″ flat camel's hair one, the kind which used to be purchased for dusting phonograph records. This is still the best one for matting with the traditional gum-arabic-bound color On the other hand, color mixed with casein and, even to a greater extent, that mixed with methyl cellulose seems to spread so much easier and to badger so much smoother than the gum-arabic color that a much smaller, ¾″ camel or oxhair brush will work even better than the 2″ one.

To place a water matt over gum-arabic tracing color takes a great deal of skill with both the matting brush and the badger blender. To do this kind of overlaying, load the matting brush with thin color. Before the test stroke is made upon a clean piece of glass, the badger blender should be close at hand. The matting brush, which must be held very nearly vertical, should just barely touch the surface of the glass when making the stroke. Never bear down on the brush. Bearing down will cause the matt to be thin and streaky in some places, wet and blobby in others. Before the test is made, be sure that the badger is absolutely clean. A badger which has dry or partially dry color adhering to the tips of the hairs will make the laying on of a smooth matt virtually impossible. There is nothing really unusual about a camel's hair matting brush except its remarkable softness, but a pure badger brush is a truly outstanding instrument. Each hair is forked on the tip. As the brush

102

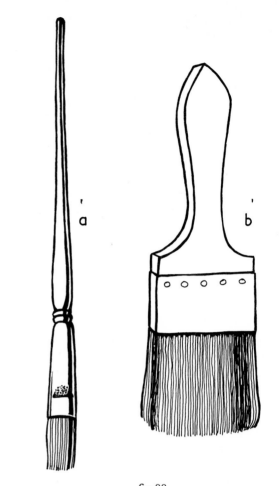

fig 88
a) a ¾″ ox or camel's hair matting brush
b) a 2″ camel's hair matting brush

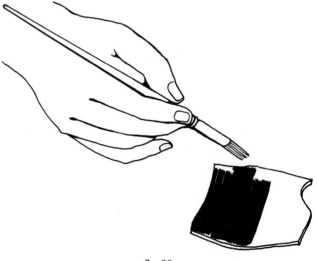

fig 89
Putting on a matt

wears down, it continues to split, which in turn causes the brush to retain its forked tip. This peculiar characteristic gives the brush a firm dense base with a very thin, light, delicate tip. Its habit of splitting makes it as good for glass painting after ten years as after ten days. About the only serious injury that can befall a badger brush under normal use occurs when the cutter neglects to groze or otherwise remove the sharp flange on a piece of glass after cutting it. Without grozing, the edge of a newly cut piece of glass is razor sharp. Since a badger-blending stroke starts outside the edge of the piece, it is extremely easy to slice a section out of the brush. Many a good badger has been ruined by such negligence. Otherwise a badger brush is about the toughest brush known to the glass painter. Our studio is at present using a badger blender which we purchased in 1930. Though a bit worn down, it is still in excellent shape. The fact that badgers are so long-lasting is fortunate, for a 4″ English brush is quite expensive.

Badger brushes are often called blenders. They are made in many sizes and shapes. Both the flat and the round ones are used for glass painting. For large work a 3″ or a 4″ flat brush will be ideal. A small round one works very well for smoothing out silver stain as well as for stippling matt color. The flat brush serves two purposes: first, to smooth out a matt, and second, to stipple it. This is a very versatile tool. It can be used to stipple a piece while wet or to continue on until the piece is dry. If it is left while the paint looks mottled, it can be rubbed. This will cause points of clear light to break out of the matt. If the matt is stippled until it is quite dry, the points of light are much smaller.

In either case, the pinpoints of light give the glass a bright and sparkling appearance. While using the badger both for blending and stippling, it is extremely important to dry the brush against the back of your hand. This must be done, not once, but continuously or the badger will soon get too wet for effective stippling.

Stippling until dry, of course, cannot be done over a traced line without completely demolishing it. The light stipple which produces the mottled effect can be put on over a traced line if care is taken.

To clean a badger, wash it thoroughly with a laundry soap such as Fels Naphtha, rinse it and, holding the handle between the palms of both hands, twirl it first one way and then the other. The action will resemble that taken by a wet dog when he is trying to shake off the water from his back and sides. Sometimes, if the paint is stubborn in coming out, the badger can be slapped against the side of your hand. Either or both ways can be used alternately if desired; as a matter of fact, all tracing and matting brushes should be washed from time to time with soap. Most emulsion paint binders, though described as water soluble,

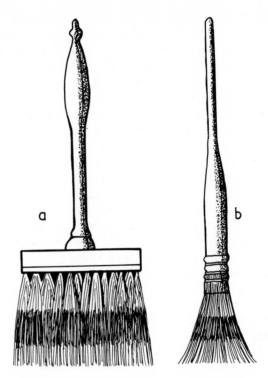

fig 90

a) a flat badger brush   b) a round badger brush

fig 91
Badgering and stippling

103

are not washed out easily with water alone. They come under the general category of polymer binders and are soluble in water when wet, but insoluble when dry. Laundry soap will cut most any of these binders even when dry. If brushes are not washed, the paint fills up the bases and quickly ruins the brushes' action.

The reader will need to know that when a polymer binder is used, he must never let the color dry out. Always take out of the main jar just enough color for immediate use; put this bit of tracing color in one of the caster saucers. If you let the color dry out, the binder will no longer hold, and new color will have to be remixed.

All glass color is heavy and will settle to the bottom of the jar in a few minutes. Every time you use the color, it should be properly stirred. If it has only been allowed to settle for a few minutes, it can be stirred with a brush. When it has stood overnight, it will be necessary to dig it off the bottom of the jar with a strong, sharp stick; using a brush will not even shift it.

If in the process of matting the badger is pressed down slightly and moved in an S-shaped sweep, the piece when dry can also be rubbed. The wavy textured result gained by rubbing adds an interesting variety to the glass painting. On a small piece no wider than two inches, little trouble will be encountered in smoothing out the matt. Like the matting brush, the badger is also held in a vertical position. It is passed lightly over the matted piece. Only the very tip of the badger is allowed to touch the painted surface. In this way the fine split tip hairs are used in the smoothing action. When a larger piece of glass is to be covered, say, a piece five inches wide, it will take five brush strokes to cover it. These strokes will have to be laid on so that their edges just barely touch. The badger then is passed over the painted surface at right angles to the matt strokes, thus blending the brush edges. The piece is slightly stippled to complete the leveling action.

Mahlstick

A mahlstick is a very worth while tool for any artist, but especially so for one who works with glass. If it is purchased in an art store, it will cost at least a dollar. One can be made for as little as twenty-five cents. Buy a $\frac{1}{2}''$ dowel stick and fit one end of it with a small rubber crutch tip. Dowel sticks come in various diameters, from $\frac{1}{8}''$ to $1''$, and are $36''$ long. The $\frac{1}{2}''$ size is best. A dowel stick can be used without the crutch tip, but with it the work in hand is less liable to be smeared or otherwise injured. The major reason for using a mahlstick is to support the artist's hand when it is held above his work. When it is used for the drawing of a cartoon, or to trace, stick light, or paint a waxed-up section

of a window, the artist will find it an invaluable tool. The proper way to use it is to place the rubber end on a convenient spot outside of the cartoon or glass section, raise the other end several inches so that when your hand rests on the stick it will be the right distance away from the work in process.

A dowel stick cut in half and fitted with a crutch tip makes an excellent alternate for an arm rest while tracing down. The tip can be rested outside the piece of glass and the other end raised several inches from the surface of the glass. This shortened mahlstick in some ways gives the painter more flexibility than the arm rest.

Texture

Many contemporary artists do not recommend using tracing brushes, but suggest, instead, all manner of brushes to apply glass paint directly to the glass pieces. This can be done if the work is nonobjective, but without the use of a tracing brush little figure painting of note can be accomplished. When a matt is put upon a piece and it is lightly stippled it will rub effectively. The longer it is stippled the less effective will be the rubbing. There is no clear satisfactory explanation why it is true, but a piece which is lightly rubbed will work much better with the scrubs than an unrubbed one. For example, when you paint a section of drapery if the pieces are matted, stippled, and very lightly rubbed, so lightly rubbed in fact that the painted surface will appear cloudy or dusty instead of pockmarked, the light areas may easily be wiped out with a fairly large scrub. This scrub should be made from a $\frac{5}{8}''$ bright brush with the bristles trimmed to about $\frac{1}{8}''$. If more pressure is exerted upon the side toward the light, the area can be made to shade from light to dark with a single stroke of the scrub. Besides

fig 92
A drapery piece made by matting, stippling and wiping out lights with a $\frac{5}{8}''$ scrub

the textural patterns which can be made by maneuvering the badger and the matting brushes there are several other ways that interesting textures can be produced. Color can be spattered upon the glass by hitting either a loaded matting or tracing brush against the mahlstick. A finer spatter can be made by spraying thin glass paint with a fixative blower. Both methods can be repeated with just clear water. If the spray is continued for a longer time, the water will run down the surface of the glass in little rivulets. A very interesting texture can be made by matting the piece and immediately blotting the surface with a paper towel. This particular matted texture can be produced in no other way. These are just a few of the possible ways of creating different textures upon glass. Use these and try other variations of your own, remembering always that the purpose is to create variety. Do not gild the lily by adding more textures to glass which already has sufficient textural variety built into its original fabrication.

Patina

In the early windows the patina, which developed upon the glass exposed to the outside, softened the intensity of the raw color causing the windows to glow rather than glitter. The effect caused by patina differs from that caused by placing a matt of similar density on the inside of the glass. The patina lowers and diffuses the light before it passes through the colored glass while the matt obscures the colored light which has already passed through the glass. Back painting a window in imitation of patina is extremely effective in eliminating distracting images of buildings, trees, or people from the outside. It is also the only way to treat a window which faces a nearby exterior wall. Paint used for back painting should be made by mixing half regular matt with half whiting. This will produce a light tan color almost exactly duplicating the color of patina. Do not make the back painting too heavy.

In the fourteenth century it was found that if a piece of glass was painted with silver nitrate or silver chloride and fired, the part which was painted would change to a bright yellow. This discovery gave rise to several amusing stories. Among the better known was the story of an apprentice boy who, while laying out glass for firing, inadvertently dropped one of his silver jacket buttons upon a piece of light-colored glass. When the kiln was fired, lo and behold, under the silver button was found a bright transparent yellow disc. Needless to say the story is very likely unfounded. The yellow made by the use of silver stain will vary from pale lemon to a deep orange depending upon either how thick a coat of silver is applied or upon how high it is fired. Also, certain types of glass accept the silver

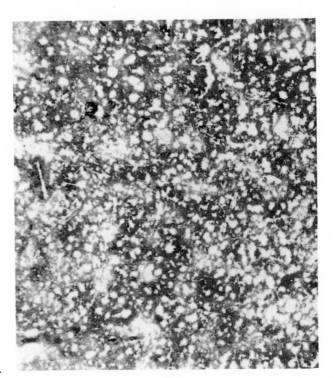

fig 93
A regular matt, stippled and rubbed when dry

fig 94
A regular matt with a badger swirl, stippled and rubbed lightly when dry

105

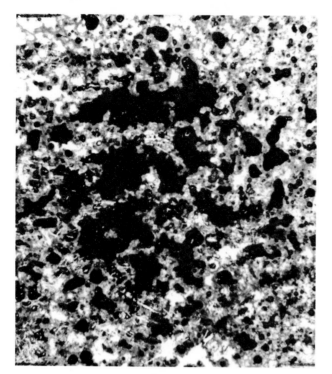

fig 95
A regular matt stippled, rubbed lightly when dry and then spattered

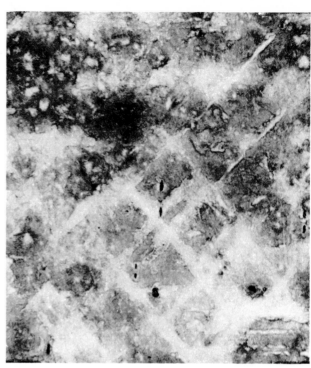

fig 96
Matted, blotted while wet with a piece of corrugated paper, stippled and rubbed lightly when dry

fig 97
Matted, dabbed with sponge while wet, and rubbed lightly when dry

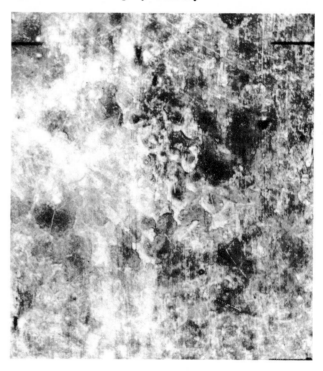

fig 98
Matted, stippled, blotted with paper when wet, and rubbed lightly when dry

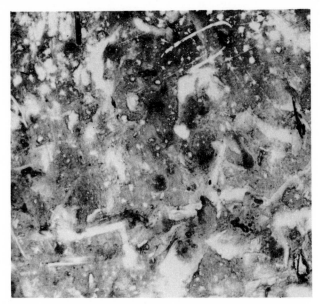

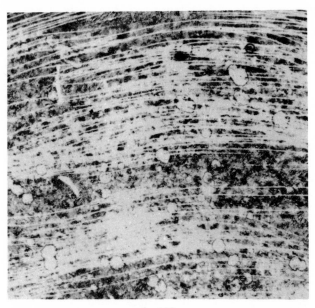

fig 99
Matted, stippled, lightly blotted with a coarse cloth while wet and rubbed lightly when dry

fig 100
Matted, stippled, rubbed lightly when dry, and brushed with a wire brush

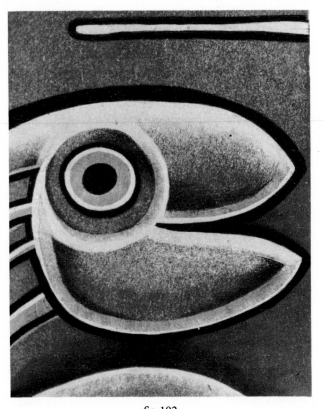

fig 101
Matted, stippled dry, details traced and lights taken out with scrubs

fig 102
Painted as fig 101, but second-painted with alcohol color. Note the increased richness over fig 101 caused by the second painting

better than others. Glass made with kelp, a form of seaweed, produces excellent staining quality, while other kinds of glass vary between staining quite dark or not at all. Those which will stain react by what is called "metaling" if fired too hard. Metaling produces an almost opaque brownish rust color which, when viewed in a surface light, shows as a light blue color. Because of this metaling characteristic it is better to fire stained pieces alone and to fire them at a lower temperature. Silver stain comes to the glass artist in the form of a yellow lake powder and is purchasable in several grades, such as silver stain light and silver stain intense. The silver is incorporated in this powder, which can easily be wiped off when fired. What remains is a clear transparent yellow. Stain is used chiefly to make hair golden, flowers yellow, or to separate and emphasize certain parts of an ornamental area. Silver stain must be applied to the reverse or unpainted side of the glass. It can be mixed with any kind of binder, but by far the best is white shellac thinned with alcohol and Cellosolve. Using this binder and thinner makes the stain immediately soluble when needed. The stain is painted on the back of the piece with a camel's hair brush and badgered smooth. The pieces can be placed painted side down over the fluorescent light and cleaned up with your pointed stick. Care should be taken not to use too heavy a coat of stain. If you do it may metal. Silver stain is much more effective in windows containing large areas of white than in full-colored ones.

First Painting

Whatever binders or methods of glass painting you may have used previously, the following procedure will prove effective if carried out as directed.

Before any painting is done the glass must be cleaned. Besides the normal visual dirt, glass collects a large amount of grease, from the air, which must be eliminated. The best way to do this is to dab a small amount of matt color on each piece. Before it has a chance to dry rub it around and off the piece. Clean all the light-colored pieces which are to be traced over the cartoon, leaving the rest of the glass to be cleaned later. Remove the cleaned pieces preparatory to tracing and matting.

1) Prepare a matt using casein as a binder. Put this in a small jar and label it "water matt, rubbing." In a second jar put some of this same matt and add more binder until it is fairly hard so that you can remove it only by rubbing very vigorously; label this "water matt, hard."
2) Cover the glass which is to be traced with a thin coat of the hard matt and stipple it dry.
3) Place your cartoon over the fluorescent light with the matted glass pieces in their proper places. Use your arm

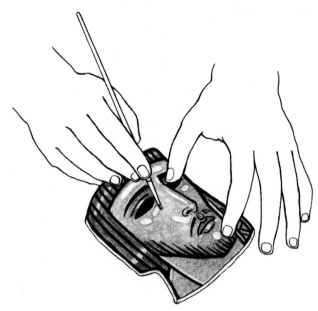

fig 103
Wiping out lights on a head by using one pointed scrub

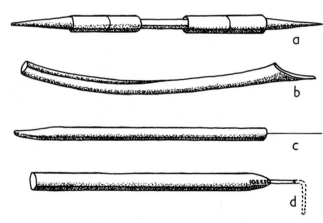

fig 104
VARIOUS TOOLS USED TO SCRATCH OUT LIGHTS
a and b) turkey quill cut as a square-nibbed pen
c) needle pushed into the end of a soft wooden stick
d) dowel with a curtain-rod support screwed into one end, broken off, and filed to a point

rest and trace the pieces.
4) When dry, take out the lights broadly with your no. 1 round, cut-down, and pointed bristle brush.
5) Soften the edges of your broad lights by stippling. This is done by using a size no. 1 or no. 6 round bristle brush, with the no. 1 cut down to $\frac{1}{4}''$ and the no. 6 cut down to $\frac{1}{2}''$ bristles. These are used to punch out tiny points of light. The operation might be described as a combination of punching and pushing while holding the brush at a slight angle back from a vertical position. If, when you

108

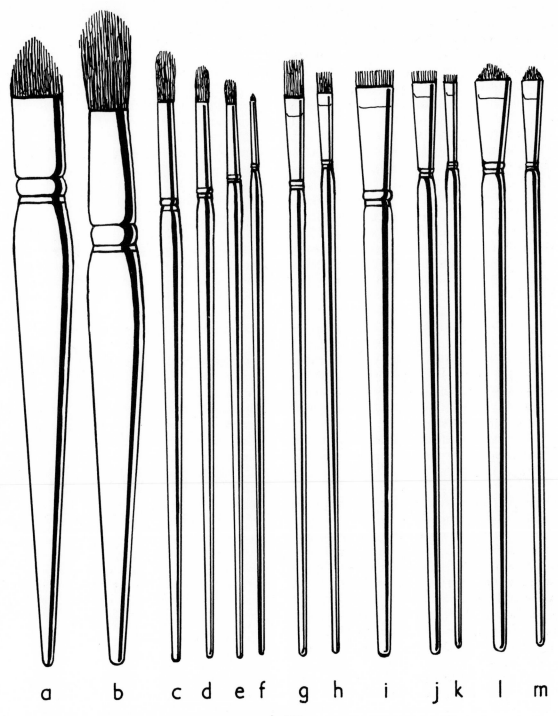

a b c d e f g h i j k l m

fig 105
ASSORTED SCRUBS USED IN GLASS PAINTING

a) a large, round, pointed bristle brush used to dry-stipple large areas of glass
b) a large, round bristle brush used to stipple and brush out large areas of glass
c) d) e) graduated round bristle brushes used to dry, stipple and brush out small areas of glass paint
f) a very small pointed scrub used to wipe out lines and to clean out small areas of glass paint
g) h) i) j) medium and small flat bristle brushes used to brush out
k) l) m) lights on drapery and for painting heads, hands, and other small details

have finished stippling, any of the areas appear spotty, you may use your needle to break up any clumps of color to even out the surface.

6) A pointed stick may be used both to correct errors in tracing or to sharpen up the edges of your painting. We call this operation stick lighting. It is extremely effective when used on hair and to accent the drawing around the nose, mouth and eyebrows. Any hard wood, such as is found in a maple dowel stick, will work well. We happen to like split bamboo which holds its point and has a slight drag against the surface of the glass. This drag makes bamboo easier to control. A sharper tool, good for scratching harder color or for making finer lines, can be made by screwing a small right-angle curtain rod holder into the end of a $\frac{3}{8}''$ dowel stick. The right-angle tip is cut off and the remaining straight metal piece sharpened with a file. The dowel can be cut to whatever length suits you best. Stick lighting tools made from almost any material can be used. An old sable watercolor brush filled with dried varnish, when sharpened to a point, has a very effective drag on the glass. One of the oldest tools is a turkey or goose quill cut like a square-nibbed pen. This is a particularly good tool, as it can be used to pick out a variable width line from fine to wide in the same stroke varying the position of the point. Just a word of warning; soak either type of quill in warm water for a while to soften it up, otherwise it will continue to split when you attempt to cut it. It should now be apparent that many of the tools used to fabricate windows will have to be made by the artist himself.

7) In order to keep the textured background glass from looking like a cobblestone street, wipe out a light approximately $\frac{1}{8}''$ wide on the dark side of the piece next to the lead. Do not do this on every piece. Occasionally take the light out on a different side and do not take any light out on others. Keep in mind that unity through variety is a valid concept. Whether or not similar lights should be taken out of the more detailed painted parts will depend largely upon the dictates of this same artistic concept. At this point most studios fire the glass.

Second Painting

1) Prepare a new matting color using white shellac as a binder and a thinner made with one half denatured alcohol and one half Cellosolve. This thinner will dry at the same speed as water which will make a color that will handle exactly like a water matt.

2) Overlay the water matt with this color. Badger it smooth and stipple it lightly. Do not brush back and forth over this color. If you do it is apt to loosen the ground color. If reasonable care is taken, you will experience no difficulties.

3) When thoroughly dry rub it lightly. It can now be dusted lightly with either a no. 1 or no. 6 uncut bristle brush. An even softer and more sensitive brush as one made of camel, ox, or sable hair can be used to dust off or to punch out the color. Since the alcohol matt is softer than the base water one, it can be lifted off without disturbing the ground color. Finally the quill or the no. 1 pointed bristle brush may be used to add a few selective highlight accents to such places as the tip of the nose above the lips and the edge of the upper eyelids as well as the drapery and ornamental details.

4) It may be found advantageous to color the hair and certain other patterns with varying shades of yellow. This can be done by painting the reverse side of the pieces with silver stain.

5) Remove the pieces which are to be stained as well as the remaining and more elaborately painted pieces. Prepare these for firing by cleaning off the wax. It is not necessary or even advisable at this time to fire all pieces. It is probable that the ones you are about to fire will need some additional painting. When they have been fired they can be replaced along with the other pieces and repainted where necessary. When the painting has been completed and finally approved, remove all of the pieces, take off the wax, and prepare the section for firing.

ADDITIONAL METHODS OF GLASS

Scratch Out Method

One type of glass painting which has not as yet been spoken of is the scratch out technique used extensively in the thirteenth-century glass painting of lettering. The piece to be lettered was covered with an opaque black tracing color and when dry the letters were scratched out of the black ground. Where the lettering is large it is not difficult to do it by tracing but when it is relatively small it is infinitely easier to do by the scratch out method. The reason is obvious. Except for straight block letters most alphabets have serifs, or sharp tails, all of which are much easier to scratch out. This method has one other distinct value, it affords the artist a chance to counterchange his forms from dark on light to light on dark. This counterchanging gives variety to a scroll or panel of lettering. It is also extremely effective when used to define ornament and representative forms. For example, if the glass used for a plant or ornamental form is light, it can be covered with the black tracing color and the form can be scratched out in thin line. The lights can be opened out until just the right amount is allowed to come through.

Painting Up

Glass-painting procedures so far have been confined largely to matting, preparatory to tracing heads, hands or intricate ornament, also to matting these traced pieces with an alcohol matt for a second painting. Little, however, has been said about painting up except the wiping out of lights on drapery. This same process is used in painting plants, trees, clouds, and simple ornaments. Broad lights are taken out with the scrub, delineating forms are traced up, and final accents are completed with the stick or quill. Painting up on the easel produces quite satisfactory results. The fact that the tracing may vary slightly from the cartoon is all to the good. The more painting up which is done, the better the panel will be.

Etching

Etching as a painting technique belongs in a category all its own. It is not known for certain when etching was first used, but flashed glass with portions of its top layer removed with a grinding wheel was mentioned as early as the thirteenth century in connection with the Canterbury windows. The interesting and important fact about etched glass is that it makes it possible to use a color such as red, a yellow made with silver stain, and a black and gray made with glass paint, all in a very small piece of glass. Flashed glass, as we have described it under glass making, was made possible by coating the original blob by plunging

111

fig 106
Patterns created by scratching lights out of solid blacks

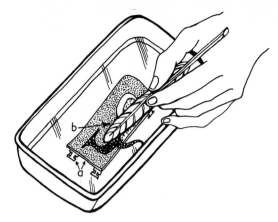

fig 107
a) shows piece of glass placed on strips of lead cames so that the glass may be easily picked up
b) shows how a feather is used to brush away the sludge formed during the etching process

it into another pot of color. When blown out it produced a sheet of glass with a thin colored flash on top of the original white, pale blue, or pale green base. What has made it more attractive and considerably easier to use in more recent times is the discovery of hydrofluoric acid to dissolve the colored layer. When it is desirable to remove a part of the colored flash from a certain area all parts except this are coated with a hot paraffin wax applied with an oxhair tracing brush. If these same areas are first covered with glass paint, the wax will be easier to remove. Wax will protect the glass from the corrosive action of the acid. For this reason the wax should be applied to the reverse side of the glass. Do not, however, cover the reverse side of the glass with paint. If you do, it will be impossible to determine when the etching is completed. After coating, the pieces are placed in a hard rubber acid-resistant tray. If short pieces of came lead are placed under the glass, it will make it easier to remove them when the etching is finished. A pair of hard rubber photographer's tongs are excellent for this purpose. The tray should be filled with enough hydrofluoric acid diluted with water to cover the pieces. Undiluted acid will etch more rapidly but will result in frosting the

glass. A solution made with one part acid to three parts water will do. Always pour the acid slowly into the water. A feather can be used to brush away the sludge formed during the etching process. If this sludge is not brushed away, the etching activity will cease. What keeps the feather from disintegrating is a mystery. A vent fan should be used to dissipate the acid fumes. If a vent fan is not available, then at least a mask along with rubber gloves and goggles should be worn while working with hydrofluoric acid. It is one of the most corrosive known acids. It will eat through any material except rubber, lead, or wax. If it gets onto your hands or skin, it will eat in and fester. Soda, lime, or any alkali will counteract its effect. After the etching is completed, the pieces should be thoroughly rinsed in water before the wax is removed. Never rinse the finished work in the sink, or pour the diluted acid down the drain. One day when we inadvertently did this the trap under our sink virtually turned into a sprinkling can. After the pieces are washed and the wax removed the painting may be carried out in the same way as with any other glass.

There is always a great temptation for artists who are deeply involved in their particular art to overinstruct, with the final result that little is left to the ingenuity or creative judgment of the individual responsible for the project.

A good deal more could be told about glass painting; however, to say more could add confusion instead of clarity. After all, given the proper tools and simple instructions on how to use them it is always much more fun to discover new ways of working for yourself. Learning to paint glass in a skillful manner requires hard work, practice, and good taste; but a reasonably good result can be made without too much difficulty.

112

FIRING

Kilns have already been discussed in some detail and a particular one recommended, but with the many kilns which are available, large and small, you will invariably end by using the one most readily accessible.

Remember two things. First, ultimately a kiln must be fired by eye if a successful result is desired and, second, to prepare yourself for this learning process it is also advisable to use the proper .022 cones. They can be purchased at any local ceramic supply store. These cones are made of a special clay which will melt at 1121° Fahrenheit, the threshold of the melting point of glass. Push the base of one of these cones $\frac{1}{4}''$ into a small wad of moist clay at a slight angle, so that when it reaches the firing point of the glass it will start to bend over in the direction in which it has been aimed. All kilns have a hole somewhere on one of their sides called a peephole. Place the clay containing one of the cones on a plate so that it will be visible through the peephole. By the time it is ready to bend over, the kiln will be red hot inside so that you will be able to see the cone. While firing watch not only the cone but also the glass itself. When first placed in the kiln the painted glass will appear to be dull-surfaced; as it fires it will become glossy. At this point the kiln should be turned off immediately as the glass will now be properly fired. The cone can be watched through the peephole but to look at the glass the kiln lid will have to be lifted. While firing it is helpful to have a flashlight handy. It will make it easier for you to tell when the glass has become glossy. Do not hold the lid open any longer than is absolutely necessary. After you have compared the bending of the cone with the glossing of the glass several times you should be able to fire by eye.

Gas- or oil-burning muffle kilns require a strong draft to supply sufficient oxygen for proper firing. When their correct heat has been reached and their fuel turned off their draft decreases. This in turn causes the temperature to rise slightly. This rise does not seriously affect ceramic ware but will cause glass to overfire. Therefore, the door of the kiln should be opened for a few seconds immediately after the fuel has been turned off to allow the excess heat to escape. This is not necessary with an electric kiln because the temperature does not rise when it is shut off. Kilns are all temperamental and no two fire alike. One thing to keep in mind is that it is better to underfire than to overfire. An underfired kiln can be fired again, but an overfired one is finished.

For the sake of clarity let us assume that we are going to use the kiln recommended earlier in the text. The following directions are given to help you fire this kiln and, incidentally, any other one.

To fire glass, you will need the following:

1) An electric kiln, preferably an octagonal one, $13\frac{1}{4}''$ deep with a diameter of $14\frac{3}{8}''$. Any gas, oil, or electric kiln can

fig 108
A multi-sided kiln

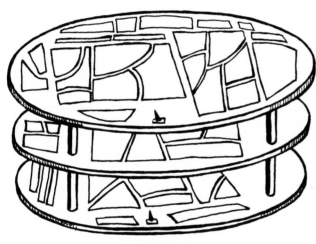

fig 109
Plates laid out for firing

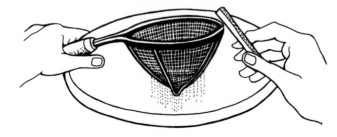

fig 110
A method of covering plates with whiting

be used but the following instructions are based on this recommended electric kiln.

2) Three round ceramic plates, 13″ in diameter.
3) One small plastic garbage can, or a similar container
4) Ten pounds of whiting.
5) One half round flour sieve, 6″ in diameter.
6) One box of twelve size .022 cones.
7) One flashlight.
8) Twelve 3″ cylindrical posts.

The accompanying illustration shows how the loaded plates are assembled. They are placed one above the other on 3″ posts. The first plate is raised 3″ above the bottom and the third or top plate will be 3″ from the lid. This 3″ space interval is necessary to allow free circulation of the heat while firing. Before the pieces of painted glass are laid out on the ceramic plates, the plates themselves must be covered with a material which will keep the glass from sticking to them. Whiting has proved to be the most satisfactory material to use. To prepare the plates place them on the glazing bench. Fill the flour sieve half full of whiting, hold the sieve about 6″ above the plate and tap the edge of the sieve with the handle of a hammer moving the sieve along with each tap. You will have a coat of the correct thickness when none of the plate is visible through the whiting. When purchasing a sieve get the deepest not the shallowest one. With a shallow sieve the whiting will bounce out when the rim is struck. Also do not load the sieve with whiting over one of the plates. If you examine one of the plates, you will note that the sifted surface is composed of many tiny cones of whiting. When a piece of glass is placed upon this surface it has just sufficient weight to flatten the cones to produce a perfectly smooth surface.

In laying out the glass keep all pieces at least $\frac{1}{2}$″ from the edge of the plate and retain a space of $\frac{1}{8}$″ between all pieces. Make a final check after you have placed each plate in the kiln to make certain that none of the pieces has moved.

Any new kiln should be tested before firing your valuable painted work. The heat circulation pattern will vary in practically every kiln. The best way to do this test is to prepare your three plates as has been suggested. Cut fifteen pieces of glass 2″ × 2″ from the same sheet. Matt them—remove a $\frac{1}{2}$″ strip with a scrub so that you will have both a clean and matted area on the individual pieces. Number the glass by scratching through the matt. Place the pieces on the center and the four corners of each plate. Record the numbers and their position on a piece of paper so that you will be able to determine just how the pieces fired in different parts of the kiln. Most kilns fire hotter at the top and cooler at the bottom. To a lesser degree they fire hotter on the edges and cooler in the center. This kiln loaded with three plates should fire in no less than one and a half hours and no longer than two and a half hours. Of course the potential voltage can be seriously affected by the amount of current which is being used elsewhere in the neighborhood. If this happens, the kiln may take longer to fire.

All of the octagon-type kilns have a three heat switch—low, medium, and high. Some of the older models are equipped with three toggle switches, which are placed along one side of the kiln. Each switch turns on a separate section of the kiln's elements—the bottom, the middle, the top. To fire the recommended octagon kiln start the firing on low and run it for forty-five minutes, then forty-five minutes on medium, and the remaining time, whatever it takes to fire, on high. With a kiln fitted with three toggle switches fire it forty-five minutes on the bottom switch, then forty-five minutes on both bottom and middle switches, and finish with all three turned on. The octagon kiln is fitted with two peepholes on its side wall, one at the top and another at the bottom. Imbed the bottom $\frac{1}{4}''$ of two cones at an angle

in separate small wads of moist clay, dry them, and place one on the bottom plate in front of the top peephole. Sometime before the kiln is fired it will become red enough inside to see the cones. If they happen to be obscured by a red haze, blow into the peephole and the cone will become visible.

This suggested firing pattern is one which we have used on several kilns. The time differential from top to bottom in a kiln is normally never too great. It will vary from slightly underfired on the bottom plate to slightly overfired on the top one. If the bottom plate continues to fire light, it can be used for the more elaborately painted pieces, such as heads and hands, as well as stained pieces which will be better if fired lightly. When the glass has been removed do not try to lay out other pieces on the plate without resifting a new surface. First take off and throw away any part of the whiting where stained pieces have been fired. The remainder can be scraped off and replaced in the whiting container. The silver deposit, which has been left by the stain, can easily be recognized by its faint yellow pattern.

In the meantime take the tin rods which you have cast, and anoint them over on both sides with wax, and rasping lead over the surface in all places which are to be soldered. Taking the hot iron, apply the tin to it in whatever place two pieces of lead meet, and you anoint with the iron until they adhere to each other. The figures being set up, you will arrange the grounds in the same manner, and of whatever color you wish, and so, piece-meal, you compose your window. The window being finished and soldered on one side, turned upon the other you will make it firm everywhere in the same manner, by rasping and soldering.

Theophilus
The Various Arts, Chapter XXVII
Of Uniting Together and Soldering Windows

GLAZING

ARTICLES NEEDED FOR THIS OPERATION

1) Glazing table
2) Two furring strips, $1'' \times 2'' \times 36''$
3) Several lengths of $\frac{1}{4}''$ cames, $\frac{3}{8}''$ cames, and any other sizes necessary to glaze the window
4) One stopping knife
5) One lathykin
6) Several dozen glazing nails
7) Flux (oleic acid)—ruby flux (acid)
8) Yardstick
9) Soldering iron, electric
10) Solder wire, 60/40—no. 12
11) Large metal carpenter's angle
12) Lead stretcher
13) Pair of pliers
14) Glazing hammer
15) Knife for cutting lead
16) No. 2 size bristle brush for oleic acid
17) Strip of $\frac{1}{8}''$ tempered masonite, $2'' \times 13''$
18) Jar of water

In a contemporary studio glazing means fitting the glass pieces into their lead cames. Tools and equipment such as a glazing bench, a lathykin, a stopping knife, a lead cutting knife, and a lead stretcher are so specialized that they need individual descriptions.

After each section of the window has been painted, fired,

and finally checked, it is laid out in its own shallow tray. Although any soft-topped table can be used for glazing, it will be time well spent if you build a special glazing bench similar to the one illustrated. The top should be made of a softwood, $48''$ wide $\times$ $84''$ long $\times$ $1\frac{1}{2}''$ thick. This will accommodate the tray of glass pieces—already laid out—the necessary glazing tools, and still leave sufficient space for glazing the section. The trays should be made as shallow

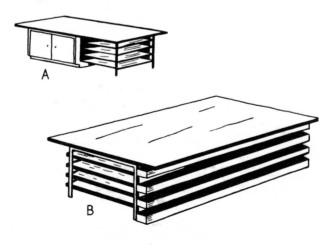

fig 111
A PERSPECTIVE DRAWING OF A GLAZING TABLE
a) top and side-front   b) top and side-rear

116

drawers, 36″ wide × 36″ long × 2″ deep and placed upon runners 4″ apart on the front side beneath the bench top. To the left of the trays a single shelf enclosed by two doors, 12″ wide × 30″ high, can be made to serve as storage space for large containers of whiting, cement, and larger tools used in glazing or cementing. On the narrow end of the bench, space for several narrow shelves is available in an area 14″ wide × 36″ long × 36″ high. Two doors, 14″ wide × 30″ high, can be hung to enclose this area. If metal shelf hardware is installed to support all of the shelves in the glazing bench, it will be possible to place them at varying distances apart when necessary. This shallow cupboard can serve as a place to store rolled cartoons or cut lines of windows not yet completed. Small glazing tools and brushes for cementing can also be stored in this same cupboard. The rear side of the bench provides adequate space to fasten four lead storage boxes placed 3″ apart. It will not be necessary to construct these as the ones used to ship the lead cames are perfect for this purpose. In glazing, ten times as many ¼″ leads are used as any other. For this reason it is better not to fasten the bottom box to the table, but to fill it with one hundred pounds of ¼″ lead and rest the box on the floor. The other three boxes can be securely attached to the bench and filled with smaller quantities of various sized leads.

The Lathykin

A lathykin is a tool designed for opening the flanges of lead cames and can be made by tapering the fore end of any hard-wood stick to a blunt point. The most satisfactory type is made in the form of a flat oval, 3½″ long × 1½″ wide, tapered to a blunt point. The wide oval end fits perfectly into the glazier's hand. The rear end of a straight stick model can be fitted with a small crutch end to protect the glazier's palm. To spread the flanges, place the lead came flange side up on the glazing bench. Wet the tip of the lathykin and push it forward between the flanges. On the first trip through the lead it is better to use a series of short forward pushes. The second time through you may use a longer continuous stroke without jamming. If you wish to have the flanges spread farther apart, push the lathykin through the flanges at a slight angle.

The Stopping Knife

A stopping knife is one of the craft's most useful tools. Strangely enough it cannot be purchased anywhere but must be made by the stained-glass artist himself. It serves as a third steel thumb which can be used for any number of glazing, cementing, or setting operations. A very simple

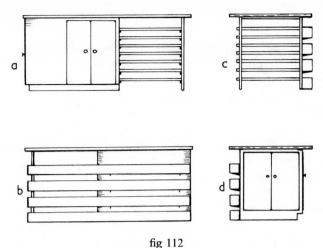

fig 112
A GLAZING TABLE
a) front   b) rear   c and d) both ends in elevation

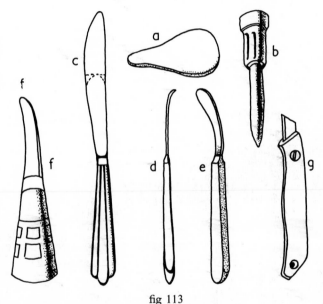

fig 113
a) an oval lathykin   b) a straight lathykin
c) stainless-steel table knife with removable parts shown
d and e) front and side views of stopping knife
f) a stopping knife made from an oyster knife
g) a lead-cutting knife

yet effective one can be made by breaking off 2″ from the tip of a stainless table knife and grinding the broken end into a half round shape. Another effective type is made by rounding off the pointed end of an oyster knife. The wooden handle is then deeply scored to hold melted lead or solder. To do this a cone of heavy paper is fastened with its wide end at the base of the handle and filled with lead or solder to form a broad-headed hammer. This broad head is excellent for pounding glazing nails in place. A tool with a wide head is less apt to break glass than a regular smaller headed hammer. The blades of both of these knives should be slightly turned upward at their tips to provide a convenient spot for the glazier to rest his thumb.

The Lead Cutting Knife

Another tool which is used in glazing is one designed for cutting the lead cames to size. Such a tool should have a thin blade and be made of top-quality steel. Many are made by breaking off all but 3″ of the blade of a 1″-wide palette knife. The wooden handle of this knife is treated in the same manner as that of the oyster knife so that it can also be used as a hammer. It so happens that our recommended knife, which has removable and replaceable blades, is both less expensive and more suitable for cutting leads than one made with a palette knife.

Lead Stretchers

The same English firm which distributes the lead mill also sells a lead stretcher. As you can see by the illustration it resembles the pincers of a giant insect. Its jaws open easily to accept the lead came but when the came is pulled back the jaws clamp down to hold the lead securely. An improvised stretcher can be made with a pair of pliers. The jaws of the pliers pass through an iron harness ring while the ring is fastened to the top of the glazing bench by a thin strap of sheet steel. The ring used must be large enough to allow the jaws of the pliers to pass through but small enough to prevent their handles from pulling through. This improvised one is easy to make while the English one, which works on the same principle, is difficult to obtain. Whichever one you use should be fastened securely to one end of the glazing bench.

The Process of Glazing

The illustration shows the left-hand corner of a glazing section. A and **B** are furring strips while c and d are $\frac{3}{8}$″ binder leads. The double dotted lines e in the center of the leads represent their hearts.
1) Arrange the cut lines on the top of the glazing bench at least 2″ from the table's edge.
2) Place the drawer containing the glass either to the right or left of your cut line.
3) Nail the furring strip **A**, which is 1″ × 2″ × 36″, along the outside edge of the base binder indicated on the cut line and a second identical furring strip **B** along the outside edge of the left-hand binder. The

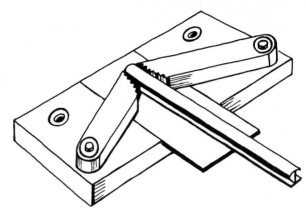

fig 114
A commercial English lead stretcher

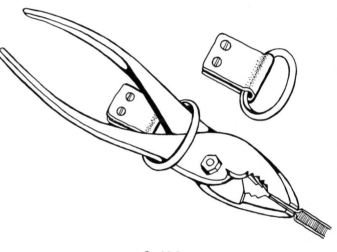

fig 115
An improvised lead stretcher

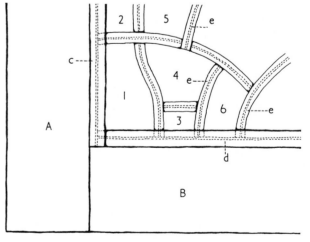

fig 116
A corner of a typical glazing section

second furring strip should be firmly pressed against the bottom strip to form a tight right-angle.

4) Stretch and straighten one piece of $\frac{3}{8}''$ lead. Put one end of the $\frac{3}{8}''$ binder between the jaws of the lead stretcher and grasp the other end with a pair of pliers. If the lead happens to be twisted, straighten it before pulling too hard. After straightening grasp the lead with your left hand about 12'' ahead of the pliers. When pulling be certain that you have a firm grip with your left hand as the lead will frequently break where it is held by the pliers. If it does, you can be seriously hurt. While the lead is still being held taut, slap it smartly on the bench top. This will remove any tendency it might have to retwist when the tension is released.

5) Open the strip of $\frac{3}{8}''$ binder lead on one side with your lathykin.

6) Cut the 72'' strip in half to make two 36'' binder pieces. Place the closed end of one, c, against the left furring strip, A, and the other against the base furring strip, B, with both their opened flanges out. If the left tip of the base binder is slightly flattened with the stopping knife, it can be pushed neatly between the opened flanges of the left-hand one to form a tight joint. If a lead line is continued for a considerable distance without being crossed by another, the entire section will be seriously weakened and may even fold along this line. If, however, it is crossed by another lead, a strong interwoven structure can be made. When the pattern is repeated several times the panel will be strengthened still more without having its appearance altered. This is one aspect of glazing which rests totally with the individual glazier. He can make a very interesting game of arranging the pattern of these crossings. In the illustration the crossing leads are indicated by the heavy lines.

7) Straighten and stretch three strands of $\frac{1}{4}''$ cames and open them on both sides with a lathykin. Cut one of the strips into six 12'' pieces, which is a convenient size to work with.

8) Place glass piece no. 1 into binders c and d so that it touches the heart of each, making certain that the glass fits properly against the cut line. If it does not, tap it with the base of your hammer. Do not pound the piece, just tap it lightly. It may be that it will need to be grozed to make it fit properly.

9) Place glazing nails at the top and side of the piece.

10) Using a stopping knife pry up binder c adjacent to the left top corner of no. 1. Pull out the glazing nail and fit the $\frac{1}{4}''$ lead over the top of no. 1 and into binder c. You will not be able to get the lead very far into the

binder, but it will be far enough to lock it in place.

11) Crease the binder down on either side of the $\frac{1}{4}''$ lead with your stopping knife and replace the glazing nail above the lead.

12) Pry up binder d at the lower right-hand corner of no. 1 and fit a $\frac{1}{4}''$ lead into the binder.

13) Remove the glazing nail; lay the lead along the glass.

14) Mark the lead at the top of no. 1 with your knife where it should be cut in order to butt neatly against the right-hand lead.

15) Swing the top lead up and cut it. To keep the lead from collapsing use a rocking motion with the knife while cutting. Make certain that the cut is made straight down. You will note that to fit properly the lead had to be cut a scant $\frac{1}{8}''$ short of the glass size. This allowance will always have to be made whenever one lead is to butt against another.

16) Return the lead to the top of no. 1 and replace the glazing nail.

17) Place piece no. 3 in the base binder d and the $\frac{1}{4}''$ lead to its left and place glazing nails at the top and sides of no. 3.

18) Pry up d at the bottom right-hand corner of no. 3 and pull out the glazing nail.

19) Place a $\frac{1}{4}''$ lead on the right-hand side of no. 3 and into binder d.

20) Butt a $\frac{1}{4}''$ lead against the left lead of no. 3 and make the right end a scant $\frac{1}{8}''$ short of the glass size.

21) Pry up d and insert lead on right of no. 3.

22) Replace first the lead and then the glazing nail. After the remaining pieces in the section have been placed in their leads the joints must be soldered. The electric iron is used exclusively in this country. Some glaziers prefer one of the pistol-type irons. While these are excellent

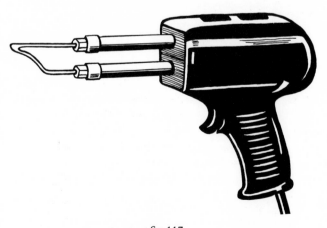

fig 117
Electric soldering iron with pistol grip

119

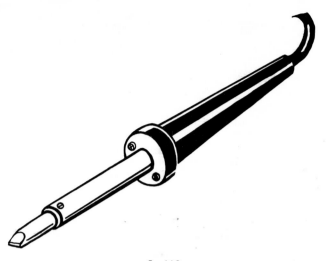

fig 118

Electric soldering iron with tip held in place with a small set screw

for soldering the copper wires which hold the reinforcement bars in place, they are a bit light for effective glazing. Soldering irons range all the way from excellent to worthless. Rest assured that if you buy a cheap one, you will be wasting your money. We have found that the best type is a medium-sized iron fitted with a replaceable tip held in place by a small set screw. Do not buy an iron with a screw-in tip. It will freeze after it has been heated several times.

23) Before an iron can be used it must be properly tinned. To do this place a small quantity of solder on a tin can lid and pour a few drops of ruby flux (hydrochloric acid) on it. Plug in the iron and let it heat for several minutes. Melt the solder into a small pool and rub all sides of your iron tip in the pool. Wipe off the surplus solder with a cloth. It should now be bright and shiny.

24) Cut off roughly 60″ of the 60/40 solder and fold it back and forth into 6″ lengths. This makes a handy package to work with. Extend a single 6″ strand to use. When it is down to 1″ length, unfold another 6″ one until the solder is exhausted.

25) Each joint in the section must be soldered. The way to do this is to dip the top of the solder into an already prepared shallow container of oleic acid. Place the solder on top of the joint and melt off $\frac{1}{8}″$ of the solder. Move the coil of solder away from the joint. Press the iron down on the joint as though you were blotting it. Hold the iron in this position for approximately one second, then lift it quickly. If you have done everything as instructed, you should have a neat shallow pool of solder covering the joint. Piling up solder does nothing to increase its holding power.

26) If your butt joint has a slight gap between it and the other lead, use the same blotting technique. However, instead of lifting the iron at once, brush it quickly over the gap, then lift it. This is known as jumping. If the gap is too wide to jump, it can be filled with small pieces of lead and then jumped. Do not feather dust or dab tentatively at the joint as novices are inclined to do.

27) After soldering six or seven joints, wipe the tip of your iron to remove the excess solder. If you keep the tip of your iron wiped clean, it will not become pitted so quickly.

28) When it finally does become corroded and pitted it will need to be filed clean and retinned. The cleaner you keep your tip, the less filing you will need to do.

29) If your heads are kept covered, they will keep for months without oxidizing. When they lose their shine you can clean the joints with a wire brush. In extreme cases you may be compelled to scrape the joint clean with a knife.

30) Leads which are used for glazing are made with high, low, or medium hearts. For most work the medium size

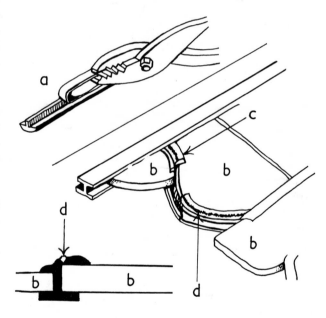

fig 119

FLANGE IN A SECTION WHERE A PIECE OF GLASS IS TOO THICK FOR A NORMAL LEAD

a) peeling off a strip from the tip of a lead came b) glass
c) strips of lead laid along the new heart of lead which has been pinched up straight and bent over glass b (lower left). b and b are glass in cross section. d is the solder joint fastening the strip of lead to the high heart came

is best. The high and low hearts are reserved for glass which is all very thick or all very thin. When using medium lead and an occasional piece happens to be extra thick, it can be taken care of by what is known as flanging. To do this bend the top flange straight up to create a much higher heart. You will then be able to insert the glass into the lead. If there is any lead remaining, crease it over the glass.

31) Strip off the top flange from a $\frac{1}{4}$" lead and lay it along-side of and touching the newly made heart.

32) Run solder along the full length of the joint to complete the new improvised high heart lead. In putting on the top and side binders you will need to be certain that the binders are on the cut lines, not over them. It may also happen that the outside binders are not quite straight. Both difficulties can be corrected by placing your 13" strip of masonite inside the flanges of the binder and tapping it. Before turning the section over to repeat the glazing process on the other side, mark the binders with the point of a nail on the right and left sides to indicate the center of the reinforcement bars. On a section 36" high you should have two bars. To turn over a section in order to glaze or cement it on the reverse side, slide it forward so that its center rests along the table's edge. Tip the section forward enough to grasp it slightly above its center. Tip it forward quickly, rotate it to a vertical position, rest it on the floor, and turn it around. To get it back on the table simply reverse the process. This identical procedure is used in handling plate glass.

Cementing

The purpose of cementing is two-fold. First, the pieces of glass used in making a window vary in thickness from a scant $\frac{1}{8}$" up to $\frac{3}{8}$". Cementing takes up the slack caused by this variation. Second, it keeps the window from leaking. In a small panel putty or glazing compound, as it is called, can be used successfully; but it takes much too long to execute a large section this way. It is better to use a cement made of whiting mixed with linseed oil in the form of a heavy paste. To this paste, approximately one half ounce of litharge (yellow lead oxide) to the quart should be added. To thin the mixture some turpentine may be used. Litharge causes the cement to harden while the turpentine helps the mixture to dry more rapidly. For this reason it is unwise to make up more than a quart at a time. A small amount of lamp black added to the cement will give it a neutral gray color. To cement a section you will need a pointed wooden

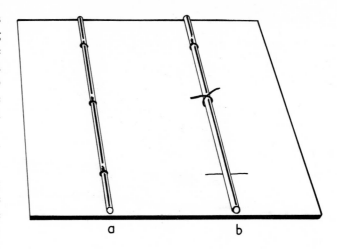

fig 120

Fastening copper wires to a section to hold reinforcement bars in place

stick, a stopping knife, two brushes, a small bit of whiting and a piece of cloth. One of the brushes should be a small scrub brush, about 2" × 4" with reasonably soft bristles, the other a coarse straw brush about 3" × 8". Both can be obtained easily from almost any hardware store.

Place your section upon the glazing table. Pour about half a cup of cement over the section. With the small brush scrub the cement thoroughly into the leads. Before you begin it is advisable to open up any of the leads which are larger than $\frac{1}{4}$". This is accomplished by running your stopping knife under the flange to raise it slightly. After all the leads are filled, close down the raised ones with the stopping knife. To remove the excess from the glass, brush the cement against the leads, lifting the brush at the end of each stroke. Scrape the brush against the rim of the cement bucket and repeat the action until the glass is relatively clean. Sprinkle the section with a small amount of whiting, rub this around the panel, and dust it off. The whiting will absorb the oil left by the cement. Use your pointed stick, running it around each lead, to clean off the cement. To finish off the cementing use the coarse straw brush to buff the surface vigorously. This should clean every vestige of the cement from the surface. Turn the section over and repeat each process upon the reverse side. All that remains to be done before setting is to solder on the copper wires which will hold the section against the round reinforcement bars.

To do this, cut off 5" pieces of 18-gauge copper wire. Solder three of these wires to the leads exactly along the lines where each of the bars will be. It will be necessary to use a flux made of hydrochloric acid. This can be purchased in most hardware stores under the name of ruby flux.

121

Setting

In the art of stained glass, setting is the accepted term for installing a window in its opening. Acute problems can and do arise during the setting process. For this reason it is advisable to employ the services of a specialist who does nothing else but install windows. He will do it more efficiently than you can and in the end the cost will be less. It may become mandatory, under certain circumstances, that you set your own work. In this case the following explanation should prove invaluable.

In a window a rabbet may vary from $\frac{1}{4}''$ to as much as $\frac{3}{4}''$, but since most have the narrower $\frac{1}{4}''$ one, we will base our setting explanation upon the $\frac{1}{4}''$ size. Naturally, if a specific rabbet varies from this measurement, the differential will have to be taken into consideration. For example, a $\frac{1}{4}''$ size will call for a $\frac{3}{8}''$ binder lead, and if deeper, a $\frac{1}{2}''$ size should be used. It is advisable to know the depth before the cartoon is drawn so that the proper binder can be indicated.

Low nave windows can be reached easily and set from a step ladder. Higher windows such as those in the transept or clerestory will need a metal scaffold such as those used by builders. They can be rented from suppliers who will not only erect them for you but will remove them when the setting is finished. High or low, large or small, a window requires at least two men to set it. If the opening is rabbeted, it will be much simpler to install than if it has a groove.

Let us begin with one which has a rabbet and assume that the opening already contains temporary glass. This glass will have to be removed and the rabbet cleaned of its old putty. In the past this was done by chipping it away with a chisel, now a special electric heating tool is made which heats and softens the old putty so that it can easily be removed with a putty knife. Once the rabbet has been thoroughly cleaned it should be given a coat of orange shellac. This is necessary to stop the linseed oil in the putty from penetrating and staining the stone work.

If the window contains tracery, the setting should begin with the very top piece. Check first this section and then the remaining tracery pieces to determine whether they fit properly. If they bind in certain places, cut them down slightly until they slide easily into the opening.

On the side of the rabbet and around the perimeter of the opening drill several $\frac{1}{8}''$ holes $\frac{1}{4}''$ back from the front of the rabbet, partially fill the rabbet with glazing compound, and firmly press the tracery piece into its opening. You will need to make several dozen aluminum wedges $\frac{3}{4}''$ long $\times$ $\frac{1}{16}''$ thick. These can be made from a sheet of $\frac{1}{16}''$ aluminum. Tap one of these wedges into each of the $\frac{1}{8}''$ holes to secure the section in the opening. Holes and wedges should be

placed roughly twelve inches apart in all sections of the window. Fill the remainder of the rabbet with glazing compound and finish by using your putty knife to fashion a neat putty bevel. Some of the glazing compound will have been squeezed out of the reverse side. Clean this off before going to the next tracery section. Repeat this process with each section until the tracery is finished. If you work from the top down as has been suggested, you will be able to do most of the setting from the outside. In most installation work it will not be necessary to erect a scaffold on the inside of the building. A second man can complete the necessary work from an extension ladder. When the tracery has been completed and cleaned begin with the top sections of the main panels. Use the same procedure as you did with the tracery. Trim each section to fit, drill holes and set the wedges and mark where the T bars are to be placed. When the top of the panel is fitted snugly into the rabbet at the top and when the bottom section is rested upon a $6''$ piece of the T bar the necessary placement of the $1''$ bar can be indicated on the stone work of the rabbet. It is necessary to use a substitute short section of the T bar for this purpose. The reason will become apparent shortly as the setting of the bars is described in detail. The section may now be temporarily removed from the opening in order to drill $\frac{3}{8}''$ holes to receive the bar.

The overall length of the T bar should be the full modified size of the opening (see both cartoon and cutline) plus an extra $1''$ ($\frac{1}{2}''$ on each end). These ends are to be

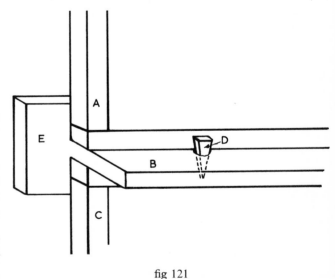

fig 121
SETTING
A) upper section of glass resting against T bar
B) horizontal member of T bar
C) lower section of window resting against vertical member of T bar
D) one of the small aluminium wedges

122

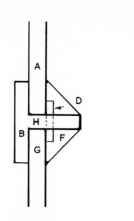

fig 122

A vertical cross-examination of the same bar (fig 121)

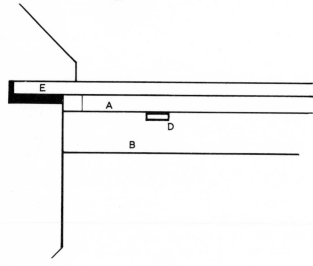

fig 123

Horizontal cross-section of the same bar (fig 121)

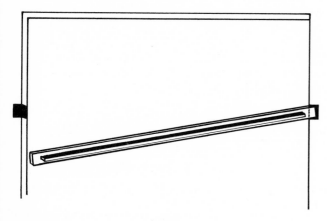

fig 124

Demonstrates the diagonal method used to get the T bar into either a rabbet or a groove

inserted into the stone work. For example, if the full modified size of the opening is 30″, then the T bar will be 30″ plus $\frac{1}{2}$″ plus $\frac{1}{2}$″, or 31″. A section $\frac{1}{2}$″ × $\frac{7}{8}$″ × $\frac{1}{8}$″ will have to be removed from each end of the horizontal part of the T bar. This will leave a vertical $\frac{1}{2}$″ × 1″ × $\frac{1}{8}$″ to be inserted in the stone work. The illustration shows the position of the upper section of glass A as it rests on the horizontal member of the T bar, B, and the lower section of the window C as it fits tightly against the under side of the horizontal member. It shows the position of one of the small aluminum wedges, D, used to hold the section of glass in place. It also displays the vertical end of the bar which will be placed in the stone work E.

Figure 122, which is a vertical cross section of the same bar, illustrates how the top section rests upon the horizontal member of the bar and also how the lower section butts against its under side and rests against its vertical member. Also shown is one of the wedges tapped through the horizontal member and the putty bevel. Figure 123 showing a horizontal cross section of the same rabbeted opening illustrates the extension necessary to hold the $\frac{1}{2}$″ end of the T bar. The black area shows the section which has been drilled out for this purpose. The dotted line describes the position filled by the $\frac{1}{2}$″ end of the T bar. You will note that the area for this end is projected $\frac{1}{8}$″ ahead of the glass section. This is done in order to make the section fit flush with the rabbet when it passes beyond the 1″ T bar. Figure 124 demonstrates the diagonal method used to get the T bar into either a rabbet or a groove. After the bar has been placed it can be slid back and forth to center it. Following this the bar can be wedged in its forward position with lead wool. Partially fill the rabbet with glazing compound, press the section firmly in place, and tap the aluminum wedges into the $\frac{1}{8}$″ holes. T bars should have at least four $\frac{1}{8}$″ holes drilled in their horizontal members to hold the base of one and the top of the other section. Do not, however, tap the wedges into the holes until both top and bottom sections have been put in place or you will have to remove them in order to get the lower sections into the T bar. Each panel should have its T bars set in the stone work, beginning with the very top section. When this has been done the glass may be wedged properly and set in its putty bed.

Setting tracery in a groove is an entirely different matter from setting the same piece in a rabbet. When a rabbet has been filled with glazing compound the tracery can be pushed directly into the opening. On the other hand, when a groove is being used the tracery section will have to be divided into several smaller pieces in order to fit into the opening. Later the pieces are reassembled by what is known as a meeting joint. If the tracery is to be set in a groove, you

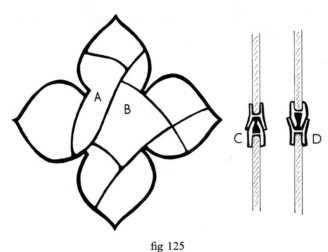

fig 125

A method of dividing up a quarterfoil section so that it can be placed in a rabbeted opening and be reassembled by using meeting joints

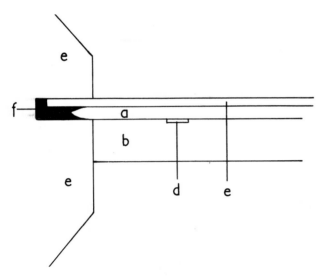

fig 126
SHOWS A HORIZONTAL SECTION OF A T-BAR AS IT IS PLACED IN A GROOVE

a) a section of the window
b) horizontal member of the T-bar
c) vertical $\frac{1}{8}$" thick by 1" member of the T-bar
d) aluminium wedge   e) stone frame   f) $\frac{3}{8}$" by 1" groove

will need to know this before the sections are glazed so that you will have the opportunity of studying and planning the shapes to be used with the meeting joints. If you look at the illustration of a quarterfoil tracery section, it can be seen readily that the lobes of the quarterfoil cannot be slid past the narrow neck back of the lobe and into the groove without being separated into A and B or similar pieces. This necessary division, far from creating awkward shapes, can

be turned into a rhythmic lead design. When a meeting joint is being made the pieces A and B are not joined by a single lead, but where the meeting occurs each piece is glazed with its own separate lead, one with a $\frac{1}{4}$" lead, the other with an $\frac{1}{8}$" one. The flanges of C, the piece with the wider $\frac{1}{4}$" lead, are opened wide with a lathykin. At this point the groove should be filled with glazing compound and piece A inserted in the groove. B should be inserted into the groove next and its $\frac{1}{8}$" lead put inside the open flanges of A. Complete the process by pressing down the raised flanges with a stopping knife. The same procedure should be followed in the other three lobes and the center of the quarterfoil. Finish by flowing solder along all the joints. Do all of the tracery sections in the same manner. Figure 125 also shows the correct and incorrect method of making a meeting joint. The overlapping $\frac{1}{4}$" part of the point should always be at the top or as nearly so as possible so that water will drain off, and not into, the window.

Figure 126 shows a horizontal section of a T bar as it is placed in a groove. The regular $\frac{1}{4}$" rabbet has been widened to $\frac{3}{8}$" in order to provide a slot $\frac{3}{8}$" wide × 1" deep × 1" high. The added forward $\frac{1}{8}$" serves the same purpose as it did with a rabbet by allowing the glass section to remain flush with the rest of the rabbet after it passes the T bar.

The setting of a section in a groove is a bit more difficult. To do this first bend the $\frac{1}{2}$" binder leads out at right angles to the section on both sides. Fill the groove with glazing compound and push one side of the section into the groove as far back as it will go. If you bow the section slightly, it will just clear the opening on the other side to permit the entrance of that side of the section into the groove. Then the flanges can be straightened on first one binder and then the other with a stopping knife. Center the panel in the opening and clean off the glazing compound which has oozed out of the groove.

Windows which have round Romanesque arches, pointed Gothic arches, or flat tops will cause no setting problems when placed in a groove, but those with cusped tops will have to be treated in the same manner as tracery pieces.

All that now remains to be done is the installing of the round reinforcement bars which must be placed and fastened on the inside of the window. These bars should be $\frac{1}{2}$" longer than the sight size of the opening and flattened a quarter of an inch on each end so that they can be pressed into the rabbet or groove along with and in front of the section. The sections were all wired for round bars at the completion of cementing. These wires show exactly where the bars are to be placed. When lined up properly, bring the copper wires up and twist the wires to tighten them around the bars. Do not twist them too much or they will twist apart. Trim off all but $\frac{1}{4}$" and fold the remaining bit down parallel to and on top of the bar.

Beginning with the twelfth century, iron has been used almost exclusively for T bars, armatures, and reinforcement bars. In the last ten years we have made a practice of substituting aluminum for iron. It costs more per pound than iron but since it weighs so much less there is little difference in the final cost. Aluminum is much easier to cut and work than iron and it never rusts away. When complex armatures which call for welding or braising are used, iron or architectural bronze is more satisfactory.

Some architects insist that a public ceremony be held in their presence for you to sprinkle the window with a fire hose to prove that the window does not leak, a performance which is both foolish and embarrassing. Very few reputable stained-glass artists will make or set leaking windows. Leaking occurs mainly through the settling of the building which may cause the window to torque. An equally frequent cause is condensation which occurs on large windows. If a window happens to show signs of this, condensation gutters can be installed.

THE EVOCATIVE TECHNIQUE

It may appear somewhat strange to the general reader to find a chapter of a book on stained glass devoted to a heretofore unknown subject called "The Evocative Technique." However, in describing the making of a stained-glass window by using the step-by-step procedure followed in a typical contemporary studio some very definite problems arise. On the surface this sequential method appeared to be a perfect way of defining this or any other craft. But after this approach had been repeated many times with only modest success, it became evident that something was seriously wrong. We discovered that the words of the explanations had been understood but not their meanings. In a sense it was putting the cart before the horse by encouraging individuals to attempt the designing of windows in a logical manner when they knew nothing about the materials, their limitations, or their proper use. The same problem of communication which had arisen with our students would certainly arise with our readers.

In casting around for a solution we asked ourselves, "How did stained glass first start?" It started when the craftsman selected pieces of colored glass, fastened them together, and placed them in a window opening. Our solution to the instructional problem was a new approach— an approach we call The Evocative Technique. This same process, which was used by the first glass artists, can be followed now with considerable ease. The final result has far greater appeal today than it had in the past, for the works of painters in the preceding decades have conditioned the world to nonrepresentational art. The simple patterns which can be made by the evocative process are not only appealing but extremely effective. This is not a new method so much as it is a new approach to a very old one. The appeal is to the senses, not to logic, to the awareness of material uniqueness, and not to ideas. Any person, regardless of his training, can be a genuinely creative artist when working with these materials. All he has to do is look, choose, and arrange. If he does not like a certain piece, he can change it. If he wants to alter the shape of a piece slightly, he can pick up his pliers and break off a corner a bit at a time (grozing), or if the piece which he chooses to remove is of considerable size, he can cut it off (cutting). Both of these processes are described as well as illustrated under *Glass Cutting*. All that is needed to start the action in this new technique is a fluorescent light fixture, a sheet of double weight window glass, a pair of pliers, a glass cutter, and some pieces of colored glass. This way of working solves one of the designer's most acute problems—how to make compositional changes with some degree of ease. If changes require a great deal of reworking, there is a tendency to settle for the first arrangement. As a result, new patterns are never tried, let alone achieved. All of the processes dealing with the making of a window are involved in the Evocative Technique with the exception of setting. We have already expressed our conviction that the most effective way to study an art is to practise it, and in the following pages we have outlined a series of projects.

Each project is different and progressively more complex than the preceding one. Those readers who may choose to forego this creative experience will unquestionably gain considerable knowledge from just reading the text on the Evocative Technique. Each project is presented in such a way as to stimulate visual or imaginative responses to crafts' materials, and to variable ways of using the materials and tools.

Every effort has been made to avoid emphasis upon the eccentricities of style inherent in the traditional or archaeological approaches repeated by so many writers on stained glass. For example, Ralph Adams Cram, the architect for many of our neo-Gothic churches, used to hold a lighted match behind the blue glass of a window. If the blue showed the slightest violet cast, he would insist that the piece be removed and replaced. Apparently he had once tried the lighted-match technique on an authentic piece of thirteenth-century blue and found that this particular blue had appeared slightly greenish.

General information on shop practice, as well as the proper way to use tools and materials, is included under separate titles such as iron, lead, glass, glass painting, firing, etcetera. The proper time to refer to these is also indicated in this section.

Project No. 1

Areas covered in Project No. 1: Exploration and selection of color, elementary cutting, grozing, glazing, and cementing.

MATERIALS NEEDED FOR THIS PROJECT:

1) One 48″ industrial type two-bulb fluorescent fixture
2) One ball-end glass cutter
3) One, preferably two, sheets of double-weight clear window glass 14″ × 20″
4) One pair of cheap pliers
5) A collection of various colored pieces of scrap glass
6) One small jar or can of kerosene
7) Six strips of $\frac{1}{8}$″ lead cames in 6′ lengths
8) Six strips of $\frac{1}{4}$″ lead cames in 6′ lengths
9) Twelve feet of $\frac{1}{8}$″ 60–40 wire solder
10) One small soldering iron
11) A one ounce jar of oleic acid flux for soldering
12) One cutting knife for cutting lead
13) A half pound of $1\frac{1}{8}$″ lathing nails for glazing
14) One 12″ × 12″ × 1″ soft-wood board (spruce or white pine)
15) A small one pound can of glazing compound (putty)
16) Several small cheap camel's hair brushes
17) A lathykin (blunt-pointed wooden tool)
18) One small scrub brush
19) A pound of whiting
20) One small vial of silver nitrate

The number of tools and materials indicated for this first project may seem rather extensive, but when it is understood that they will be used again and again in carrying out additional projects, the number of needed items should not appear excessive.

To start work, place the fluorescent light fixture upon a sturdy table. Since this light fixture is your most expensive single purchase for the first project, this and any other substitutes should be discussed at greater length. Most fixtures are made with relatively narrow bases; they are meant to be hung from the ceiling so when placed upon a table they tend to rock back and forth while being used. This fault can be rectified by arranging short lengths of 2″ × 4″ pieces of wood along both sides of their reflectors. There are many types of 48″ fixtures available, nearly all of which are fitted with fancy grills or dividers placed over their reflectors supposedly to diffuse the light and improve their appearance. For our particular purpose these lights are quite useless unless the grills are removed. Industrial fixtures which have no grills are the simplest, cheapest, and best for the purpose at hand.

There are two types of industrial fixtures which are suitable for our use. The first one is the simple two-tube reflector model. This can be used as it comes from your electrical dealer and only requires the 2″ × 4″ supports. The second type has no reflector but relies upon its white

fig 127
Two-tube fluorescent light fixture with reflector

enameled base for its reflective power. If the second type is used, it will have to be placed in a shallow wooden box fitted with a plywood floor and mounted upon short legs so that air can circulate around and under the fixture. The first type also works better if mounted in a similar box. Measured from inside the box it should be $12\frac{1}{2}''$ wide $\times$ $48\frac{1}{2}''$ long $\times$ $5\frac{1}{2}''$ in depth. The legs can be approximately $5''$ in length.

A cheaper light can be constructed by removing the floor of the same light box and placing a sheet of white drawing paper upon the table underneath the light box. The standard incandescent lamps with simple reflectors can be placed at either end of the box with their lights directed diagonally upon the white paper. The light will be reflected upward and illuminate your panel. This light will prove adequate, but not as satisfactory as the fluorescents. You can possibly acquire old fluorescent fixtures from an office or factory which is being modernized. No matter what kind of fluorescent fixture is used, put 40-watt cool white bulbs in the fixture. They are color corrected, which means that the color will appear the same as in daylight. The $48''$ fixture will accommodate both pieces of $14'' \times 20''$ window glass over the lights. They will provide a space for laying out a panel as well as a convenient area for spreading out the small pieces of colored glass about to serve as a palette.

Carefully study the pieces of colored glass which have been scattered randomly over the new palette. Pick out a piece which happens to attract your eye. Set this upon the window glass reserved for the new panel. Again return to the palette, choosing a second piece which will go well with the first one. In choosing consider color, size, and shape. Now pick a third and a fourth one. This process of selecting pieces of color constitutes a series of steps in a creative act. In selecting the first piece of glass you are making a creative decision. Each selection thereafter will expand and implement the first selective creative action. Each piece which is added should relate to the already growing composition as the selective process continues. After a number of pieces have been selected and placed you will notice that they can be joined in certain places but not in others. Continue selecting and joining the pieces where it can be done successfully. It will also be apparent that where they do not join gaps will form. Do not be alarmed by this—later these gaps will be filled out with lead to create black areas. These black areas will turn out to be assets, not liabilities, for areas of black placed in juxtaposition with colors add to their brilliance as black velvet does to an opal. At a certain point in the arranging a piece may seem out of place or wrong in color. If so, reject and replace it. When it becomes evident that no matter how the pieces are arranged certain ones will have points projecting which cannot be accommodated, use

the grozing pliers to chew off the projections, a bit at a time. When the projections are too large to groze use the cutting wheel and cut off the unwanted piece. (At this point read the section on cutting which describes in detail both cutting and grozing.) After all of the selecting, rejecting, grozing, and cutting has been completed, and the results seem reasonably satisfactory, restudy the panel to see whether the movement of line is interrupted thus causing a certain amount of disorganization. It may be that by moving a piece a bit to the left or the right or a bit up or down the continuity of line and the compositional unity will be greatly improved. When all the adjustments which seem necessary have been made, the glass pieces may be put into their leads. There is no point in endlessly rearranging the glass. There comes a time where one's attention span and interest have become exhausted. If the process is continued, all that will happen is what occurs with so many painting students, namely, to paint one painting on top of another.

Select a piece of $\frac{1}{8}''$ came lead, wrap it around one of the pieces of glass so that the ends of the lead butt. Notice that a lead came is shaped like the capital I. When wrapped, the glass will fit between the upper and lower flange of the came. The wrapping process will necessitate cutting the lead to fit. It is very easy to cut $\frac{1}{8}''$ lead with either a sharp knife or a pair of cheap scissors. As soon as you begin working with $\frac{1}{4}''$ or larger leads you will have to use a cutting knife such as the one suggested in the list of tools and materials needed for this project. These knives have removable and replaceable blades. A known brand will cost at least a dollar; however, quite satisfactory ones can be purchased at any one of several discount stores at very reasonable prices. In making a cut rock the knife blade back

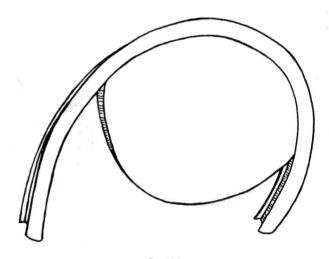

fig 128
Wrapping $\frac{1}{8}''$ lead around glass piece

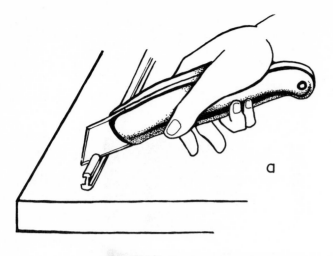

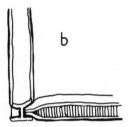

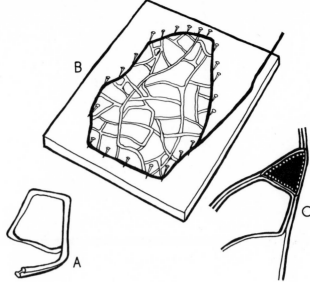

fig 130
GLAZING PROJECT 1
A) single piece wrapped for glazing assembly
B) placing and nailing wrapped pieces with $\frac{1}{4}$" binder shown in place
C) placing and soldering a piece of sheet lead in place of a glass piece

fig 129
a) how to rock the lead cutting knife to avoid crushing the lead
b) method of fitting one binder lead inside of another

and forth over the lead. If you attempt to press down with the blade without using the rocking motion, the lead will collapse. When the lead has been cut to fit, place the wrapped piece of glass upon the 12" × 12" board. In putting the wrapped pieces upon the board, make certain that they start and are kept at least 1" from the edges of the board. In the wrapping process, a certain amount of pressure must be used to force the glass tightly into the lead. Continue to wrap and replace each piece upon the 12" × 12" board as it was on the window glass before wrapping. Press the wrapped pieces tightly together. In order to hold them steady while soldering, drive a glazing nail into the board touching the edge of the wrapped piece at the top of the panel. Now drive another nail against the piece at the bottom of the panel, then one on the left and one on the right side of the panel. Continue to drive glazing nails around the perimeter of the panel 1" apart. Just a word of warning: do not, under any condition, use a plywood board. Its wood is too hard. Nails will be difficult to drive in, and even more so to pull out.

(Before proceeding further read the section on glazing. This covers such procedures as the cutting and stretching of the lead, the making and using of the lathykin, soldering the joints, and the correct flux to use for soldering the lead and copper wire. It also explains how to tin an iron and many other important directions on glazing.)

The pieces should be spot soldered. Later, solder may be flowed between the adjoining $\frac{1}{8}$" leads, but for the present it is better to make certain that all pieces are securely fastened. It is now time to fill those gaps between the pieces of glass with sheet lead about $\frac{1}{16}$" thick. If there is no sheet lead at hand, pieces cut from any available tin can will serve as well as lead.

Make patterns of the shapes which need to be filled. The patterns, and shortly the pieces of lead or tin, should reach to about the middle of the $\frac{1}{8}$" lead cames. This will allow solder to cover both the lead cames and the edge of the sheet lead or tin. A simple way to make the patterns is to use a china marking pencil with a very sharp point. Draw a line through the middle of the lead surrounding the gap. Place a piece of paper over the marked lead. Rub the paper vigorously with a hard stick to transfer this line to the paper. Then the paper can be used to carbon the pattern shape onto the piece of sheet lead or tin. Two pieces should be carboned and cut at the same time, one for the front panel, the other for the back. Solder one piece to the front,

129

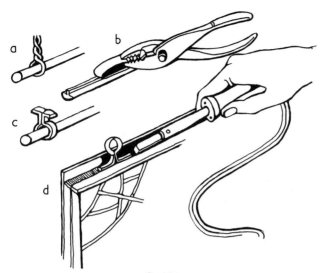

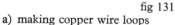

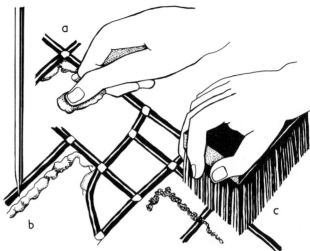

fig 131

a) making copper wire loops
b) stripping top flange from ¼″ lead for loop
c) making lead loop
d) top binder opened to show method of placing either lead or wire loop

fig 132

a) wiping putty into the lead flange
b) separating the putty from the flange with a pointed stick
c) brushing the putty away with a coarse straw brush

saving the other for the back when the panel is soldered on the reverse side. Solder may be flowed between all the adjoining ⅛ leads to finish off the top side. Remember that flux must be applied to every part of the lead which is to be soldered. The panel should have a ¼″ binder for the glazing to be finished. This binder must be run completely around the perimeter of the work. The addition of the binder will make the panel much more rigid. If a free form or round shape has been used, a simple strand of lead can be run around the panel. However, if a rectilinear form has been used, four separate strands of binder leads will be necessary, one for each side. It is very nearly impossible to maintain a square corner with a single strand of lead. Before a binder can be put on, the lead will have to be straightened, which means that at first all of the twists must be removed. When this has been accomplished the lead will need to be stretched to complete the process. Because the binder must overlap the leads used in the already glazed panel, it will have to be opened with a lathykin. (This process is also described under glazing.) Most panels when completed will be hung in a window. This will mean that a loop for hanging will need to be affixed along the top edge. This loop can be made of a piece of stout copper wire but one made from ⅛″ or ¼″ lead came will look better. For a small panel a piece of ⅛″ lead came can be cut in half the long way. If the panel is heavier, the top flange stripped from a ¼″ came can be used. Stripping is done by making a cut immediately beneath the top flange of the lead. By getting a firm grip with the pliers upon the free cut end of the flange one can

strip the top flange off the came. A loop can be made by wrapping either the ⅛″ or the ¼″ lead around a small round dowel. The strip used should be at least 2″ in length and shaped as illustrated. To locate where the loop should be soldered hold the panel by the top edge between the thumb and first finger. Move the fingers one way and then the other until it balances. When the panel is fairly large it may be advisable to use two rings. In this case one should be fastened upon either corner of the top. To mount the ring or rings make sure that the outside of the binder is opened wide, the flat places on the ring set down into the binder, and the ring soldered in place. It is better to spot solder, first one side and then the other, returning later to solder each side thoroughly.

The panel must now be puttied. At this point there is always the rueful complaint, "Why do I have to putty it?" There are several good reasons for so doing. The putty will compensate for the varying thickness of the glass pieces and keep the panel from rattling like a pair of castanets. Also, believe it or not, there are many light leaks in an unputtied panel. Finally, if the panel should later be glazed into a window and exposed to the elements, it will keep it from leaking. To putty a panel take a small quantity of glazing compound between the thumb and first finger. Partly push and partly wipe the compound between the lead flange and the glass. The wiping is done in much the same way as one would clean a shoe on a foot scraper. When all of the leads are filled use a small pointed stick to remove and clean up the excess compound. Always keep

130

the pointed stick upright, at no time try to dig under the lead flange as the stick is drawn around the inside of each lead. The excess compound loosened by the pointed stick can be picked up with the wad of compound in much the same way that we use a blotter. After removing the excess putty sprinkle the panel with a bit of whiting, rub this around and off with a rag or some paper toweling. The whiting will soak up any oil deposited from the putty while acting as a polishing agent. Buff the panel vigorously with the small scrub brush in much the same manner as you would use a shoe brush. Make certain to brush at right angles to the lead, never parallel to it. Turn the panel over and repeat the same routine. Remember that the panel must be soldered, puttied, and cleaned on both sides. Buffing will greatly improve the appearance of the panel by darkening the leads as it polishes them. The leads may be darkened still more by covering them with the silver-nitrate solution.

Project No. 2
Simple Glass Painting

New areas covered in Project No. 2: Simple drawing suggested by the shape of the piece, elementary glass painting, and firing.
1) Glass paint one half pound tracing black
2) Glass paint one half pound matting brown
3) One no. 1 oxhair tracing brush
4) One $\frac{3}{4}''$ camel's hair matting brush
5) One round badger brush
6) One two ounce bottle of casein emulsion
7) One palette knife with a 3″ blade
8) Three small jars, one for water, one for tracing color, and one for matting color.
9) One set of glass caster cups (4 cups)
10) One sharpened hard-wood stick
11) One small needle mounted in a soft-wood stick
12) Two no. 1 round bristle brushes
13) Two no. 2 round bristle brushes
14) One no. 24 round bristle brush
15) One no. 5 round oxhair brush
16) One arm rest
17) One kneaded eraser
18) One stick of Koh-I-noor compressed charcoal grade no. 2
19) One charcoal pencil 2B
20) One Blaisdel Nu Way 536T eraser pencil
21) One small bottle of fixative
22) One fixative blower

As attractive and as stimulating as color can be in stained

figs 133 and 134
Examples of project 1, designed and executed by students

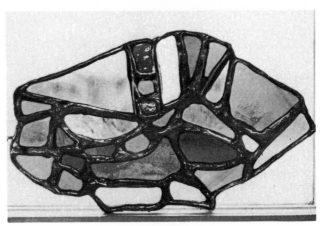

fig 133

fig 134

glass, it was not until the eleventh century, when the artist discovered and utilized monochrome enamel to define representative forms, that the art of stained glass really became significant. It is very likely that the first painting done on glass was restricted to small decorative rosettes or to similar simple forms. There is little doubt, however, that in a very short time glass painting became much more extensive and definitive in its representations. A present-day student may follow in the footsteps of the first stained-glass artists without in any way being compelled to imitate the archaisms of the early artists. Since the art of stained glass had sprung into existence almost overnight in the eleventh century, due to the introduction of enamel and

131

the demands of architecture, it had neither a long gradual evolutionary span nor entrenched traditions. The subject matter and design forms were not sacrosanct as they had to be drawn, of necessity, from other existing arts. Present-day artists can follow exactly the same pattern as their eleventh-century brothers by adapting contemporary forms to the medium. For adapted they must be. A form taken from another medium should not be *imitated* but *transcribed* into the new medium. (Before attempting to do any painting read the section on glass painting from the beginning, through simple and elementary painting. Learn how to mix the tracing color, which is used for the linear details, then the matting color, a thin transparent paint used to define the tones. After the tracing color has been mixed put it into a jar and fasten the lid. Do the same with the matting color when it is neither too hard nor too soft. This, of course, will entail matting a piece of glass, stippling it, and testing it by rubbing.)

When the paint is ready, return to the palette of glass pieces. Choose several light-colored ones, place them upon a sheet of white drawing paper and outline each piece with a pencil. Make a drawing upon each outlined piece. Draw whatever catches your fancy, or intrigues you—an animal, a bird, an insect, a flower, a head, hands, abstract forms, in fact anything so long as it is defined by a trace line and covered with a light-toned matt. A charcoal pencil will do for the lines and tone while a hard-pointed eraser will work wonders for picking out highlights.

After the drawings have been completed spray them with fixative and place them on the sheet of window glass covering the fluorescent fixture. Take a small quantity of matting color from the jar. Put it in a glass caster cup. Add water a bit at a time until the color is thin enough to spread properly. Using the ¾″ flat camel's hair brush, cover the pieces with glass paint, smooth out the matt with the badger blender, and stipple the pieces until dry. Unless the matt is thin enough or the surface stippled enough, the matt will be too dark to see through when the glass is placed over the drawing. Before tracing take a small quantity of tracing color from the tracing-color jar, put this also in a glass caster cup, again add water until the color has the proper consistency to be used for tracing. To support the tracing hand while working use an arm rest.

This will be the time of reckoning. It can never be imagined how many things can go wrong at the same time. It is almost certain that before a pleasing result can even vaguely be attained the pieces will have been matted and retraced at least a half a dozen times. There are several different ways of doing the matting and tracing but ultimately they all present their own particular difficulties. It may as well be accepted that this can well be the most

132

fig 135
An example of a fourteenth-century fragment window

frustrating experience in making stained glass; however, you, like hundreds of others before, will learn to master the technique in a relatively short time. There is very little to be gained by burdening the reader with critical suggestions. However, there are two actions that can cause endless trouble and should be avoided. The first is the novice's attempt to extend each brushful of paint indefinitely; the other is his failure to continue adding water to the tracing color. This must be done so that the color will retain its proper consistency. Try loading the tracing brush after each stroke, also restir the color each time the brush is reloaded. When the painted pieces are found acceptable, relax—the rest of the project is mostly downhill.

It has been stated several times that glass painting is more a process of removing than of adding paint. To remove the paint prepare one of the no. 1 brushes by trimming the bristles to a length of $\frac{3}{16}''$. After trimming burn the cut end with a match and sand it to a point. Be sure that just the tip is burned or only a brass ferrule will remain, instead of a brush. This slightly pointed brush will prove excellent for wiping out lights. To get into tight corners a pointed stick can be employed.

In this first painting operation it should be understood that the prime purpose of the matt is to protect the trace lines from obliteration by halation. At least a $\frac{1}{8}''$ band of matt should be left next to the trace lines. This narrow strip of matt keeps the light from spreading, thus the edge of the matt is made to appear lighter as it approaches the clear area. This gives the forms painted an appearance of being slightly rounded. With the removal of all the matt except for that portion which was left to protect the trace lines, a very simple but effective painting method has been completed. No more painting should be done on this project. All that remains now is to fire the pieces and then to glaze the panel.

Instructions on how to prepare a plate for firing, how to lay out the pieces, as well as how to determine when the pieces are properly fired, are all described in the section on firing. (Before attempting to fire the pieces, read the section on firing.)

When the fired pieces have cooled they may be removed from the kiln, wrapped with $\frac{1}{8}''$ leads as in project no. 1, and arranged on one of your $14'' \times 20''$ sheets of clear window glass. Pieces of colored glass should be added to the ensemble and similarly wrapped with $\frac{1}{8}''$ leads. Both the colored and the painted pieces should be assembled on your glazing board in the format of your choice, soldered together, and finished in the same manner as in project no. 1.

In many older windows, especially the fourteenth and fifteenth century ones, odd fragments were gathered up and glazed into windows. Fragment windows can be, and often are, quite charming. When not studied too closely they take on the appearance of a designed window.

Project No. 3

New or special areas covered in Project No. 3: Indicative form; simple creative designing of a cartoon, advanced painting, traditional glazing.

Additional materials needed:

1) Four pieces of $8\frac{1}{2}'' \times 11''$ carbon paper
2) One piece of thin paper; one piece of heavy paper; both pieces should be 2" larger in all dimensions than the drawing
3) One fairly hard pencil
4) One small roll of Scotch drafting tape
5) One 12" ruler
6) One B4 Speed ball-pen point
7) Two furring strips
8) A one quarter pound petroleum wax or beeswax

Did you ever find yourself gazing at the cloud formations and watching the images form and dissolve only to reassemble themselves into new and different configurations? Did you ever observe the patterns and figures defined by the frost upon a window? If you have, you have watched indicative form in action. Indicative form is the figurative aspect of the Evocative Technique. It is the ability to recall and recreate images, one of the necessary major elements of visual expression. It is with this kind of visual form that our third project is concerned.

Rather than starting with an idea or predetermined image, start by selecting a piece of light-colored glass roughly 6" or 7" in its longer dimension, preferably a piece of irregular or eccentric shape. Do not alter the piece in any way; contemplate the uniqueness of its particular shape and visualize the kind of form that would be appropriate to fill it. Allow your imagination free rein. While still in the process of contemplating the piece, place it on a sheet of white drawing paper, trace a line around it, and construct a freehand rectangular panel around the piece. With a 2B charcoal pencil draw $\frac{1}{4}''$ lead lines around each of the pieces including the outside binder of the panel. If no interesting or seemingly valid idea has yet come to mind, try placing an irregular tone over the middle piece. Rub this with your finger to produce a variable tone. Cut up your kneaded eraser into four parts; keep one out to work with and put the other three away for future use. Use the kneaded eraser to pick out the larger lights and the hard-pointed eraser for minute lights. Keep the kneaded eraser pliable; it can be altered easily for broader or finer work by pinching it into various shapes. Doodle upon the charcoal tone with both the kneaded eraser and the hard-pointed eraser, and finally with the 2B charcoal pencil. The first time that this type of approach is attempted the solution may prove to be somewhat evasive; however, the more times that it is tried, the easier it will become. The drawing which is in the process of being worked upon is called a "cartoon"; a small one, to be sure, but nevertheless a bona fide cartoon (see Glossary). Do not do any drawing on your cartoon with a regular lead pencil. There is no part of glass painting that can suitably be interpreted with a lead pencil!

In making your drawing, try to revive the nebulous images seen in clouds and frost. Be concerned with the suggestions which may appear by accident on the irregularities of your drawing. If you continue making marks and smearing around while at the same time picking out lights with your erasers, sooner or later your drawing will begin to take shape. When it does, follow what is happening—you will be moving in the right direction. To the non-artist this entire operation may appear to have come directly from the familiar Ouija board. However strange as it may seem, it is the method followed by many artists when starting a creative composition. It is also the major reason why most artists are literally terrified when they first face a large blank canvas. There is very likely no more difficult operation for an artist than the starting of a composition. One of the typical critical gambits which you will hear when one painter looks at another's work is "you have a good start."

This new way of making a drawing, by developing it from a nebulous and somewhat vague original form, will offer an opportunity for a broader and more sophisticated approach to the actual painting. While in the previous project the small pointed scrub was used only for wiping out the thin lights, it may now be used to wipe out broad lights. The painting can then be carried on by employing some of the longer-haired scrubs to stipple the edges of the remaining matt. If the matt is stippled and thinned out as it moves toward the clear places, it will give the forms a rounded appearance. Although there are many different ways of carrying out this stippling action, the major purpose is to punch out more tiny lights like the ones started on the previously stippled wet matt.

In the drawing you will need to suggest texture and form as well as protection of the trace lines against halation, the optical corrosion of the line caused by the spread of light. This will be an exercise in more advanced designing and glass painting.

Unlike the first two projects where the pieces of glass were wrapped with lead, this third project is to be cut and glazed in the traditional manner. The lead lines and the

figs 136 and 137
EXAMPLES OF PROJECT 3 BY STUDENTS
(INDICATIVE FORM)

fig 136

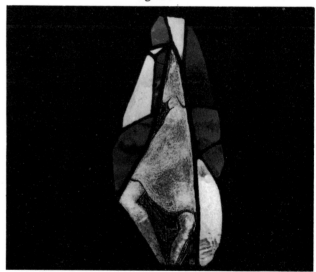

fig 137

binder lead should be drawn ¼″ wide with the charcoal pencil. When the cartoon is completed spray it with fixative. The sequential steps to complete this panel are as follows:
1) Make two carbons of the lead lines
2) Number the patterns
3) Trace ¼″ false lead lines on one of your 14″ × 20″ glass plates
4) Use your B4 Speedball pen to draw over your lead lines on the carbon which is to be used to make the patterns
5) Make the patterns by cutting on either side of the broad

134

line made by the Speedball pen. This operation will cut out a strip $\frac{1}{16}''$ of black paper which in turn means that $\frac{1}{32}''$ will be removed from each piece. The patterns will be the correct size for cutting the glass

6) Wax the patterns to the plate in their proper place
7) Select and cut the glass
8) Wax up each cut piece
9) Matt the glass
10) Place the glass over the cartoon and trace the pieces
11) Paint the pieces
12) Remove the pieces, clean the wax off the back, and prepare the plate for firing
13) Fire the glass
14) Glaze the panel
15) Cement the panel (putty)
16) Mount the rings for hanging the panel
17) All of these processes are extensively covered under the proper heading:

Numbers 1 through 6 under "The Cut Line"
Numbers 7 and 8 under "Glass Cutting"
Numbers 9 through 11 under "Glass Painting"
Numbers 12 and 13 under "Firing"
Number 14 under "Glazing"
Number 15 under "Glazing" (Cementing)
Number 16 under "The Evocative Technique," Project No. 1

Project No. 4
Module Panel

New or special areas covered:

The architectonic importance of the horizontal and vertical demands in a stained-glass structure. How to create transitions between lead and glass by the use of paint.

Additional Materials Needed:
1) One celluloid angle 45°
2) One small box of hard pastels
3) One piece of thin paper, one piece of heavy paper; both pieces should be 2″ larger in all dimensions than the drawing

Project no. 4 has been planned to offer you an experience in a simple controlled design. The panel should be a rectangle 9″ × 12″, divided into nine basic modules 3″ × 4″. These modules may again be subdivided as follows: one section divided horizontally into two pieces 2″ × 3″; another vertically into two pieces $1\frac{1}{2}'' \times 4''$, and a third vertically and horizontally into four pieces $1\frac{1}{2}'' \times 2''$. By studying the illustration you will see that in addition to the four examples shown, an almost endless series of different compositions can be created. Only the four

original modules should be used and these must be kept to a horizontal and vertical structure. The importance of carrying out this project lies in the fact that a stained-glass window demands a high degree of emphasis upon the horizontal and vertical aspect of its design if it is to fulfill its mission as a handmaiden to architecture. To do this it must affirm, not deny, its architectural setting. Anyone who has seen a cathedral stripped of its windows as, for example, at the time of the Second World War, can truly appreciate the insistence of the architectural format upon the windows. This effect is amplified by the addition of the necessary horizontal structural T bars and round reinforcement bars. If there is one error followed by many contemporary stained-glass artists, it is the general disregard for this fundamental consideration. There are always sufficient needs for curved and diagonal lines in a window composition to balance off the horizontal dominates. It is neither necessary nor desirable for the artist to go out of his way to increase the problem purposely by adding sweeping curves and diagonals to his composition.

Using a 3″ to the foot scale, lay out a series of rectangles for making trial sketches of your panel. In case you do not have a scale rule, a rectangle $2\frac{1}{4}'' \times 3''$ will represent your 9″ × 12″ panel accurately. Try a number of different combinations. Color them with your hard pastels and draw the lead lines with the 2B charcoal pencil. After doing several of these compositions, line them up and study them. You may find one of your designs particularly satisfying, but usually you will end by combining the better qualities of several sketches. Your final selection should be laid out full-size and colored. If you still wish to modify the hue or value of some of the colors, do so. When finished fix the full-size drawing, and all of the smaller sketches, then make two carbons of the lead lines of the 9″ × 12″ panel, one for glazing and the other for patterns. The outside binder lead line must be considered as any other lead line of the composition. If the $\frac{1}{32}''$ is not taken off at each side of these outside pieces they will all be too small and the exact value of the modules will be lost. Being modular only one of each pattern will need to be cut. All the pieces can be cut over one of these four patterns.

Project No. 5

Project no. 5 is more of a continuation of no. 4 than a completely new one and is planned as an exploration of four different ways in which an identical modular panel may be modified by the use of painting alone.

We have taken Figure 141 from Project no. 4 as the original modular form:

Figure 142 is the same panel with the addition of

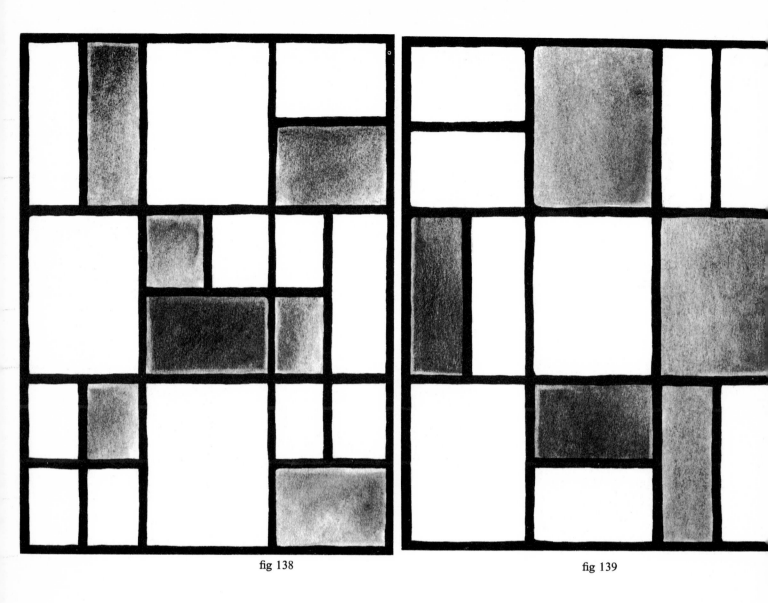

fig 138

fig 139

figs 138-141
EVOCATIVE TECHNIQUE PROJECT No. 4. FOUR DESIGNS MADE BY FOUR DIFFERENT MODULAR
ARRANGEMENTS

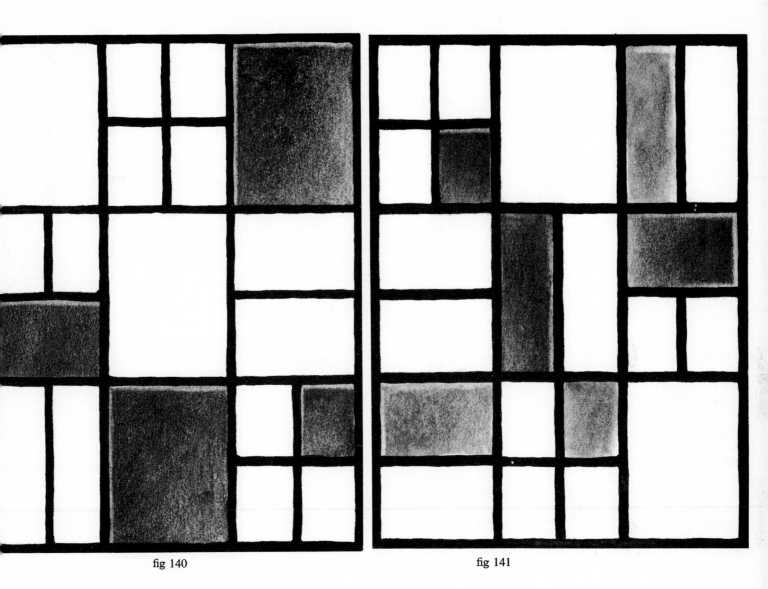

fig 140   fig 141

137

fig 142
A design composed of horizontal and perpendicular line and tone
patterns using fig 141 as the selected modular breakup

fig 143
A design composed of curvilinear line and tone patterns

fig 144
A design composed of diagonal line and tone patterns

fig 145
This is a design composed of naturalistic forms

fig 146

Window in Christ Church, Cincinnatti, Ohio, designed and executed by the authors. This window, 35′ wide by 47′ high, utilizes the same modular construction as the smaller examples

painted lines and tones to affirm the original horizontal and vertical forms. The addition of these line and tone forms helps to relate the lead, glass, and the paint more effectively.

Figure 143 is again similar, except that curvilinear forms are used which tend to create contrast and greatly change the appearance of the original modular form.

Figure 144 varies in that diagonal forms are used to contrast the original structure.

Figure 145 alters the appearance of the previous panels by introducing an entirely new element—by replacing the geometric forms with naturalistic images. Since they are familiar, recognizable forms, they attract attention to their subject content which, in turn, affects the original panel still more.

Using less black, lighter tones, and thinner lines will create less of a contrast and so will preserve more of the effect of the original structure. These drawings are meant to be used as suggestions of what can be done and should not be copied. Rather, use your own imagination to produce varied panels using a basic model.

The large west front window in Christ Church, Cincinnati, Ohio, which measures thirty-five by forty-seven feet, is an example of how the same structure can be used in a very large window as well as a small panel.

NEW AND RELATED TECHNIQUES

For a number of years the use of stained glass as a contemporary medium has been vigorously resisted by many modern architects. The unfortunate and incorrect concept that it is suitable only for a medieval church has been a considerable factor. Reacting to the gross over-decoration of the Victorian Age, modern-minded architects have tended to strip their structures of all decoration, thus creating barren, rather than functional, interiors. Fortunately, in more recent times the architects have come to recognize this error and at present are using and encouraging exploration of the medium. Stained glass is not limited to the making of traditional church windows. It has already been used effectively for two- and three-dimensional purposes. By far the most widely used new technique is the one called *Dalle-de-Verre* by the French, and slab, chunk, or faceted glass by the English and Americans.

Dalle-de-Verre

In the late 1930s, A. Labouret, in collaboration with Pierre Chaudiere, another Frenchman, created a series of windows using heavy, thick pieces of faceted glass. Not only the edges but in many instances entire pieces were worked over in this manner. The extensive faceting gave a sparkling effect but precluded the use of painting in all but a few pieces. These windows, considered important enough

at the time to be reproduced in full-color on the cover of the Christmas edition of the French magazine, *L'Illustration*, for some unknown reason were apparently not too well received. It is possible that the early approach of World War II may have been a contributory factor. During this same period other windows of note expressing a distinct contemporary trend were being made. Although these windows were strongly influenced by contemporary easel painters of the time, they still retained the techniques of the old glass. Among the better Swiss windows are those designed and executed by Hans Stocker and Otto Staiger for the church of Saint Antonius in Basel. They are simple, modern in feeling, and soundly structured. There are also a series of nave windows in the Trois Ave Marias church in the French city of Blois, markedly different from those in Saint Antonius, but equally good. By and large, however, most European windows in the period from 1930 through 1938 appear unconvincing and somewhat superficial.

In the 1960s or slightly before, probably due to the popularity of nonobjective art, the use of *dalles* was revived in France. It has now rapidly spread to Germany, England, and the United States where the technique of imbedding glass in cement or epoxy resin can be classified correctly as a recent innovation. *Dalles* (French for slabs) vary in thickness from $\frac{3}{4}''$ to $1\frac{1}{2}''$. Their dimensions are not standard but are determined by the maker. Those made in the

142

fig 147
Annunciation from the Trois Ave Marias, Blois, France

very simple and bold. This, of course, can be a desirable feature under certain circumstances; however, where subjects such as those included in the Passion series are required, abstract treatment is incapable of expressing the drama of the particular incidents. Faceting, spoken of in glowing terms by the devotees, sometimes can be of questionable value. When considered critically, most windows benefit by being muted and modified rather than intensified.

In a slab-glass window the pieces are fastened together with concrete or epoxy resin. The earlier French windows were set in concrete, but when introduced into the United States the extremes of weather proved disastrous. It was found that the co-efficient of expansion between the two materials was so different that the pieces loosened and in some cases actually fell out. This difficulty has now been remedied by the production of special mixtures of concrete. Epoxy resin compounds are frequently used in this country to hold the pieces together. Whether the glass is set in concrete or epoxy makes no difference in how a window is made. As in traditional stained glass, a sketch is followed by a cartoon showing the individual pieces. Two carbons are made from the cartoon, one is cut up into patterns and laid out upon a large board; the other is retained for laying out the pieces when all of the glass has been cut.

The selection of the color is made by one of the studio's artists who places the pattern on the selected glass while another craftsman cuts the glass roughly to shape. He scores the piece with a standard glass cutter and taps directly beneath the cut line on the slab to break it. Some studios use a thin anvil with a sharpened edge, placing the glass directly over the anvil's edge where the break is to be made. A brick mason's hammer is used to strike the slab directly over the anvil's edge. Either way works equally well. After the rough cutting has been completed the pieces are returned to their proper place on the large board where still another craftsman proceeds to cut the pieces to the pattern. To do this, a special anvil made by covering a wedge-shaped block of wood with a sheet of lead is employed. The rough-cut piece, with its pattern on top, is placed against the slanting side of the anvil where the glass is chipped with a brick mason's hammer to fit the pattern. It is surprising how well this hammer and anvil work. When a piece is to be faceted it is made to stand on its edge and is struck a glancing blow with the hammer. The hammer can be a conventional brick worker's one or a similar commercial one made with a carboloy tip. The carboloy-tipped ones come in different sizes and can be purchased from various suppliers. The brick mason's hammer is adequate if a limited amount of slab glass is to be cut, but a commercial type with the much harder tip, though

U.S.A. by Blenko are 1″ thick × 8″ square, while those made on the continent are somewhat larger. The average weight of a single slab is around ten pounds. There are advantages and disadvantages in the use of this technique. Windows made in this manner are less costly than traditionally made stained glass, especially that of painted figure windows. To make a painted window requires the employment of a number of highly skilled artist-craftsmen for many more man-hours than for one made of *dalles*. Although the original price of this glass is about three times that of regular antique glass, the elimination of painting, firing, and glazing reduces the ultimate cost of the window. One disadvantage in the use of *dalles* is that the design of a window is restricted to broad color areas. Since there is no painting to modify or define the forms, details must be kept

143

fig 148
Dalle de Verre. Cutting the patterns

fig 150
Dalle de Verre. Selecting the glass from the sketch

fig 151
Dalle de Verre. Rough cutting the glass

fig 149
Dalle de Verre. Laying out the patterns

fig 152
Dalle de Verre. The finish cut

144

fig 153
Dalle de Verre. Faceting

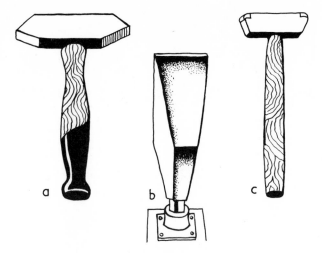

fig 154
Dalle de Verre. The anvil and hammers used for finish cutting and faceting

more expensive, will retain its sharp breaking edge for a much longer time.

When the cutting of the *dalles* has been completed a shallow wooden tray is constructed whose inside measurements must correspond to the exact dimensions of the projected section. A railing 3″ high will need to be placed around the perimeter of the tray to contain the epoxy mixture when it is poured. The cut line is placed in this shallow tray and on top of this is laid a thin sheet of transparent plastic, coated either with rubber cement or a special latex compound. The latex can be applied to each piece with a brush if so desired. The worker who is about to clean and arrange the glass in the tray should wear a pair of rubber or plastic gloves, both to protect his hands and also to keep dirt and grease away from the pieces once they have been cleaned. The pieces should be washed with

acetone and wiped dry. Any grease or dirt, especially the oil present on human skin, will act as a resister to the epoxy mixture. The plastic being transparent allows the underneath cut line to be seen and followed while putting the glass pieces in their proper place over the cut line. The coat of rubber cement or latex adheres slightly to the under side of the glass and keeps the epoxy mixture from running under the pieces while being poured. Before the epoxy is poured, a light coat of sand should be sprinkled over the plastic and around the pieces of glass. The sand which will adhere to the newly poured epoxy while creating a barrier will also eliminate the unpleasant shiny surface of the epoxy mixture. One of those large flour shakers can be used for the sand or a satisfactory substitute can be made by punching holes in the lid of a coffee can. Care should be taken that the excess sand is removed from the glass. The pouring can be done from a can with its rim pinched into a proper pouring spout. When the pieces are placed close together a better device can be made by fashioning a cone from butcher paper, cutting off the narrow tip and using this for a spout. If the hole is cut small enough, the cone will only pour when it is tapped or pressure is exerted against its sides. Still another device, which is equally good to use, is a plastic bag. Put some epoxy into the bag and snip off a small corner. The epoxy can then be squeezed in between the individual pieces of glass to the desired depth. If the edges are faceted, they will need to be covered with moist clay around the faceted parts to keep the epoxy from adhering. The epoxy may be purchased in several colors, such as limestone, mortar, adobe, gray, charcoal, and black. Regular light-colored sand will appear the same as the base material upon the lighter colors but a charcoal-

fig 155
Dalle de Verre. Dusting the panel with sand to keep the epoxy from sticking to the board and to make it a better and more interesting surface

fig 156
Dalle de Verre. Pouring the epoxy mixture

fig 157
Dalle de Verre. Cleaning and pointing up the panel

colored sand will need to be used with black or gray. Since the underneath side of the glass will, when finished, become the outside and since a light stone color is usually preferred for this side, a natural-colored sand should be shaken over the glass and followed by whatever color epoxy is selected. If a light color is also desired for the inside, the full 1″ of epoxy can be poured at once. If the charcoal gray or black is selected, then pour only $\frac{1}{2}$″ of the light color and finish with $\frac{1}{2}$″ of the darker color. If black or gray has been used for the inside, shake charcoal-gray sand over the top before the epoxy has time to set up. Most mixtures set up in from four to twelve hours at room temperature, although it is better to let them stand overnight before being moved. When thoroughly matured the sections can be cleaned and

fig 158
Dalle de Verre. Window set up for final inspection

146

any epoxy which has inadvertently gotten on the glass can be removed by chipping it away with a chisel. Some studios use a shallow bed of moist clay upon which to rest their pieces for pouring. There are also those who prefer using a thin sheet of polyurethane foam for the same purpose. When either of these last methods is used the cut line cannot be seen so the pieces will have to be placed largely by guess.

Almost any effect which can be achieved through the use of *dalles* can be accomplished by using antique glass and variable sizes of lead cames—to say nothing of the enormous advantage possible by the addition of painting. Like any other technique there are variations which could have been suggested but they would not have differed in principle from those which we have already offered.

Setting this type of window will depend to a great extent upon how the window opening has been prepared by the architect and builder.

In the final issue, making a window of *dalles* is in reality just another way of making a stained-glass window. What is intriguing is that using *dalles* opens up some possibilities which would be difficult, if not impossible, to achieve by working with lead cames and antique glass in the traditional manner. There are two new possibilities, one is two dimensional, the other three dimensional. To deal with the second possibility will carry us directly into an exploration of stained-glass sculpture, which we shall discuss shortly.

In addition to windows made for churches, traditional stained glass, as well as *dalle-de-verre*, can be used for a number of other purposes. Small medallions hung or glazed into a domestic window add a touch of color to the room's décor.

Colored antique glass with or without painting and framed with wood or aluminum can act as an almost perfect room divider. The semi-transparent antique glass permits persons on either side of the divider to see movement on the opposite side yet still separates one area from another. *Dalles* set in epoxy and similarly framed with wood or aluminum can also be used effectively as room dividers. However, when *dalles* are used the areas, because of the translucency of the glass, appear more separated.

By using the same bank of fluorescent lights described under Studio Equipment, light areas of different sizes can be designed. The areas must be ventilated but this presents no difficulty. Murals created for hotels and other public buildings can be illuminated in this fashion.

Quite often in an urban location a church will find one or more of its windows blocked out by the erection of a high building. When this happens the wall can be closed and the window illuminated by a bank of fluorescent lights. In Catholic churches, where Stations of the Cross are mandatory, stained glass so illuminated will lend a note of distinction to the Stations.

It can be easily demonstrated that the use of these lights serves the dual purpose of providing illumination for the room, as well as an artistic purpose. Nowhere do they illustrate this duality better than when used for light and decoration in a theatre. Rheostatic controls are now available which make it possible to lower the lights during a performance and to raise them again during intermissions and at the end of the show.

By using this same fluorescent light source we have produced several large stained-glass signs for restaurants. The signs have proved to be particularly effective. They are designed to be seen at night when the outside light is low.

Applique Technique

There is another way that traditionally made stained-glass windows can be modified—by the introduction of the appliqué technique. This method differs from the traditional one in that certain 'pieces have bits and pieces of colored glass attached to their front surface before the panel or section is glazed. The smaller pieces of glass must be applied with the panel in a horizontal position, otherwise the applied pieces will slide off. You will have a greater degree of success if the backs of the larger applied pieces are coated with English flux no. 75. The flux is in powder form and must be mixed with water before applying it to the back of the piece. Small bits and crushed glass will adhere without a flux. Whenever possible use the same kind and thickness of glass for both base and the appliqué pieces. It is also wise to design your panel to tolerate the crackling of the base piece which will almost certainly occur. To finish the pieces, fire them slightly harder than normal glass painting. A less satisfactory and less permanent technique can be used to fasten the small pieces to the base one. This is done by applying a transparent adhesive, such as white glue epoxy or Eastman no. 910 to the back of the pieces instead of English flux no. 75. In this case the pieces are left unfired. It will be quite surprising for you to find that pieces mounted in this way will also cause cracking of the main piece. The cause is the same 'in both cases. The co-efficient of expansion and contraction is different in thicker or thinner pieces and also in larger and smaller ones. You will, however, find that the smaller the applied pieces are the less the cracking will be. When either of these methods are combined with glass painting in small panels the final result is rich. For larger windows which are seen at long range the extra labor will be wasted.

147

Laminated Glass

Several glass firms have attempted to develop or enlarge the appliqué technique into a large-scale process. The most successful technique now in use was developed by the Willet Studios of Philadelphia. It is a chemical process of laminating plate, colored, clear, and mirrored glass called the Farbigem process, which was invented by a Dutchman.

Willet bought the process and are the sole users of this technique. The technique is quite difficult, since fusion is very precarious where the co-efficient of expansion of different glasses varies. Epoxies are not advisable for the lamination, since they are not always reliable as far as long-range adhering is concerned.

Lamination of glass can be done in such a way as to give three-dimensional effects. For instance, shapes of plate glass as much as $\frac{1}{2}''$ in thickness can be built up, one shape upon another. Cylinders of glass protruding from the surface of the base plate can also be very effective. Mirrors backed with black glass, for example, will give a change of design, the front differing from the back. A panel used as a room divider would be most intriguing done in this fashion. The possibilities are numerous not only in design but also in surface textures. Cracking, similar to crackling in pottery, will vary the appearance of the surfaces. The effect of this contemporary technique is a very sophisticated one and best lends itself to domestic buildings such as office buildings, hotels, etcetera, for decorative panels and murals. Innovations with lighting devices further enhance the beauty of these forms.

Sculpture Relief

Some examples of etched glass made in the past might possibly be considered as very low relief but they certainly are not significant as works of art. On the other hand, examples of outstanding merit have been produced in cut glass, which is a true form of low-relief sculpture. Undoubtedly the best-known makers of these miniature pieces of sculpture are Steuben Brothers. Their works carved in crystal glass, depicting animals, birds, and humans, either singly or in compositions, have been designed by some of the world's leading artists. Though executed upon bowls and goblets they should not be dismissed as purely utilitarian pieces but appreciated as sculptural works of art.

It was not until the late 1920s that any relief work of note was executed on a large scale. At this time figures and compositions were carved in low relief for store fronts and other commercial buildings. Sandblasting made possible the execution of these larger works. A sheet of plate glass can be covered with a special rubberized adhesive material

fig 159
An example of shallow relief made by sand blasting

closely resembling heavy-duty adhesive shelf paper. On this surface single figures or compositions can be drawn. Areas to be sandblasted can be cut easily, removed, and later replaced. If a small nozzle is used on the air brush, the blast can be directed to a very small area. By spraying against the cut edge of the adhesive material a graded depth of carving can be made—the deeper the cut, the darker the form edge will appear. A whole figure may be outlined in this way, while later the drapery, mouth, nose, and hair may be handled in a similar manner.

Very few sheets of antique glass are sufficiently thick to use as a base for sandblasted relief carving, but they can be used for casting pieces. A mold can be made of a modeled relief form by casting it in a special plaster called hydrocal, which is currently used to make aluminum tire molds. A piece of antique glass can be laid over the shallow mold and both placed in the kiln. When the glass has reached a temperature of 1100° Fahrenheit it will soften and sag into the mold. If the mold is made too deep, the edge where the glass first starts to sink into the mold will become stretched too thin for safety. A deeper casting may be made by crushing scrap glass of a desired color into finely broken pieces which can then be used to fill the molds. When this glass has been heated to a temperature of 1200° Fahrenheit it will melt and produce an excellent slightly translucent casting. These reliefs can be hung in a window as plaques or can be introduced as medallions into a leaded window. *Dalles* which are 1" thick may be carved by sandblasting into a fairly deep relief. Again, these may be used as

148

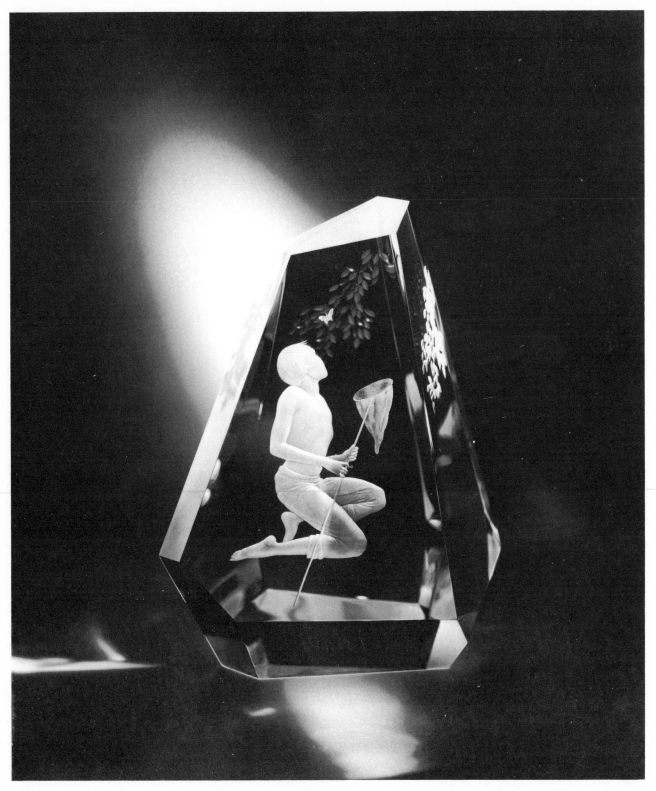

fig 160
An example of Steuben carved glass

fig 161
A glass sculpture by James Metcalf

and making furniture. They both have, however, retained their interest in glass and have adapted its use to their own two- and three-dimensional techniques. Glass is particularly suitable for making a new kind of varicolored sculpture and James, the sculptor, has carried out several experiments with glass as a medium for sculpture.

On a recent visit to the studio he fashioned a stained-glass piece of sculpture using Yin Yang forms. These forms were made by carving out the soft porous bricks used as liners for a kiln. After the carving was completed, the brick forms were covered with powdered graphite mixed with water and applied with a soft brush. When dry the graphite was rubbed to produce a highly polished surface. The graphite is necessary for two reasons: one, to fill the pores of the bricks and, two, to keep the glass from adhering to the bricks when fired. These concave and convex forms were covered with sheets of glass and placed in the glass kiln. When the temperature of glass reaches about 1000° Fahrenheit it becomes soft and if, as was done in this case, it is placed over either a convex or concave surface, it will sag and take the form of the shape beneath it. When cool the various forms were joined together with lead cames and assembled into a sculptural form. Before firing, certain pieces were decorated with gold leaf; when fired, this gold leaf fastened itself to the glass. In the finished sculpture this pattern appeared visible as gold when light fell directly upon the piece and as gray when light passed through the glass from behind. Since the pieces were varied in color, the bizarre effect was enhanced as well as changed with every step and every different position which the viewer took as he walked around the piece. As one can see readily, the effective possibilities can be almost limitless. Colors can be varied; form shapes can be changed. Lights can be placed inside or outside or both. Sculptures can be made by combining glass, lead, bronze, and iron in the form of a mobile. This may be looked at by walking around the piece or by having it turned by a small motor.

More and more the technique of stained glass as a means of painting with colored light will find its way into the contemporary scene where new and dramatic uses can continue to be found for it.

individual pieces of sculpture or added to a regular *dalle-de-verre* window.

Stained-glass Sculpture

The unlimited possibilities for three-dimensional usage have just begun to appear. Our two sons, James and Robert, who had previously worked for a number of years in the family studio, have more recently followed their own particular fields: James in sculpture and Robert in designing

BIBLIOGRAPHY

ARMITAGE, E. L.: *Stained Glass: History, Technology and Practice*, Newton Centre, Massachusetts, 1959

ARNOLD, H.: *Stained Glass of the Middle Ages in England and France*. London, 1913

——: *The Glass in Balliol College Chapel*, 1914

ASHDOWN, C. H.: *History of the Worshipful Company of Glaziers, of the City of London, otherwise the Company of Glaziers and Painters of Glass*. London, 3d ed., 1909

AUBERT, MARCEL: *Stained Glass, Twelfth- and Thirteenth-Century French Cathedrals*. New York, 1951

BAKER, JOHN: *English Stained Glass*. New York, 1960

BEYER, VICTOR: *Stained-Glass Windows*. Chester Springs, Pennsylvania, 1965

CONNICK, CHARLES: *Adventures in Light and Colour*. London, 1937

DAY, L. F.: *Windows: A Book about Stained and Painted Glass*. New York, 1909

——: *Stained Glass*. London, 1903

DIERICK, ALFONS: *The Stained Glass at Chartres*. New York, 1960

DIDEROT, DENIS: *A Diderot Pictorial Encyclopedia of Trades and Industry*. New York, 1959

DRAKE, M.: *A History of English Glass Painting*. London, 1912

FISCHER, J. L.: *Handbuch der Glasmalerei*. Leipzig, 1914

FREUND, MIRIAM K.: *Jewels for a Crown—Story of the Chagall Windows*. Reprinted New York, 1963

GAUDIN, FELIX: *Le Vitrail*. ,

GRODECKI, LOUIS: *Chartres*. New York, 1963

HEINERSDORFF, G.: *Die Glasmalerei*. Berlin, 1914

HUTTER, HERIBERT: *Medieval Stained Glass*. New York, 1964

JOHNSON, JAMES R.: *Radiance of Chartres*. New York, 1965

LABINO, DOMINICK: *Visual Art in Glass*. Dubuque, Iowa, 1968

LEYMARIE, J.: *Jerusalem Windows of Marc Chagall*. New York, 1967

MACLAGAN, C. P. D.: "*The Old Stained Glass of All Saints, North Street, York.*" Published as an excerpt from: SHAW, P. J.: *An Old York Church, All Hallows in North Street: Its Mediaeval Stained Glass*, 1908

MARCHINI, G.: *Italian Stained-Glass Windows*. London, 1957

RACKMAN, BERNARD: *Ancient Glass of Canterbury Cathedral*. London, 1926
READ, HERBERT: *English Stained Glass*. London, 1926
REYNTIENS, PATRICK: *The Technique of Stained Glass*. London, 1967
RHODES, DANIEL: *Kilns*. Philadelphia, Pennsylvania, 1969
SHERILL, CHARLES HITCHCOCK: *Stained Glass Tours in France, England, and Italy*. New York, 1908
STAINED GLASS ASSOCIATION OF AMERICA—Quarterly Magazine.
SOWERS, ROBERT: *The Lost Art*. New York, 1954
——: *Stained Glass: An Architectural Art*. New York, 1965
THEOPHILUS: *The Various Arts*. Translated by Robert Hendrie. London, 1847
von WITZLEBEN, E.: *Stained Glass in French Cathedrals*. New York, 1968
WESTLAKE, N. H. J. FSA: *History of Design in Painted Glass*. London
WHALL, C.: *Stained-Glass Work*. The Artistic Crafts Series of Technical Handbooks. London, 1905
WINSTON, CHARLES: *Memoirs on Glass Painting*. London, 1865

CAME LEAD
Bruntons Ltd.
5 Miles St.
Vauxhall, London SW8

British Insulated Callender Cables, Ltd.
21 Bloomsbury St.
London WC1

COLORING FOR EPOXY RESIN
Golden Valley Colours, Ltd.
Wick, Bristol

GLASS
James Hetley & Co. Ltd.
Beresford Ave.
Wembley, Middlesex

Claritude Ltd., Importing Agents for St. Gobain
19 Dunraven St.
Park Lane, London W1

KILNS
Wild Barfield Ltd., Elecfurn Works
Otterspool Way
Watford By-pass, Hertfordshire

Catterson Smith Ltd.
Adam Bridge Works
Exhibition Ground
Wembley, Middlesex

GLAZIERS' TOOLS
Sharratt & Newth Ltd.
287-289 Goswell Road
London EC1

PUTTY AND WHITENING
Dussek Brothers
Oil and Rosin Refiners
Thames Road
Crayford, Kent

RESINS: EPOXY AND POLYESTER
James Beadel & Co. Ltd.
Frodsham House
Edwards Lane
Speke, Liverpool 24

POLYESTER RESIN
Bakelite Ltd.
12 Grosvenor Gardens
London W1

British Resin Products Ltd.
Devonshire House
Piccadilly, London W1

C.I.B.A.
Duxford, Cambridge
W. A. Mitchell & Smith Ltd.
Church Path, Church Road
Mitcham, Surrey

Alec Tiranti Ltd.
72 Charlotte St.
London W1

SANDS
A. Elder Reed & Co. Ltd.
Riverside House
Carnwath Road, London SW6

SOLDER AND SOLDERING IRONS
James Hetley & Co. Ltd.
Beresford Ave.
Wembley, Middlesex

STAINS AND PAINTS
Messrs. James Hancock & Son
Diglis Ceramic Art Color Works
Worcester 9

James Hetley & Co. Ltd.
Beresford Ave.
Wembley, Middlesex

Johnson Matthey & Co.
Ceramics Division
78 Hatton Gardens
London EC1

TOOLS
Buck & Ryan Ltd.
101 Tottenham Court Road
London W1

INDEX

Abbeys: Cluny, 28; Saint-Denis, 28; Vézelay, 28
Aging, 69; see also Breakage and Lead, rhythm
Alabaster, 16
Aluminium, 125
Ambulatory, 29
Angers, Cathedral of, 30, 31, 96
Annealing, see Lehr
Antique glass, 42, 44, 147; buying, 83, 84; casting, 148; cutting, 83
Applique, 147
Armature, 49, 50, 51, 125
Ascension window, Le Mans, 24, 26
Augsberg, 26

Back painting, 105
Badger, see Brushes
Bauhaus School, 36
Beam compass, 71
Beeswax, 83, 135
Binders: casein, 98, 99, 108; gum arabic, 98, 100; matt, 99, 100; metal, 68, 70, 119, 121, 130; paint, 98, 99, 100; polymer, 100, 103, 104; treacle, 99
Blenders, see Brushes
Blenko Glass Company, 38, 39, 42, 143
Blowing, glass, 39, 42, 44
Breakage: value and history, 69; see also Lead, rhythm
Bronze, architectural, 125
Brushes: badger blenders, 101, 102, 103, 104; cementing, 121; cleaning, 103-4; matting, 99, 102, 104, 105; rigger, 98; scrub, 104, 134; tracing, 73, 98, 101, 102, 104, 105

Bubbly glass, 44
Buckling, 49, 68
Burne-Jones, Edward, 34, 35, 36
Byzantine, 16, 17, 18, 24, 26; church, 29

Cames, 45, 50, 116, 147; elementary techniques, 128, 129; extrusion, 47; stripping, 130
Canterbury, 32, 111
Carbon paper, 71, 72, 73
Cartoon, 53, 67-70; color, 70; drawing wall, 54; materials and tools, 67; simple, 132, 133, 134
Casein: colors, 64; black, 73; binders, 98, 99, 108
Castagna, 34
Cellosolve, 100
Celtic, 18, 26, 27; enameling, 18
Cement and cementing, 121; elementary, 130, 131; room, 53, 54
Ceramic: kiln, 61; painting, 101; suppliers, 98
Champlevé enamel, 18, 24
Charcoal, 51, 67, 70
Chartres, Cathedral of Notre Dame, 15, 20, 23, 28, 29, 30, 31, 50, 51, 69
Chaudiere, Pierre, 142
Cheeks, lead mill, 47
Chemicals, 37, 38, 39
Chiaroscuro, 20, 133
Christ Church, Cincinnati, Ohio, 141
Christianity, 19, 28, 29
Chunk glass, see Dalle-de-Verre
Clerestory, 19, 29, 30, 50, 67, 97
Cloisonné, 18, 24

155

Cluny, Abbey of, 28
Color: chemicals, 37, 38, 39; early, 37; flashing, 44;
    selection, 82, 83, 128
Concrete, 36, 143
Condensation gutters, 125
Cones, kiln, 113, 114, 115
Connick, Charles, 35
Constantinople, 16, 17
Contemporary, 35, 36, 142-150
Contraction, 147
Copper, 121; oxide, 96
Corrosion, 69
Cram, Ralph Adams, 127
Crown, 42, 44
Crucifixion window, Poitiers, 24, 26
Curves, 80, 135; paper curvature, 71
Cusped tops, 65, 66, 124
Cut line, 71-75; equipment and materials, 70, 71;
    numbering, 71, 72; scissors, 74; tracing, 73
Cutter, 77, 78, 79, 80, 82; care of, 84; sharpening, 84
Cutting, 76-86; curves, 80; dangers, 76, 79; elementary,
    128, 129; gauge, 84, 93; methods, 77-81; tools, 76;
    wheel, 77
Dalle-de-Verre, 36, 142-147, 148
Dangers: cutting, 76, 77, 79; easel, 56; etching, 112;
    eyes, 76; handling, 59; leaking, 121, 124; to badger
    brushes, 103; wax, 75; with polymer binders, 100
Decorative uses, modern, 147
Dom, Cathedral of, Augsberg, 26
Drafting tape, 66, 67, 68; on pliers, 82
Drawing: elementary, 132; room, 53; wall, 54-5
Dürer, Albrecht, 34

Easel, 56, 57
Egypt, 15
Enameling: brown, 19, 96; early, 18, 24, 96; see also
    Champlevé and Cloisonné
English: Bede, 17; contemporary, 35, 36; flint glass, 38;
    flux, 147; Gothic, 27; Late Period, 33-35; Middle
    Period, 32, 33; muff glass, 42; Silchester, 16
Epoxy resin, 36, 143, 145, 146
Erasers, 67, 70; hard pointed, 134; kneaded, 133, 134
Etching, 111, 112; room, 53
Evocative technique, 126, 127, 133
Eyes, protection of, 76
Expansion, 68

Faceted glass, 36, 142
Farbigem process, 148
Favrile, 35
Firing, 113-15, 133; cones, 113, 114, 115; equipment, 113,
    114; metaling, 108; room, 53; see also Kiln
Five Sisters, York, 32
Fixative, 64, 70
Flashed, 44, 83
Flashing, 44
Fluorescent, see Lighting
Flux: oleic acid, 116; paint, 96, 130; ruby, 120, 121;
    see also Soldering

Fracture, 79, 80
French: antique glass, 42; contemporary, 35, 36, 142;
    Gothic, 27, 28, 29, 30; Late Period, 33-35; Middle
    Period, 32, 33
Furring strip, 116, 118, 119

Gauge, cutting, 84, 93
German, 16, 20, 26, 27, 35; antique glass, 42; Bauhaus
    School, 36; Dürer, 34
Glasmalerei, 19
Glass: applique, 147; cleaning, 108; colors, 38, 82, 83;
    components, 37, 38, 39; cutting, 76-80, 82; effects of
    age, 69; kelp, 108; laminated, 148; room, 53;
    temporary, 84, 93, 94; types, 38, 39, 108; wastage, 83
Glazing, 116-125; bench, 116, 117; early, 33; elementary,
    129, 130; materials, 116; nails, 119; room, 53, 54
Gothic, 26-30, 34; abbeys, 28; cathedrals, 29; English, 27;
    French, 27, 28, 29, 30; origins, 27; revival, 34, 35, 98
Graphite, 150; see also Sculpture
Grisaille: English, 32; French, 31
Groove, 65, 122, 123, 124
Grozing, 76, 77, 82, 103, 126, 128
Gum arabic, 98, 100, 102
Guthrie, John Gordon, 35, 69
Gutters, 125

Halation, 97, 134
Hand-blown, see Antique glass
Hearts, see Lead
Horizontal, 123, 135, 141
Hydrocal, 148

India stone, 76, 84
Industrial Revolution, 34
Ink, India, 64
Installing, see Setting
Irish, see Celtic
Iron, 49-51, 125; armature, 49, 50; charcoal, 51; grozing,
    76, 77, 82; saddle bars, 49; soldering, 119, 120, 121;
    T-bars, 49, 64
Italian, 20, 26; artists, 27, 32, 34; Renaissance, 31, 32

Kiln, 60-2, 113-15; ceramic, 61; electric, 60, 61, 62; flash,
    60; heating, 115; loading, 114; muffle, 60, 113;
    testing, 114, 115; voltage, 61; see also Firing
Knife, 74; lead cutting, 118; stopping, 117
Kraft paper, 71

Labouret, A., 142
La Farge, John, 35
Lakeman, Ernest, 69
Lamination, 148
Lasting nails, see Glazing
Lathykin, 117, 119, 124
Lead, 45-8; cames, 45, 50, 116, 147; cheeks, spindles and

wheels, 47; crossings, 119; extrusion, 46; hearts, 121; mills, 46; rhythm, 69, 124; scrap, 47; stretchers, 118; wrapping, 128, 129
Leaking, 125
Lehr, 39
Le Mans, 24, 29
Lighting: decorative, 147; fluorescent, 54, 55, 127, 128, 147; reflectors, 127, 128; table, 58, 127; wall, 55
Lobe, 124

Mahlstick, 104
Marko, 42
Matt, 99, 100, 110, 133; water, 101
Matting, 102-4
Medallion, 50, 147, 148
Meeting joint, 123, 124
Metaling, 108
Methyl cellulose, 99, 100
Middle Ages, 26-30, 52, 63, 87
Middle Period, 31-3
Module panel, 135, 141
Mcnte Cassino, 17
Morris, William, 34, 35, 36
Mosques, 17
Muff glass, 42
Mullion, 51

Nave, 29
Nails, glazing, 118, 119, 129
Needles, 100
Negro lead pencils, 64
Norman slab, 42, 43

Offices, studio, 53
Opal glass, 35
Oil, 44
Origins: Byzantine, 16, 17, 18; Egyptian, 15; Roman, 16, 17; Syrian, 15

Packing room, 53
Paint, 98; color, 96; permanence test, 96
Painting, 95-112; alternatives, 111, 112; ceramic, 101; early, 95-6; elementary, 131, 132, 133; first, 108, 109; materials, 100; pigments, 88; preliminaries, 108; second, 110
Painting up, 111
Pastels, 67, 70
Paper: carbon, 71; cartoon, 66, 67, 68, 71; curvature, 71; cut line, 71; kraft, 71
Patina, 69, 105
Patterns, 71, 72, 74, 93
Pencils: charcoal, 70; negro lead, 64
Periods: classified, 20; contemporary, 35-6; Gothic, 26-30; identification, 21, 23; Middle, 31-3; Late, 33-5; prestyle, 23-6, 27
Pigments, 87, 96, 98
Plasticine, 75

Plate glass, 38; color selection, 82; studio, 58, 59
Pliers, 76, 77, 80, 82
Poitiers, 20, 24, 26, 29
Polymer, 100, 103, 104
Pre-Raphaelite, 34, 35
Prestyle, 23-6, 27
Projects, 127-141; cartoon, 133, 134; cementing, 130, 131, 134; color exploration and selection, 128; cutting, 128, 129; drawing, 132, 133; firing, 133; glazing, 129, 130, 134, 135; grozing, 126, 128; module design, 134, 141; painting, 131, 132, 133, 134
Putty and puttying, 130, 131; removal, 122

Quarter foil, 124

Rabbet, 65, 122, 123, 124
Racks, 57, 59
Raphael, 34
Read, Herbert, 20
Relief, sculpture, 148
Reinforcement bars, 68, 70, 72, 121, 124, 125
Renaissance, 26, 31, 33, 52; Italian, 32
Resin, see Epoxy resin
Reynolds, Joshua, 34
Rickman, Thomas, 20
Rigger, 98
Roman, 16, 17, 18, 19; church, 17, 28, 29, 31
Romanesque, 26, 124

Saddle bars, 49
Saint-Denis, Abbey of, 28, 29
Sainte Chapelle, 51
Sandblasting, 148, 150
Scissors, 74
Scrap lead, 47
Scratching, 102
Scratch out painting, 111
Sculpture, 150; relief, 148
Scrubs, see Brushes
Setting, 122-5; dalles, 147; tracery, 122, 123, 124
Silver stain, 32, 105, 108
Sketch, 63-4; colors, 64; scale, 63
Slab, see Dalle-de-Verre
Smear shading, 88
Soldering, 119, 120, 121, 124; elementary, 129, 130; flux, 116, 120, 121, 130; irons, 119; spot, 129, 130
Sowers, Robert, 50
Spun rondel, see Crown
Staiger, Otto, 142
Stains, 105, 108
Staples, 71
Steel heart lead, 48
Steuben, 148
Stick lighting, 110
Stipple, 103, 104, 108, 109, 110
Stocker, Hans, 142
Storage, 53, 58, 59, 83; glazing, 116, 117
Stretchers, 118

Studio, 52-62; drawing, 53; drawing wall, 54; easel, 56; etching, 53; firing, 53; glass work, 53; glazing and cementing, 53, 54; kiln, 60-2; lighting, 54-6; offices, 53; packing and storage, 53; procedure, 52-3; selecting table, 57-9
Suger, Abbé, 28, 29
Supplies, Sources of
Swiss, 142

Tape, drafting, 66, 68
Tapping, 79, 80
T-bars, 49, 64, 68, 70, 72; setting, 122-5
Template, 53, 65-6
Temporary glass, 84, 93, 94, 122
Texture, 104-5, 110
Three dimensional, 142, 147, 148, 150
Thumb break, 79
Thumb tacks, 71
Tiffany, Louis Comfort, 35
Tinning, 120
Torque, 125
Tortillon stumps, 67
Tracery, 122, 123, 124
Tracing, 73, 101, 102, 104, 105
Transept, 29
Treacle, 99
Turpentine, 74, 99, 100
Two dimensional, 142, 147

Tables, 65-6; drafting, 54; layout, 54; selecting, 57, 58; sight and full, 65

Uccello, 34
United States, 35, 36, 47, 141, 143, 148

Vertical, 123, 135, 141
Vézelay, Abbey of, 28
Viollet-le-Duc, 28
Vitraux, 19

Wastage, 83
Watercolors, 64
Wax: bees, 83, 135; petroleum, 135; sculptors, 75; soft or thumb, 74, 75, 83
Waxing, 82, 83
Wedges, 122, 123
Westlake, N. H. J., 19
Whall, Christopher, 35, 56, 98
Wheel, cutting, see Cutter
Whiting, 114, 115
Willet, William, 35
Winston, Charles, 34, 35
Wire, 116, 121

York Minster, 32, 33, 34
Young, Henry Wynd, 35, 66, 84